Terrorism Miscellany

Terrorism Miscellany

P. M. Kamath

GYAN

First Published, 2017

Published by

Gyan Publishing House
5, Ansari Road
Daryaganj, New Delhi-110002
Phone: 9811692060
E-mail: books@gyanbooks.com

Printed at: G. Print Process, Delhi.

Cataloging in Publication Data—DK
Courtesy: D.K. Agencies (P) Ltd. <docinfo@dkagencies.com>

Kamath, P. M., author.
Terrorism miscellany / P.M. Kamath.
pages cm
Collection of articles wrote during the period from 1995 to September 2016.
ISBN 9788121213509

1. State-sponsored terrorism—India—History. 2. State-sponsored terrorism—Pakistan—History. 3. India—Foreign relations—Pakistan. 4. Pakistan—Foreign relations—India. 5. Terrorism—Prevention—International cooperation. I. Title.

HV6433.I4K36 2017 DDC 363.3250954 23

Contents

Foreword

This publication by Dr Kamath includes chronological history of terrorism in India by Pakistan in the framework of bilateral political history and domestic situations in those countries. The role of United States in particular and that of former U.S.S.R, to a lesser extent, has been skillfully interwoven by the author in the act of terrorism. It has also been linked with international policy of United States and its domestic issues. The author also discusses the role of Afghanistan politics and Kashmir problems. It is very interesting how the author has related the terrorism of Pakistan with the situation of Kosovo and Muslim Jihad which is faced presently by the world.

Human rights and displacement of civilians as migrants are also highlighted. The content of this book is not only relevant for India-Pakistan but also for other terrorism afflicted countries in the world. This material helps the theoreticians in Peace Science to quantify the magnitude of these incidents and build a quantitative theoretical model, which can be used to predict the future scenarios. Dr Kamath also discusses Nuclear Weapon issues and how it influences the terrorist activities by Pakistan. He has blamed the United States policy for not taking appropriate stronger actions to stop the continuation of terrorism by Pakistan. This volume is indeed different kind of study in the field of Political Science and International Relations.

Manas Chatterji
Professor, School of Management
Binghamton University - State University of New York
Honorary Distinguished Professor
Poznan University of Poland, Poznan, Poland
Guest Professor, Peking University, Beijing, China
Honorary Visiting Professor, Central University of
Finance and Economics, Beijing, China

Preface

In 1990s I was invited by Mid-Day's then Editor Shri Nikhil Laxman and his Deputy, Shri Sai Suresh to contribute weekly an article on Education. Since I was teaching in the Department of Civics and Politics, University of Bombay and involved in guiding students on their M. Phil and Ph.D. dissertations, I also began to contribute regularly articles on the subjects of my academic interests. Simultaneously, I also began to contribute to other news papers as well. More specifically, a student under my guidance did a Ph.D thesis on terrorism. To be a successful guide, one has to be abreast with the latest on the subject of the thesis that gave me a wider vista on it.

The *Terrorism Miscellany* is a collection of 60 such articles I wrote during the period from 1995 to September 2016. I recall the words of Late Shri Rama Krishna Hegde former Chief Minister of Karnataka—an intellectual, who later became Minister of Commerce in the Atal Bihari Vajpayee government. While releasing my book *Indian Politics under Mrs Gandhi: Reflective Essays (1993)*, he had said that every essay in the collection, though written between January 1970 and November 1984, is still relevant to the current readers. I venture to make a similar claim that though articles in this *Miscellany*, were written between 1995 and September 2016, are relevant to the readers, interested in the grave problem of senseless terrorist attacks imposed on India from externally by Pakistan with or without collaboration of the Islamist groups nationally. Pakistani Army exploiting debilities of democratic facade in Pakistan, with complete—at different times—connivance or convenience of the United States which wants to maintain its military ties with Pakistan and at the same time, cultivate economic ties with India.

Many have motivated me to work and complete *Terrorism Miscellany*. A munificent grant from well known industrialist, Shri Adi P Godrej to the VPM's CIS for this project set the wheels moving. I am extremely grateful to him and the Godrej Co. for their support. My thanks are also due to Prof C. J. Pai for his help in reading the manuscript. I am also grateful to Ms Anita for her help in compiling the articles and typing the Introduction. Yet, if there are any flaws in the content of the *Miscellany*, I alone is to be held responsible for it.

Mumbai **P.M. Kamath**
16 September 2016

Introduction

When I was in the US on my fourth visit to that country in 1987 with a 3 months study grant from the Ford Foundation, my friend and a close associate, Prof Krishen D Mathur from the University of District of Columbia arranged a luncheon meeting with a Professor from New York, Dr.Yonah Alexander who was then heading a Centre for Studying Terrorism in New York City University. With my academic interest in the study of US national security policy, I was keenly interested in the study of terrorism. Though US did not experience any major terror attacks then, India had already seen the rising of its monstrous head in Punjab with Sikh separatists using it as an instrument to achieve their goal of so-called Khalistan, an independent state for Sikhs.

India's neighbour Pakistan was then headed by a Military General– fourth Military Dictator and the first after the end of the war between West Pakistan and East Pakistan that resulted in the birth of Bangladesh in 1971. However, seeds of division of Pakistan were sown right at the time of its birth in 1947. Pakistan, carved out of the Indian State, was created with two geographical parts, West Pakistan and East Pakistan with over 1609 km of Indian State's presence in the middle. West Pakistan had no territorial contiguity with the East. But Pakistan's vivisection in 1971 was entirely blamed on India.

Hence, Pakistan's Military Dictator, Gen. Zia-ul-Haq was keen to settle score with India. The word 'revenge' frequently appears in the speeches of Pakistan's leaders, particularly, with those drawn from the military and those associated with terrorist organisations based in Pakistan. Thus, General Zia embraced Khalistani movement right in the beginning by providing them military training, weapons and by financing the movement. Pakistan thought its planned support, will create a new liberated state of Khalistan, thus securing its twin goals: First, revenge for India's role in the liberation of East Pakistan and second, creation of a buffer state between India and Pakistan, serving its goal of achieving strategic depth for a state that had not yet become a nation.

Then one factor that increased Pakistan's leverage with the US was the Soviet Union's military intervention in Afghanistan in December 1979. Until then the US was blamed by Pakistan for not helping it against India over the Bangladesh War of 1971. President Gerald Ford in 1976 US elections was succeeded by Jimmy Carter, who was more concerned with human rights issues than Nixon or Ford. The US-Pakistan relations had touched the lowest point and Islamabad saw anti-US riots in which two American lives were lost.

All of a sudden the Soviet intervention in Afghanistan made the US hyper-active in pursuit of its Cold War against the Soviet Union. The US called the Soviet military intervention the greatest threat to World Peace. President Carter sought Pakistan's co-operation against the Soviet Union in making their collective opposition to the Soviet Union as a Freedom War. Zia also turned it into an Islamic *Jihad* to motivate and incite the Islamic countries to join in its war against the Soviet Union. In return, Carter offered $400 million military aid to Pakistan. Zia rejected that as peanuts; Carter's successor, Ronald Reagan, in 1981 turned peanuts into walnuts by raising it $ 4 billion that became acceptable to Pakistan's military General, Zia.

There was thus a mutual Pact between US and Pakistan during the Reagan Presidency. Though the US Congress aimed to impose controls and conditions on Pakistan, such as–Presidential certification that Pakistan was not pursuing actively its nuclear weapons programme, Reagan went on certifying that Pakistan was not on the path of developing Nuclear Weapons, though the US administration knew the truth to be the contrary; Pakistan, with the US blinking, continued hectically on its nuclear path. During the next eight years, Pakistan's state like Satan, on one hand had a well trained and experienced terrorist-Army, on the other hand a nuclear-armed regular army which came out globally from the gloomy days after the 1971 defeat in the war over Bangladesh.

Then came an end to the Soviet occupation of Afghanistan when, Mikhail Gorbachev, last Soviet Communist Party's General Secretary and President of the Soviet Union decided to withdraw from Afghanistan in May 1985. Thus, the US–Pakistan duo who introduced terrorism in South Asia had a problem of 'surplus' of well-trained terrorists fully brainwashed in Islamic terrorism. The then American President, Ronald Reagan must get all credit for planting seeds of smooth disintegration of the Soviet Union-over which the then Vice-President, T.W. Bush had presided over formally as one-term (1989-1993) President, succeeding Ronald Reagan.

With total co-operation of General Zia, US turned Pakistan into the Global University of Terrorism. In this it was aided by 'surplus' trained terrorists. Hence, Pakistan decided to pump them into Jammu & Kashmir (J&K). J & K has been an integral part of India. It was an act of unwarranted internationalism of Nehru that placed the Pakistan's blatant aggression against India on the agenda of UN Security Council. The Super Powers, the US and the Soviet-Union in turn made it a Cold War issue to sub-serve their own interests. The West, led by the US, embraced Pakistan as it was looking for a foothold in South Asia for its geopolitical reasons. Thus, India perforce was forced by circumstances to seek the Soviet-Veto support, as the US was turning a victim of Pakistani aggression, India, into an aggressor. Though it must be admitted that Nehru could not have ideologically ever considered the option of aligning with the US.

In this background, "India is not fighting a war in Kashmir" (*Times of India, Sunday Review* 5/2/1995) was critical of Indian policy of considering the then brewing internal terror activities as something done by 'misguided youths.' I have dealt in detail how the Americans in the 1970s dealt with adequate force the then developing internal terror activities by Black Panthers including a demand of their own state.

Contrary to that, India saw the first signs of growth of 'insurgency' in 1987. In 1989 under a weak PM, Vishwanath Pratap Singh, the federal government gave-in to the demand for the release of captured terrorists. Delhi easily succumbed to terrorists demand for the release of Sheikh Abdul Hameed, a JKLF "area commander," Ghulam Nabi Butt, younger brother of the late Maqbool Butt; Noor Muhammad

Kalwal; Muhammed Altaf; and Javed Ahmed Zargain, in return of the then Home Minister, Muffi Mohammed Sayyed's kidnapped daughter—Rubiya Sayyed.

Subsequently, the Congress government in 1991 did not come out with a clear policy against growing threat of terrorism, as it was under constant pressure from anti-India American administration that was then represented by Robin Raphel, Assistant Secretary of State for South Asian Affairs-a person completely committed to Pakistan. It is not an exaggeration to say that she was the spokesperson of Pakistan within the US Government. Indian policy suffered since the beginning from lack of a national perspective, in favour of parties in power, playing politics at the cost of national interest.

PM Narasimha Rao's policy towards Pakistan promoted terrorism in Kashmir is the focus in "India's Kashmir Policy: All Rhetoric and No Action" (*The Sunday Observer*, 10/6/1995).As the title of the article makes it abundantly clear that there was lot of tough talk during the Rao tenure, but no action; for instance, PM often reiterated the government's long held position that Kashmir is an inalienable part of India but the PM and his then Home Minister, S.B. Chavan often considered terrorists as 'misguided youths'. This was largely due to vote bank politics since the Congress Party always depended on Muslim vote. Rao was also defensive on India's human rights record. From the Rampart of Red Fort on 15 August 1993 he had loudly asked: "While Pakistan is carrying out false propaganda about human rights violation in J & K, only two days ago terrorists from that country killed 17 people by pulling out them from a bus, do they mean that those who have been victims of their bullets have no human rights? Do only terrorists have human rights?" Yet, he did not aggressively react when *Al-Faran*, a terror group inscribed on a dead body '*Al-Faran*'. There were also no government protests when Hindu Kashmiri Pandits were uprooted from the Kashmir valley!

"US doublespeak on terrorism must end" could not escape my attention and my next piece (*The Blitz*, 7/12/1996) asked for an "end" to such behaviour. Bill Clinton did advocate 'zero tolerance' against international terrorism. His slogan just did not encourage Indians to say a thank you to Bill Clinton in 1996 as he was very generous to Ms Bhutto of Pakistan, when she pleaded for the US assistance to tackle problem of terrorism in Karachi, while encouraging it in J & K. The US as the only Super Power, arrogated to itself the right to declare according to its national interest, Iran, Sudan and Libya as 'terrorist states'; while taking Pakistan out of it where George, T.W. Bush had placed it earlier. Not only that but Clinton also certified that Benazir regime had given up direct support to terrorists. His Assistant Secretary of State for South Asian Affairs, Robin Raphel had temerity to advise India to draw a lesson from terrorists' attacks during 1996 Republic day! As a spokesperson of Pakistan she stressed the need to "resolve the problem of the Kashmir conflict" amicably!

The brief tenure of PM, Inder Kumar Gujral saw unilateralism on the part of India in extending olive branch to Pakistan by creating a liberal regime for Pakistanis to obtain Indian visas, enabling ISI sponsored terrorists to come from the front door, while using the crossing the borders stealthily in the night, exactly at a time when its President F.A. Leghari in March 1997 was accusing India of "repression and Human Rights violation in Kashmir" in Organisation of Islamic Countries (OIC). The latter obliged by calling for "right of self-determination to the people of Kashmir." The need really was for reciprocity in international affairs, which is the heart of International Politics, so argues "Never Say Die" (*Mid-Day,* 14/5/1997).

"The Burden of refuge" (*Mid-Day*, 5/7/1997) highlights the tragic problems faced by internally displaced persons (IDP) in J & K; in this case, the Pandit community of over 2,50,000. Pakistan promoted terrorists in J& K aimed at ethnic cleansing; hence, killed original inhabitants of the State-Kashmiri Pandits; destroyed their homes and forced them to move internally to Delhi, Jammu and other safer places in the country fearing for their life. It was not a major concern for the short-lived governments then in India.

In the 1990s as the Pakistan-promoted terrorism became more aggressive, with Pakistan continuously refining terrorism as an Instrument of State Policy. There was a slow realisation in the US administration that terrorism is a double edged instrument; it can be turned against the US as well. Pakistan was a close ally of US, but Pakistani terrorists recognised only their cause–promotion of terrorism. Hence, American-civilians employed in American Oil Company were gunned down by the terrorists in Karachi. It was claimed as in retaliation to Pakistan handing over, suspected Pakistani terrorists, Mir Ajmal Kasi and Ramji Ahmed Yousef for conspiring to bomb world Trade Centre in 1993. They were swiftly convicted by the US courts. This background was discussed in "Taking on terrorism" (*Mid-Day*, 6/1/1998). The UN General Assembly for the first time also passed a resolution moved by the US, comprehensively defining terrorism as "criminal acts" and "unjustifiable" whatever may be the cause "political, religious, ethnic or ideological."

But pertinent questions also were raised as how India tackled terrorism. Then as in 1989, there were 32,000 terrorists languishing in prisons, without speedy trial and justice. That gave human rights activists to cry foul rather than create confidence in general public on Indian willingness to take on terrorism for lack of political will power.

In "Is India serious about curbing terrorists?" (*The Sunday Observer*, January 18-24, 1998) the tone and tenor is again of regret on India's lack of will-power to take on terrorism. However, it analyses fresh changes in the US approach to the problem of Pakistan promoted terrorism in India. The US Ambassador in India, Thomas Pickering, had in October 1997 clearly stated during the US and India strategic dialogue: "Both of us are committed to work together to enhance our capacity to fight terrorism, whether it is sponsored from the moon or from any corner." The US did not, of course, clearly name Pakistan! He had earlier in 1991 for the first time as the US representative in UN had said that UN resolutions on Kashmir were no longer relevant and the matter should be resolved by the two countries bilaterally. Though US has moved closer to Indian stand on terror, India because of religion of terrorists did not demonstrate sufficient nerve to act as shown by the fact that a JKLF leader had the temerity to equate himself to Mahatma Gandhi, though he had confessed of killing of six J & K officials!

Any discussion on terrorism cannot escape a solution to Kashmir dispute willingly created by the idealistic fault-line in Nehru's Foreign Policy. As nuclear armed neighbours, what could be the way to resolve the long simmering conflict? In the background of PM Vajpayee's bus trip to Lahore, I stated my oft-repeated position in "Division of

Interest" (*Mid-Day*, 27/2/1999) for reaching an understanding between two countries by turning LOC into an international border.

After the end of the Cold War, the US arrogated to itself under Bill Clinton Presidency, right to promote, albeit, selectively human rights globally. This approach was implemented by the US under the broader framework of North Atlantic Treaty Organisation (NATO) to support Kosovo Liberation Army (KLA), which was fighting to secede from Yugoslavia. KLA was designated as a terrorist organisation by Yugoslavia. Then why support terrorists ignoring moderates within Kosovo, who were willing to accept genuine autonomy for the province where a majority were ethnic Albanian Muslims? It was the concern in "Kosovo now; Kashmir next?" (*Mid-Day*, 13/4/1999) as the American intervention in Liberation of Kosovo was seen as a threat to national security and integrity of multi-ethnic, multi religious states like India or the Russian Federation.

"Double trouble" (*Mid-Day*, 4/6/1999) basically focuses on double standards practised by the US in dealing with International terrorism. Terrorists in Afghanistan, in the 1980s were trained by the CIA. Osama Bin Laden, who came to Afghanistan to fight against the Soviet occupation of Afghanistan, was a freedom fighter. However, after the Soviet withdrawal from Afghanistan in1985, Osama changed the cause and wanted to fight against the Americans and Jews and everyone else perceived to be on the US side! Then he became an International terrorist. Similarly the US presided over the disintegration of Yugoslavia. In Kosovo, Kosovo Liberation Army (KLA) was for Clinton administration a force of freedom fighters. But in its earlier Avatar, KLA known as Ushtria lirimtare-e-Kosovës was declared by the US Drug Enforcement Agency as the terrorists in 1998. In 1999 they became freedom fighters! It is this contradiction of 'your terrorists are my freedom fighters' that is preventing the nations in the UN to agree on a broad definition of terrorism.

Kargil war was an outcome of Pakistani state-sponsored international terrorism. The next article on "Blame Game" (*Mid-Day*, 21/8/1999)focuses on Indian politics as it was then, mired in blame game between the then ruling NDA under PM, Atal Bihari Vajpayee and long–governing Congress Party led by Sonia Gandhi, then leading the opposition. While it is the democratic right of the party in opposition in the sense of letting the government know where exactly it has gone wrong, merely opposing because it is in opposition on such vital issue of Pakistan externally promoting terrorism, author points out that if the issue is of apportioning blame for all wrong decisions, often present decisions have the past history of wrong decisions in the background. Then the Congress party from its inception-Mr Nehru onwards have to be blamed for allowing Pakistan to keep Kashmir as an issue to trouble India. Terrorists taking control of Hazartbal Mosque in 1993 or occupation of the Charar-e-Sharif shrine in 1995 during the Congress rule had the effect of making terrorists bold to attack India with impunity.

Next two articles "Save Children from Terrorists" (*Weekend Observer*, 4/9/1999) and "Spare the Child" (*Mid-Day*, 7/9/1999), in this book deal with saving children and women from the scourge of international terrorism. Terrorism promoting nations like Pakistan or leaders of terrorist groups, may dismiss such killings of children as collateral damage. Hardened criminals and criminality promoting State—Pakistan, cannot hear the cry of children globally. For instance on 27 January 1998 Pakistani sponsored terrorists, killed 25 men, women and children of two families from Kashmiri Pandits. Only survivor–Vinod Dhar (14 then) cried loudly, "Where should I go now?."

The UNSC had highlighted the global need to save children from terrorists: It aims to control mercilessly killing innocent children and recruiting them as terrorists at young age. Articles refer to Pakistan's *Lashkar-e-Taiba* training 80,000 young children for jihadi terrorism. However, it is obvious that UN efforts to save children stuck by double standard followed by the US—only surviving super power, had only limited impact. This is illustrated by examples of innocent children being killed in American bombing indiscriminately to punish Osama Bin Laden on his suspected hideouts to punish him for terrorist bombings of American Embassies in Nairobi and Dar-es-Salaam. Can other nations like India retaliate by attacking sources of terror attacks? George Fernandes, the then Defence Minister had asked: "Why is it that Americans keep quiet when other countries are affected by terrorism, but apply a different set of rules when they are at the receiving end?"

Indian fight against terrorism had a setback when an Indian Airlines flight IC 814 was hijacked by Pakistani terrorists, to gain freedom to imprisoned anti-Indian terrorism–brains, like Maulana Massood Ahzar and General Secretary of Harkat-Ul Mujahideen (HUM), Mushtaq Ahmed Zaqar both Pakistanis and Omar Sayeed Sheikh, a British national-put in prison by Indian government in 1999, in exchange for safe return of 159 passengers and crew. Appeal of PM Vajpayee to the US to declare Pakistan as terrorism-promoting state was disapproved by the author since the act is based on the US domestic law. The need was to mobilise the UN on the matter as US might be tempted to use its domestic law to interfere in Indian protection of human rights as argued in "Pakistan as a terrorist State" (*Free Press Journal*, 12/1/2000).

Another article, "Pledge to commit" (*Mid-Day*18/1/2000), seeks to highlight the Indian policy paralysis on terrorism and to suggest making it the last and final occasion when India is pushed to release hardcore terrorists captured at the cost of several innocent lives. The incident of hijack brought out two obvious failures: of a) airline security and b) intelligence machinery. Slackness of airline security is narrated by personal experience of my boarding AI flight 128 from Chicago on 24 December 1999. Plenty of intelligence warning was available in the public domain for discerning agents of RAW. AQ had warned that it would target India soon after increased cooperation between the US and India was announced by counter-terrorism experts. Since the US was a target as well, it had made several moves to warn the general public. But the Indian inaction has gone unexplained.

"Divide and Rule" (*Mid-Day*, 29/4/2000) focuses on changing scenario in the J& K with Dr Farook Abdulla as CM and Shri L.K. Advani as the Home Minister in the Federal Government. Serious objections are raised to Mr Advani describing Hurriyat as an Indian dissident group. Isn't it that dissident group members advocating merger of J & K with Pakistan and working for Pakistan in India cannot be Indians? During March 2000 and soon after Bill Clinton's historic visit to India there was a plan floated by Kashmir Study Group to divide J&K on religious lines. This needed to be opposed, the article argues on two grounds: One using terror, separatists have made 3.5 lakh Kashmiri Pandits, IDPs. The process is continued by terrorists under the instructions of their masters by attacking Sikhs in the village Chattisinghpora. The Sikh population in the Kashmir valley of 35000 had come down because of Sikh migration. Second, any further reorganisation of states within the Indian Union will seriously affect the mosaic of India. In this context, author extends support to Dr Abdulla when he said: "Any such move (opening the settled issue) will not only create one Bosnia but many Bosnias in J&K as well"

Then comes a major turning point in the US approach to international terrorism after the 9/11 attack on the symbols of US military might and economic power as represented by the Pentagon (Washington, DC) and the World Trade Centre (New York), respectively. Until then, the US attitude was one of safety of American main land well-protected by Atlantic Ocean on the East coast and Pacific Ocean on the West. In "War on terrorism: impact on India"(*FPJ*, 19/10/ 2001). I anticipated the probable changes in the Taliban-ruled Afghanistan after US began its war against Afghanistan on 7 October 2001 because it refused to hand over Osama Bin Laden then hiding in that country. Taliban rule for the first time had made Afghanistan a client-state of Pakistan. Hence, Musharraf then ruling Pakistan, was able to promote terrorism training camps in Afghanistan, in addition to such camps in PoK. I had then advocated that along with extending support to the US in its war against Taliban in Afghanistan, if India attacks terror-training camps in PoK, it is not a violation of Pakistan's territorial integrity, since the entire J & K had joined India in 1947.

"What is Central: Kashmir or American Interest?" (*FPJ*, 30/10/ 2001), takes the argument further by referring to Musharraf's formulation that "Kashmir remains at the heart of Pakistan–India tension." After the change of President in the White house, with Republican George W. Bush had sent his secretary of state, General Colin Powell to Pakistan and India. General Powell agreeing to the centrality of Kashmir in maintaining good relations between the two neighbours clearly indicated that "issues must be resolved through peaceful, political and diplomatic means and not through violence and force." While the US was interested in punishing Bin Laden for an AQ attack on the US, it was reminded by India that AQ bases elsewhere like Pakistan and PoK could rise to hit the US interests again!

But Indian political leadership was found wanting. Hence the next article "Why do our politicians lack will to fight terrorism?" (*Free Press Journal*, 21/12/2001), in the immediate background provided by the 13 December 2001 terrorist attacks on Indian Parliament—so soon after October 2001 attack on J & K Legislative Assembly, Srinagar, as an attack on Indian Democracy by terrorists controlled by Pakistan's dictatorship. But it is a testing of the Indian will power by a nuclear armed Pakistan. India failed to draw a lesson from the US attack on Taliban-ruled Afghanistan to attack terror bases in PoK. Pakistan's terror was extended the nuclear umbrella and India was unwilling to breach it by an attack on terror camps in PoK. If Pakistan goes on suicidal path of using nuclear weapons, in second strike India could have flattened Karachi and Islamabad. But that demanded a national will to get rid of Pakistan promoted terrorism in Kashmir just as India was able to get terror banished from Punjab under the Chief Minister, Beant Singh and KPS Gill as the Police Chief.

"Pakistan sponsored terrorism and China" (*Free Press Journal*, 1/1/2002) focussed on the issue of China's non-cooperation controlling Pakistan sponsored terror. Then, for the first time India and China had set up a joint consultation mechanism on terrorism in October 2001. Yet, China always played a dual game. While arguing with India that UN is the right forum to end the scourge of global terrorism, China was not willing to help India in fighting Pakistan sponsored terrorism in South Asia in the background of Pakistan-sponsored attack on Indian Parliament in December 2001. It is now a set pattern that whenever there is a crisis, Pakistan goes to Beijing for advice and support. When the intrusion of terrorists in Kargil came into open, Musharraf–Jiang Zemin summit took place in Beijing. It related the Kargil conflict to Kashmir as the "core issue" responsible for Pakistan-India and regional tensions!

Even today India is extremely concerned with the attitude of non-cooperation of China in controlling Pakistan-sponsored terrorism in India. Prime Minister Narendra Modi expressed India's anguish and concern at China's refusal to support India in getting custody of Lakhvi declared as a terrorist by the UNSC. This was followed by similar Indian efforts against Maulana Masood Azhar after the Pathankot attack of January 2016.

How did the US view Pakistan promoted terror is the content of the article on "American moment of decision on terrorism" (*Free Press Journal*, 25/2/2002). President George W. Bush was keen to improve relations with India. In his State of the Union message to Congress, he not only equated India in importance with Russia and China but described relations with India as unparalleled in the history of Indo-US relations so far. But on the problem of Pakistan sponsored terrorism, US duality of approach was still obvious. President Bush while openly praising Pakistani co-operation in fighting international terrorism, the US was only using private pressure (so it said) on Pakistan, not to promote Islamic Jihadi terrorism against India! Another weapon the US was slowly learning to use was its huge economic and military aid package to bring about a friendly change in Pakistan's attitude towards promotion of terrorism. During February 2002 visit of Musharraf to Washington DC, though he was pressing to retire $3 billion debt, US agreed to do so only $1 billion. US had also persuaded General Musharraf to deliver a national address on 12 January 2002 pushing down the idea to develop Pakistan "as a modern, moderate state"

In the background of US suffering 9/11 terror and Pakistan inflicting such humiliating acts of terror like October 2001 attack on Srinagar Legislative Assembly and attack on Indian Parliament in December 2001, "Evolving a strategy against cross-border Terrorism" (*Free Press Journal*, 19/3/2002) lays down six guidelines for India-US Co-operation in the broad field: fight against International terrorism.

Turning attention to domestic terror with international ramifications in "Godhra terrorism: Is it Political or Communal?" (*Free Press Journal*, 6/4/2002), I have focussed on three possibilities: First, Congress aiming to destabilise Gujarat ruled by the BJP, second, Pakistan's ISI, to divert attention from emerging increasing clarity on its role in promoting cross-border terror, and third a possible role of the disgruntled elements within the BJP to discredit Chief Minister Modi. But failure of IB in not being able to predict either the Godhra attack or the post-Godhra riots was a glaring fact that the administration needed to improve.

Despite Pakistan promoting cross-border terrorism, India is interested in a stable democratic, modern Pakistan. But "Criminals in India are favoured guests of Musharraf" (*Free Press Journal*, 19/4/2002), highlights Musharraf's continued commitment to promotion of cross border terrorism and internal domestic terror in India. To subserve the latter motive, declared criminals are sheltered in Pakistan like Dawood Ibrahim and his henchmen, on whom it has conferred its citizenship. In a lighter vein after citing an American example of pre-civil war era, I have said "India can offer to Musharraf to transfer all our criminals for the safe custody of Pakistan!" But, he has been selective, preferring those who had ISI links and backing.

"Ramifications of violence on Indo-Pak relations" (*Free Press Journal*, 23/4/2002), refers to distortions in presenting 1992 post-Babri riots. Thus many Muslims abroad thought that in those riots only Muslims were killed though many Hindus also lost their lives. A scholar from Quaid-I Azam University, Islamabad lamented that policy of Hindutva wants to tolerate no other minority. "They are killing Muslims in Gujarat, burning churches and Sikhs are not safe in India." But if so, they clearly forget that the Muslim population would not have grown from a mere seven percent in 1947 to around 12 per cent in 1990s. On the other hand, non-Muslims constituted 14.1 per cent of Pakistan population in 1951; were reduced by Pakistan to 2 per cent in 1990s. Author blames Congress policy of 'Peculiar Secularism' under which it is open to treating Muslims as the vote bank, while branding the BJP as a communal party.

"Will the US fight India's war against Terrorism?"(*Free Press Journal*, 1/6/2002), was provoked by 4 May 2002 attacks in Jammu on women and children raising the war clouds in India-Pak relations. Though by 2002 Americans had come to accept the fact that Pakistan is the epicentre of global terrorism; Frank Pallone, a Pro-India Congressman then had said that Pakistan globally fights terrorism, while locally promoting it. But as of then, US president was not interested in Indian cause of ending Pakistan promoted terrorism. His sole interest in 2002 was to capture Osama Bin Laden then hiding in Pakistan with the help of General Musharraf. Musharraf was using hiding Osama to get continued Military and economic aid from the Bush administration. Musharraf on the other hand was very vocal in publicly promising that Pak occupied territories are not used to promote terror against India and was interested in discussing all issues including Kashmir dispute. India was placed in peculiar dilemma whether to act against PoK terror camps or exercise "restraint" as then advised by the US.

Has Pakistan become a responsible state after it acquired nuclear weapons? Not in the least, with nuclear weapons, it thinks it has been conferred immunity from any punitive action by India or the UN. Its Ambassador to the UN, Munir Akram, in June 2002 on the very second day of presenting his credentials, stated that his country will not hesitate to use the nuclear weapons, if India tries to cross Pakistani borders in pursuit of terrorists anywhere in Pakistan. The article, "Different options to end Pak-sponsored terrorism" (*Free Press Journal*, 7/6/2002), discusses options available under the nuclear status of Pakistan. This is also in the background of Indian commitment not to be the first to use nuclear weapons. Under her commitment to No First Use (NFU), India will only use nuclear weapons massively as weapons of self-defence, in second strike.

Under these circumstances, the author indicates surgical strike to destroy all terrorist camps in PoK as one option. This should be welcomed by Musharraf as he has announced to make Pakistan "a moderate state." Second, the US and EU could threaten to use economic sanctions; and third, in the larger interest of the South Asia, US could take up the responsibility to bomb the terror camps to make Pakistan a democratic, secular Republic as well.

"Time to pursue uniform policy against international Terrorism" (*Free Press Journal*, 5/7/2002), focuses on continued use of double yardstick by American administration on the issue of terrorism. In mid-2002, George Bush was blunt in telling Palestinian people to elect new leaders and "not to compromise by terror." I raised the issue: Will Bush apply the same yardstick to General Musharraf in Pakistan? Pakistan was promoting terrorism in J & K as well as in other parts of India. Musharraf, on the other hand, in July 2002 had said, that he had informed "President Bush nothing is happening across the line of control. This is the assurance I have given. I am not going to give you an assurance that for years nothing will happen." If Pakistan continues to promote cross border terrorism, some years hence, it may be difficult to get a Pakistan "uncompromised by terror!"

"Post-election Kashmir Scenario: Implications for Indian foreign relations" (*Free Press Journal*, 30/10/2002), discusses political scenario post-2002 elections in Jammu & Kashmir. The turnout was 44% on the face of gun-culture promoted by Musharraf's Pakistan and his agents in J & K, All Party Hurriyat Conference (APHC). Musharraf had described the elections as a farce in UNGA. It was countered by PM Vajpayee by drawing global attention to the fact that those words do not go well with Musharraf, who had to "adjust voting and counting procedure" to win a referendum to continue in power by legitimising it to become President after usurping power as the Military General in 1999! Pakistan has justified its promotion of terror in J & K on the ground of its claim for the state. I raised the question: Can the issue be resolved by converting cease-fire line into the international border between the two?

In the background of unabated terror attacks against India, the 24 September 2002 attack on Akshardham temple in Gandhinagar, Indian secularists see only the domestic roots of communalism created by jihadi terrorists in India. But it has international origin. The US succeeded in driving the Russians out of Afghanistan by turning what was actually their war against suspected expansion of communism in Afghanistan. It was religious war-*Jihad*. It is this which is the root cause of South Asian communalism. It is observed: "This phenomenon has given rise to overt linkages between global ethno-religious identity and tensions.... and domestic communal disharmony....." Pakistan promoted terrorism is aimed at creating a wedge between "Hindus and Muslims within the country." Author suggests, in "UN must make all nations pursue secularism" (*Free Press Journal,* 22/11/2002), by borrowing Bill Clinton's noble thought from his address to the Joint Session of Indian parliament that it is "difficult to be a democracy bordered by nations whose governments reject democracy." Isn't it necessary, hence, for the UN to make all nations pursue secularism? Isn't it a great challenge to India to be a secular state, when surrounded by states swearing by one or the other religion?

"Islamic Pakistan posing a greater threat to the world" (*Free Press Journal*, 14/12/2002), takes up the issue of nuclear Thieves-Market promoted by Pakistan under Musharraf by supplying technology to North Korea to build a nuclear arsenal" and in return its providing missile technology to Pakistan that can reach "every strategic site in India." Zia used Islam to legitimise his overthrow of democratically elected Zulfikar Ali Bhutto government in 1978; Musharraf promising to build a "modern and moderate" Islamic state, in reality promoted religious strife in India which reverberated in Pakistan. The article anticipated, at the end of 2002, that "international Islamic terrorists will have free play in Pakistan Politics." Pakistan-Taliban controlled terror attacks in Pakistan since 2006, culminated in the December 2014 attack on Military School in Peshawar. It shows Islam imposed tragedies on Pakistan.

Author draws a comparison between Indian Kashmiris and Sri Lankan Tamils in the next article "What can Indian Kashmiris learn from Sri Lankan Tamils" (*Free Press Journal,* 17/12/2002). After prolonged negotiations under what was called Oslo Talks between Norwegian peace makers, LTTE and the Sri Lankan Government, LTTE had agreed for a federating unit-status to Tamils in the 'Sri Lankan Federation' rather than insisting independence. Indian Kashmiris could strengthen federal structure as it is not a new concept for India. However, there were two important developments globally, that are relevant even today in the case of Kashmiri separatists. One is the fact that Irish Republic Army (IRA) that was fighting for merger of Ulster as a Catholic majority area with Ireland from England, sued in September 2002 to remain within England. It happened largely because, under European pressure, the US stopped sources of funding to the IRA. In the like manner, LTTE was also under financial strain, there is a lesson to the Government of India: all these years, heaven knows why, Hurriyat leaders–in reality agents of Pakistan—were funded by Pakistan in J & K, were also funded by India, though they were political spokespersons for Pakistani cause! Cut off all external funding and see the change emerging.

"US must act against Pak, the real epicentre of global terrorism" (*Free Press Journal,* 11/3/2003), continues to argue that unless the US, which has Pakistan as its partner in the US-led war against international terrorism, cannot be won as it is simultaneously involved in funding, protecting, promoting and sheltering terrorists who act globally and regionally. The fact of provocation then in writing the article was the fact that early in 2003, Khalid Mohammad the third in command in AQ, after Osama and Ayman al-Zawahiri was arrested in Pakistan. He was believed to be responsible for WTC bombing in 1993, 1998 bombing of US embassies and attack on USS Cole in Yemen in 2000.

PM, Vajpayee was mildly critical of the Bush administration when he said in Lok Sabha that President Bush has his own priorities in fighting global terrorism. But it is true that international opinion on Indian problems with Pakistan promoted terrorism is shaped by domestic attitude to the subject. Then, unfortunately barring the BJP, splinter parties in the Lok Sabha and the main opposition then, as it is now, is concerned with protecting its vote bank. Every party works to have a slice of Muslim vote-cake. Hence, the opposition was critical of government's possession and its use of strong law like TADA and its newer version POTA (Prevention of Terrorism Act). But sound advice to the US administration was given by Jessica Stein, Harvard Professor who had said in her book *The Ultimate Terrorist* that by withdrawing from Afghanistan after the end of the Cold War, the US allowed Pakistan to become the *Jihadi* University for the entire world. But now if the US fails to get at the real epicentre of terrorism, Pakistan might replace Afghanistan as its main concern. Better US goes after the epicentre rather than acting against periphery.

American neglect of terrorism and Indian weakness in tackling it emboldened the Terror University to take its terror industry to hinterland of India after Punjab, J & K and Delhi. Its expansion further is discussed in "Terrorism at our doors-how do we counter the threat?" (*Free Press Journal*, 19/3/2003).Though Mumbai experienced impact of terror on 12 March 1993, the 13 March 2003 serial bomb explosions in the Central and Western Railway trains literally brought it to every Mumbaikar's doorsteps. The article also argues that political parties need to look after public good rather than oppose stern action just because terrorist attacks are carried out by Muslims. Congress used stern action against Sikh terrorism as it had already lost political base to Akali political parties, but it was too hesitant to act against Muslims!

The duality of approach by the US and Pakistan to international terrorism comes out clearly in "Pakistan must learn to dictate to terrorists: Sooner the better" (*Free Press Journal*, 20/5/2003). President

George W. Bush and his Secretary of State introduced conditionality for enabling Palestine to full-statehood when they said: Disarm terrorists to promote peace in the Middle East. What about South Asia? Pakistan performed its role as a US partner against international terrorism by the right hand while promoting it elsewhere by using its left hand! How can Pakistan be an ally in its war against Al Qaeda while at the same time promote cross-border terrorism against India with whom the US desired increased economic co-operation?

In this background part–time National Security Adviser of Vajpayee made a suggestion of trilateral co-operation between India-US and Israel in Washington DC in early in 2003. Indian Muslim voices were quick in opposing India cooperating with Israel! Can Muslim intellectuals be requested to make a direct appeal to their counterparts in Pakistan to prevail upon the latter to learn the evil influence of terrorism? Then Foreign Minister of Pakistan Khurshid Mohammad Kasuri had admitted that Pakistan had influence with terrorists crossing Pakistan-India borders. But he said: "When a suicide bomber goes on a Pakistani martyrdom mission, he does not take permission from anyone." Mr Kasuri, neither will they take permission from ISI, whenever they attack targets within Pakistan! Now there are more Pakistani suicide bomb attacks inside Pakistan than in Afghanistan or India.

I attended a seminar in Islamabad organised by the Institute of Regional Studies in 2003. I traced the origin of terrorism in South Asia to the Americans equating their war to drive out Soviets from Afghanistan to a religious war—an Islamic *jihad*. This has given fillip to religious identity in the region. Yet, "What do people in Islamabad speak about Kashmir Issue?" (*Free Press Journal*, 18/6/2003), states that by and large, Pakistanis speak only of state terror by India in, what they call India held Kashmir! In discussion with knowledgeable people, it was clear that they wish to settle the problem peacefully. We were of the opinion that turning LOC into the international border was one option that has a better chance to succeed.

"Weed out anti-national elements: Muslims must help" (*Free Press Journal*, 30/8/2003), draws attention to spreading of Pakistan promoted terrorism beyond J & K, in Indian cities like Delhi or Mumbai. Under global pressure to end cross-border terrorism, Pakistan, switched to use terrorist sleeper-cells created within the local population. Musharraf-Kasuri Combo had said that just as they cannot control birds flying from across the border into India, they cannot and do not control every terrorist entering into India. Yet Musharraf did admit in August 2003 that "freelance elements" were operating and had promised to keep a watch on them. But now that local Muslim boys are trained, financed and allowed to freely operate inside India as in the case of IM (Indian Mujahidin) or SIMI (Students Islamic Movement of India), India cannot blame Pakistan! Hence, the appeal to Indian's Muslims to act against "misguided boys" under the Congress and United Front regimes. But was it effective, when the then CM, Sushil Kumar Shinde and Deputy CM, Chagan Bhujbal in Maharashtra were alluding to Gujarat riots as the cause of terror surfacing in Mumbai?

Globally Israel can be considered as a Nation, worst affected by terrorism. It has experienced terrorism since its birth in 1948. "A strategic triangle in the offing: War against terrorism" (*Free Press Journal,* 19/9/2003), discusses what we can learn and that includes not only 'dos' but 'don'ts' in the background of first ever visit by an Israeli PM, Ariel Sharon. Among the many areas two nations co-operate one is: Israel's willingness to train Indian personnel in the fight against terrorism. Counter-terrorism agreement was signed during the visit. Strategic triangle here refers to a possible trilateral co-operation against terrorism between India, Israel and the US.

However, the article also draws how certain sections in India consider Sharon a *persona non-grata* for his stern action against terrorism. These Indian Muslims and 'peculiar secularists' opposed any co-operation between India and Israel on the subject of terrorism; they voiced their opposition to first-ever-state visit to India by the then Israeli PM, Ariel Sharon, because his hands are reddened by Palestinian blood. But these very people advocated negotiations on terrorism and visit of Musharraf to Agra on 15 July 2001, though his hands too were more reddened with Indian blood by spreading tentacles of terrorists beyond J & K.

"Cross-border Terrorism now localised: Will it again be internationalised?" (*Free Press Journal*, 28/4/2004) is a perspective that focuses on Indian PM Vajpayee and General Musharraf's joint–statement on 4 January 2004 in Islamabad soon after Pakistan made a commitment that "it will not permit any territory under Pakistan's control to be used to support terrorism against India in any manner." As a matter of fact, it was a slow development under the US prodding; first in January 2002 Musharraf in his address to the nation said that cross-border terrorism will end and subsequently in June 2002, he had promised to US Deputy Secretary of State, Richard Armitage that cross border terror and training camps will be ended! Peace remained fragile, but terrorist attacks were localised and domesticated!

In May 2004 the Congress-led United Progressive Alliance (UPA) assumed power at Delhi. But Pakistan continued to be a favourite of the US and was given the status as Non-NATO ally. Terrorism had begun in India under the Congress rule and there was the fear of once again its turning international. In the meanwhile, soon after National Elections, Congress-men proposed Sonia Gandhi to be the PM but she humbly declined. Rajiv Gandhi had fought 1984 general elections on the ground of threat to national security soon after the assassination of Mrs Gandhi. But his successors in the UPA appeared to subordinate fight against terrorism to political interests of the party in power. "Don't play politics with National Security: UPA soft on Terrorism?" (*Free Press Journal*, 8/6/2004), focuses on this issue. There was the demand for abrogating POTA on the ground of its misuse; remedy to prevent misuse is naturally to plug legally such opportunities rather than the withdrawal of POTA.

"Terrorism, a non-issue to Pakistanis and their US supporters" (*Free Press Journal*, 15/8/2005), that is something I learnt in Washington, DC in July 2005 at the Fifth international Peace Conference organised by Kashmir American Council (KAC), which was co-sponsored by Association of Humanitarian Lawyers. KAC is the brain child of Dr Ghulam Nabi Fai. Its announced theme was the "The Kashmir Dispute and Building a peaceful South Asia." In my own presentation, I placed greatest emphasis on elimination of Cross-border terrorism as a pre-requisite for building peaceful South Asia. The Washington Conference, in reality, had one theme: of India-bashing. It was natural as a majority were, ministers and leaders from Pakistan, Pakistan Occupied Kashmir and Pro-Pakistan Kashmiris living overseas. Mine was the lone voice pointing out Pakistan's use of terror to grab Kashmir. Pakistan calls its engineered violence in J&K as "Kashmir Freedom Struggle!" Musharraf, however, bemoaned that it is not accepted by anyone outside Pakistan.

Musharraf and his supporters in India have never lamented the fact that 35,000 Kashmiri Pandits were forced out of their homes but cry over Indian violation of human rights in J & K. I continued with the above theme in "Return to the Valley" (*Indian Express*, 16/9/2005), by stating that International Conference on Kashmir at Washington, DC was on violation of human rights by terrorists. While making a big demonstration at Indian violation of human rights to protect unarmed civilians from harm, no one talked about violations of human rights of Pandits in J&K. Mufti Mohammad Sayeed who had become CM of Kashmir had raised a rhetorical question: "The Pandits were a miniscule minority of 2 per cent of the population and if we can't rehabilitate them, then what meaning does our secularism or *Kashmiriyat* have"? The article makes the plea to settle the Pandits in their old habitats and not in any newly created colony.

Plea for enabling Kashmiri Pandits to return to their original homes was reiterated with more supporting evidence in "Why new colonies for Pandits? Let them go back to their old homes" (*Free Press Journal*, 20/9/2005). Going back to the Conference organised by KAC, first it came out according to a Belgium based international lawyer at the Conference, under humanitarian law developed by the UN, indigenous people have a right to take up the arms against the occupying people! My query for exact reference to source was not answered by him. Though the existence of such a law is a doubtful proposition, Kashmiri Pandits are genuinely indigenous people and not necessarily Kashmiri Muslims alone, whom the Barrister was referring to. Second, Lara Rise, then Senator in Norwegian Parliament said at the Conference that Professor Bhatt, and then Hurriyat chief told him that his outfit stood for pluralistic society. Both these facts should help J & K to see that not only Kashmiri Pandits return but are also well settled in their respective homes.

In any democratic governance the crucial factor is timely and adequate co-ordination of policy on terrorism. "What Maniyappan's murder told us" (*Indian Express*, 5/12/2005), tells us that there is crucial lack of co-ordination between agencies handling national security. Ramankutty Maniyappan, an engineer of Border Road Organisation, was killed by terrorists of Afghan Taliban in November 2005. But NSA's public statement had to be publically corrected by the then Defence Minister, Pranab Mukherjee, placing the UPA government in bad light.

"Stop bragging, bring to book blast culprits" (*Free Press Journal*, 19/8/2006), makes a case for National Security Adviser (NSA)-then, M.K. Narayanan to follow early traditions of anonymity, when NSAs in the US were not making a public statement one day and changing it next day. Article draws a comparison between Indian failures in concluding investigations, trial and punishment early of terrorists involved in 1993 bomb blasts in Mumbai (judgement came only in 2015),with speedy investigation and punishment in 9/11/2001 by the US. British, US ally in war against terror, on 10 August 2006 discovered a plan by global terrorists–Al Qaeda to blow up flights to US in mid-Atlantic after the planes have taken off from the Heathrow Airport. They had a list of 24 suspects. Soon after that the first thing the British Government did was to freeze their funds. Nothing of the kind was done on the 7/11 train bombing case in Mumbai! Investigations in India are hampered also by political interference. After 7/11 train blasts, Muslim MPs complained of terror against innocent Muslims!

"Don't give in to blackmail" (*Hindustan Times* 16/10/2006), takes a critical look at the surprising facts of the then CM, Ghulam Nabi Azad and Mehbooba Mufti, president of Progressive Democratic Party (PDP) of J & K pleading for clemency for Afzal Guru for masterminding Parliament attack of 13 December 2001. It recalls golden words spoken by PM, Narasimha Rao from the ramparts of the Red Fort on 15 August 1993: "Do they [terrorists] mean that those who have been victims of their bullets have no human rights? Do only terrorists have human rights? They have a right to kill others and they have human rights so that nobody should kill them! This is a warped logic beyond comprehension and we are not prepared to accept it." There is the need for immediate end to looking at the religion, caste, language or region of the convict in the administration of criminal justice. Let us not make administration of justice be governed by these factors to protect democracy and promote integrity of the nation.

General Musharraf had the longest tenure as the ruler of Pakistan at the crucial phase that was graduating in the use, conduct and manoeuvres of terrorists and terrorism in his country. "Musharraf warns West, clings on to Al-Qaeda and Taliban" (*Free Press Journal*, 16/10/2006), points out his bragging that it is the ISI co-operation that enabled the US to win the war against the Soviet Union in the Afghanistan. He also wanted to change his image that of a pro-west dictator. To that end, he entered into an agreement with Al Qaeda and Taliban ceding authority to them over North Waziristan, where foreign terrorists were enjoying right of free movement without firing on or disturbing life of Pakistanis! He thought it would help him to win the 2007 elections as a Civilian!

Indian governments have from time to time claimed non-involvement of Indian Muslims in the acts of international terrorism. It was a shocking incident that a Bengaluru-born highly educated Ph.D. in fluid dynamics, Kafeel Ahmed was arrested for the failed terror attack at Glasgow airport in Britain. Two of his cousins–both medical doctors- Mohamed Haneef and Sabeel Ahmed were detained for questioning, the former in Australia and the latter in London. It broke the myth of non-involvement of Indian Muslims in international terrorism at a time when a debate was going on in India on the question whether 'Indian Muslims' or 'Muslim Indians' was correct phrase to be used! "Alleged terror link of few Muslims: All Indians suffer" (*Free Press Journal*, 24/7/2007), highlights above development of that time in July 2007.

"Musharraf under fire from moderates too" (*Free Press Journal*, 11/8/2007), highlights the predicament of Pakistan's military ruler in 2007. His American support was waning, despite his military action in July to flush out foreign terrorists of Al Qaeda holed in Lal (Red) Masjid on pressure from President Bush. Then Musharraf made the biggest mistake of his life in sacking the Chief Justice of the Supreme Court, Iftikar Ahmed that not only alienated lawyers in the country but moderates too. Prior to Musharraf's usurpation of power in Pakistan in October 1999, Islamic fundamentalists constituted less than five percent. His support and use of Islamic terrorists against India left him with Islamic terrorist throughout his country!

Provocation to write "Why Naxals alone? Islamic terror is equally a security threat" (*Free Press Journal*, 27/2/2008), was a query to the then PM, Manmohan Singh on his observation that internal security threat posed by the Naxals is the greatest national security threat faced by the nation. The UPA Government's single important policy has been to enlarge its minority vote bank. Creation of Department for Minority Affairs at the Centre and in states has promoted religious divisiveness in the country. Pakistan-promoted Islamic terror, in different phases since 1984, if we say, has practically moved all over India, it is not an exaggeration. Every state, every village, town and city today has sleeper cells—as demonstrated by the emergence of Bhatkal, a small temple town of the same name. The internal groups act on various grounds as agents of their external political masters. No internal terrorist group, whether Naxals or Pak or domestic Indian terrorists, can survive without external support of two permanent adversaries of India—Pakistan and China!

There is a strong case to declare Pakistan as a 'terrorism promoting state' or place it in the US terror watch list. As a matter of fact, President George T.W. Bush, before he left the presidency after serving in the White House for one term (1989-1993), had placed Pakistan on the terror watch list. However, President Bill Clinton removed it under the charming influence of Benazir Bhutto, during her brief stint as a democratically elected PM. "Pak deserves being placed on terror list" (*Free Press Journal*, 24/5/2010), made a case once again in May 2010 to place it back in the list. The greatest irony of international politics is: Pakistan is the Terrorism University—home for thousands of home-grown and foreign terror groups, yet is strategically an important partner of the US in its war against international terrorism! Can Pakistan state that terrorists aren't there? Musharraf told American officials and Presidents, whenever he was pressurised to do more to control terrorism emanating from Pakistan and Pak-controlled territory, he asked them to enquire with the CIA to find out the quantum of dollars given to Pakistan by it as prize money for capturing the terrorists!

In the next article, "Ghulam Nabi Fai that I knew" (*Free Press Journal Weekend* 31/7/2011), I return to Dr Ghulam Nabi Fai, as he was arrested on 18 July 2011 by American Federal Bureau of Investigation (FBI) on the ground as an American citizen he was working as an "unregistered lobbyist" for the Pakistan government to influence US government and general public in favour of Kashmir's self-determination. He is supposed to have received 4 million dollars from Pakistan's ISI. I had the unique opportunity to get into the largest lobbyist in favour of Kashmir's self-determination, when I attended International Kashmir Peace Conference in Washington DC in July 2005 convened by him. It was a great honour, in retrospect, to be speaking at the conference on non-viability of self determination to Kashmir, where with the exception of Dr Subramanyan Swamy and this author, everyone else was drawn globally, spoke on inevitability of 'self determination' for J&K!

"Terror of 13/7: Lessons to be learnt", (*One India One People (OIOP)*, August 2011), analyses terror attacks that took place in commercially busiest areas of Mumbai on 13/7/2011 in which 20 were killed and 131 innocent Mumbaikars were injured. An established pattern of the UPA government's responses to such acts is to promise strong action against terror attacks and literally wait till the next one. The Home Minister, P. Chidambaram visiting Mumbai described the terror attacks "coordinated" one as though uncoordinated would have seen a lesser number of casualties! PM Manmohan Singh spoke of his determination to see that "perpetrators of the Mumbai bomb blasts shall be pursued relentlessly and brought to justice quickly." UPA government having linked dialogue to normalise relations soon after 26/11 Mumbai attacks, Prime Minister delinked connectivity between terrorism and dialogue during *Sharm-el-Sheikh* nonalignment summit in July 2009. Hence, the then Foreign Minister, S.M. Krishna said, despite terrorist attacks, dialogue will continue! By 2011 PM Manmohan Singh had made visiting Pakistan to normalise India-Pakistan bilateral relations as his mission before completing his second term! By then the general public had one prominent question: If US could prevent attacks on its homeland, why can't India?

"Delhi Terror of 7/9, *(Freedom First*, October 2011) deals with terror attacks near Delhi High Court soon after Mumbai attacks of

13/7. While it was beyond any doubt, that these attacks were orchestrated by ISI controlled terror groups, the then Indian PM was unwilling to name Pakistan; he said "It is a cowardly act. We will deal with it. It is a long war. We will not succumb." Pakistan's civilian democratic facade had by then also started a new alibi for their in-action: Pakistan too is a victim of terror attacks. Article makes a plea that terror attacks be considered as an attack on India and Federal government act with a law similar to TADA or POTA; if these acronyms offend political concerns of opposition, let new law be called as "Nation Protection Act" as after 9/11 the US called their law "Patriotic Act."

In the absence of a strong federal government, as it happened during UPA II's last three years, Indian state governments increased their parochial approach towards those facing death sentences confirmed by the Supreme Court. It is that issue, which is dealt with in "Clemency for terrorists-undesirable in every way" (*One India One People*, December 2011). Such demands were raised by Tamil Nadu state government with regard to killers of former PM Rajiv Gandhi, facing death sentence were all Tamils. Similar regionally motivated pleas to save the life of Devinder Pal Singh Bhullar were made in Punjab and Afzal Guru convicted for Parliament attack on 13 December 2001. If the law makers and the people of different states say: "The man you want to send to gallows may be a terrorist; he is our man, hence deserves to live," is an invitation to the disintegration of the Indian Union. The article makes a suggestion to disqualify such advocates from contesting elections in the country.

The Supreme Court had upheld death sentence awarded to lone Pakistan terrorist—Ajmal Kasab captured by the extraordinary bravery shown by Police Constable Tukaram Ombale. He was finally executed in November 2012 after four years of hearings, appeals, clemency pleas. Pakistanis were troubled! That was publically expressed by Imran Khan as a politician; he asked for a "tit for tat" to take revenge by hanging Pakistan held Indian prisoner-Sarbjit Singh! The article on "Ajmal Kasab and Imran Khan" (*One India One People*, January 2013), tries to inform Imran Khan how Sarbjit Singh's case is different from Ajmal Kasab, if he can understand, as hatred filled minds always advocate irrational ideas!

Terrorism has emerged as an international amoeba, constantly changing its shape and giving rise to new terrorist creatures under a new name. In early May 2014 Islamic State of Iraq and Syria (ISIS) became an additional terrorist group. It is truly Islamic, has no territorial boundaries to operate and proposes to bring back a Sunni Caliphate. "Inertia of ISIS will prove dear" (*Free Press Journal*, 6/11/2014), highlights how it is likely to come to India via Pakistan. It draws attention to growing attraction of ISIS to Indian youths as reflected in the first group of four men who went to fight side by side with ISIS. It concludes: "We must prepare to safeguard our country from this far more brutal terrorist group calling itself ISIS. Its brutalities overshadow even the crimes of the Pakistani Army like the beheading of Indian soldiers within India, or the ISI and their creation LeT promoted Mumbai attacks of November 26, 2008." Current head of NIA Alok Mittal has called it "biggest terrorist organisation" in India with seven to eight thousand members!

By December 2014 Pakistan's promotion of terrorism had come full circle to haunt it. It was almost in a situation that deserved the description of 'He who mounts a tiger cannot dismount it'. It will only devour him. On 18 December 2014 *Tehreek-e-Taliban* (TeT) or the Pakistani Taliban attacked the Army School in Peshawar in which 148 were killed of which 132 were school children whose life was cut short by terror attack. What was their crime? "Terror lessons Pak holds out" (*Free Press Journal*, 27/12/2014), not only highlights this aspect but also discusses lessons, if any, that India can learn from the stern actions actually taken or proposed to be taken by the Pakistani government led by Nawaz Sharif to control home-grown terrorism on the Pakistani soil!

Indians sympathise with the loss of Pakistani children's lives; several leaders led by the PM, Narendra Modi have extended their sympathies to the victims of terror attack. It was executed with a purpose, according to the spokesman of TeT, Mohammad Umar Khorsani, as "revenge" against government's acts of targeting their families in North Waziristan tribal region. Military men ought to "feel the pain", as he said. But the swiftness with which Pakistan acted against terror groups operating against Pakistan was worth emulating by India. Pakistani PM, Nawaz Sharif had said that there is no distinction as good terrorists and bad terrorists and vowed to end all acts of terror. But he, by his actions, continued to indicate that some terrorists are more equal than others by releasing on the very day of Pak Taliban attack, Zaki-ur Rehman Lakhvi second in command in planning and executing of Mumbai terrorist attacks 26/11! He was able to walk free on the streets of Lahore!

It indicated that Terror against India will continue. That was the case when Pakistan's Terrorist Army, since Musharraf had called terrorism as the first line of defence of Pakistan. Later, it was *Jaish-e-Mohammed* led by Maulana Masood Azhar released by the NDA government in December 1999 when his terrorists attacked Pathankot Air Base on 2 January 2016. "What use this bonhomie?" (*One India One People,* February 2016) examines the Pathankot terrorism emanating from Pakistan in the back drop of PM Modi trying to improve India-Pakistan relations by his dramatic visit to Lahore on 25 December 2015 on his return journey from Afghanistan. It was an act of personal diplomacy to greet Nawaz Sharif on his birthday and also wish his grand daughter on the day of her wedding. Pathankot attack in retrospect is an act of terrorist group executed by its protector and promoter in Pakistan–military and its instrument ISI to disapprove Nawaz Sharif's bonhomie with Modi. But it could have been anticipated as the attack came after dry-runs earlier in Gurdaspur in July 2015. Pakistan PM, Nawaz Sharif did promise action, but despite Indian co-operation in sharing information on the involvement of *Jaish-e-Mohammad*, Pak Military has created obstacles for Indian return visit to Islamabad.

With "Can Pakistan dismount the terror-tiger?" (*One India One People*, September 2016) as of now, conclusion is inevitable that terrorism will emerge as the ruling ideology of Pakistan. All hopes generated after gruesome attack on military School in Peshawar in December 2014 that Nawaz Sharif, PM and his Army General, Rahil Sharif, would work jointly to curb and eliminate all terror groups operating within Pakistan were belied after Pathankot airbase attack in India. On 8 August 2016 when 74 lawyers were brutally killed in Quetta by a group consisting of a faction of ISIS and Pakistan Taliban, so soon after Rajnath Singh, Indian Home Minister, at Islamabad appealing to Pakistan to stop using terror as an instrument of policy, has belied that hope even domestically in Pakistan. Why this attack? Terrorist group claimed that democracy is anti-Islamic and against Caliphate and lawyers are "considered as custodians of Pakistani democratic system."

Can we Indians draw our own the single most important lesson from this-Miscellany on Terrorism? If only political parties in the 1990s had treated terrorists as terrorists instead of "misguided youths," nation by now would have learnt not to treat anyone community as its 'vote bank.' Even now it is not too late!

1

India is not Fighting a War in Kashmir

(Times of India, Sunday Review 5-2-1995)

A comparison of Kashmir insurgency with Black Panther movement in America would have helped us to understand why we have failed to contain it.

Two recent developments in Jammu and Kashmir suggest that we are nearing success in our efforts to contain the insurgency, and Pakistan's proxy war there: first, the confirmation on January 12 by the home secretary that preparations to hold elections are continuing; and second, the news that villagers on the international border fought the terrorists and killed some of them.

Skeptics in India and abroad are likely to see the elections in J&K as yet another pipe-dream. A former J&K governor, Jagmohan, feels they would be untimely. Robin Raphel, US assistant secretary of state for South Asia, does not set much store by the poll. And an American journalist, Ethan Casey, has tried to compare India's effort to revive the political process in J&K to America's dream, during the Vietnam war, of winning the hearts and minds of the South Vietnamese.

However, South Vietnam was not an integral part of the US; it was not even a mandated territory. The US troops, sent there as President Johnson's advisors, turned the insurgency into an American war.

India is not fighting a war in Kashmir. Here, a purely domestic uprising has been turned into a low-intensity conflict by Pakistan through training, equipping, financing and encouraging cross-border terrorism in the name of Islam. Now, it has also started supplying the manpower. However, domestic support to insurgency seems to be declining, going by the news of villagers beating up militants.

As one who has studied American foreign policy for the last 30 years, I propose that the insurgency in Kashmir is more comparable to the American Black Panther movement in the late 60s and early 70s. Such a comparison will help us understand why we have failed to contain insurgency in Kashmir in five years, while the Black Panther movement was crushed in less than four years. It will also educate Indians, who see an American hand in our starting the electoral process in J & K, on how the Americans have dealt with insurgency in their own states.

The Black Panther movement was led by American Blacks converted to Islam demanding, among other things, a state of their own. Never very strong, the movement was sporadic in its activities. The Black Panthers were involved in bombing public buildings, arson, looting banks, hijacking, kidnapping and assassinations. The government suspected that they got material and moral support from Arab and North African countries, particularly Algeria, in addition to Marxist regimes in the Caribbean and elsewhere.

The Black Panther movement was viewed by the White House — particularly the Nixon administration — as one of the most serious domestic crisis around. In July 1970, the Huston Plan empowered the FBI to infiltrate the movement; many people were arrested on mere suspicion, many were shot dead under suspicious circumstances while some disappeared without any trace. As Nixon was eliminating Black Panthers, Panthers themselves "helped by killing each other as fast or faster than the police were killing them," in the words of one American commentator.

Having originated in the 60s when Lyndon Johnson was president, the Black Panthers were completely annihilated by 1974 under the Nixon administration, as part of a bi-partisan effort to nip Black Panthers' terrorism in the bud. In the protection of national integrity, there was no party politics.

In contrast to the American response to the Black Panther movement, the Indian government has always been more concerned about the political fallout of any move than about preserving national integrity. Hence, successive governments have failed to apply harsh measures to curb Kashmiri insurgency.

Kashmiri insurgency began in 1987, when the Congress was at the Centre. The insurgents become bold when a Kashmiri, Mufti Mohammed Sayyed, became the home minister in 1989. When the Congress returned to power at the centre in 1991, the problem had gone out of control.

India can draw important lessons from the American experience: first, it is not too late for India to treat insurgency in Kashmir as a national problem. The militants are unlikely to win an electoral battle, as they have not won the battle of bullets. The silent majority consisting of Shiaites, Buddhists, Dogras and Hindus will be able to throw up a political alternative by isolating terrorists.

However, India can successfully complete the political process only if political parties put national interests above their partisan interests. As of now there are only two forces: those of national unity and those representing national disintegration. Elections can be successfully held if all national political parties like the Congress, the BJP and the National Conference come together to fight seccessionist forces.

Second, civil liberties are for those who have been respecting the rights of other human beings. Terrorists surrender their rights the moment they take recourse to violence against civil society and the state. They are not 'misguided youths' as described by Governor General Krishna Rao. They are terrorist agents of Pakistan, Pakistanis from occupied Kashmir, Afghanistan and other Arab countries. There is no case for Pakistan to treat terrorists of another country as their freedom fighters. As Mr Picco, the UN assistant secretary general for political affairs, wrote, "Terrorism is a criminal manifestation of intolerance. Appeasement of intolerance has always bode ill for humanity." India has learnt it in the case of Sri Lanka. Pakistan will be forced to learn it if we treat terrorists in Kashmir as Nixon treated Black Panthers in the US.

Finally, if Indian policymakers hesitate to order harsh measures against the people in J&K, they should consider Nixon's words: "When the issue juxtaposes the lives of innocent citizens and the possible curtailment of personal liberties we all cherish, the answers are never easy." Nixon's actions provided an effective answer.

2

India's Kashmir Policy: All Rhetoric and no Action

(The Sunday Observer 10-6-1995)

The policies followed so far have not sent clear signals to the terrorists in Kashmir and their patron-promoters outside that India mean business when it proclaims its determination to safeguard its territorial integrity...

Each Independence Day since 1993 has seen fine rhetoric from Prime Minister P.V. Narasimha Rao on India's Kashmir policy. Speaking from the ramparts of the Red Fort in 1993 about Pakistan's promotion of terrorism in that unfortunate state, he said: 'Pakistan may do whatever it wants, but Kashmir is an inalienable part of India.'

On Independence Day 1994, Rao declared that 'if there is an unfinished task before India, it is to get Pakistan to vacate that part of Kashmir it continues to occupy'. The rhetoric then was heightened because just one day earlier, Pakistani Prime Minister Benazir Bhutto had described Kashmir as 'part of the unfinished agenda of Partition'.

On August 15 this year, Rao reiterated India's position that 'Kashmir is an inseparable part of India. He described Pakistan-Occupied Kashmir as being 'under forcible occupation'.

Is this rhetoric matched by even half as strong action? The answer is no. Of course, I do not suggest that India should have gone to war to recapture PoK. But the policies followed so far have not sent clear

signals to the terrorists in Kashmir and their patron-promoters outside that India means business when it proclaims its determination to safeguard its territorial integrity and crush terrorism.

The Hazratbal incident of 1993, the burning of Charar-e-Sharief, a secular symbol, in May and the ghastly murder of a Norwegian tourist, Hans Christian Ostro, by Al-Faran, all these are the fruits of a weak-kneed policy.

If the prime minister means to effectively handle the Kashmir crisis, he needs to take certain steps immediately. First, the government must have a clear perception of who it is dealing with: Pakistan's agents, trained, equipped and financed from abroad and including foreign mercenaries, are terrorists, plain and simple.

However, by and large the government fights shy of calling them terrorists. Only once in 1994, while proposing extension of President's rule in Jammu and Kashmir, did Home Minister S. B. Chavan say in the Lok Sabha that the government was dealing with 'terrorists, pure and simple'. They are not militants as referred to by Doordarshan, nor are they 'misguided youths' as Governor K. V. Krishna Rao referred to them during the Hazratbal crisis.

Even if there is a mix of all three, the secessionist movement today is largely in the hands of terrorists. They need to be tackled as such, with all the strong-arm methods necessary.

But the government let foreign mercenaries go scot-free after the Hazratbal crisis without exposing them to the international media. This gave credence to the propaganda that the government was only playing with public opinion by referring to the presence of foreign mercenaries.

Second, we need to recognise the significant role played by Islamic extremism in sustaining terrorism in Kashmir. Are all those who participate in terrorism, in creating chaos in Kashmir, Islamic fundamentalists or Islamic extremists? The government needs to distinguish between Islamic fundamentalists, in the sense of those who try to go to the roots of Islamic precepts and practices today with a view to reform them and Islamic extremists. The extremists are those who try to forcibly impose Islam on others and use terrorism for this purpose.

It is relevant here to quote what former British foreign secretary Douglas Hurd said: 'We have no quarrel with Islam, nor are we opposed to Islamic revival. What we are opposed to is terrorism dressed as religion.'

We need to use strong-arm methods with the extremists led by the Jamaat-e-Islami, Hizbul Mujahideen, Harkat Ul-Ansar, Al-Faran and scores of others. Unfortunately, however, Prime Minister Rao is unwilling even to recognise the threat emanating from Islamic extremist forces in the sub-continent.

This leads to the third task. Rao and the Congress are unable to distinguish between terrorists and Muslims, the latter being sought after as a vote bank. India is not fighting Muslims. In Kashmir, India is fighting terrorists who happen to be Muslim, as it did in Punjab where it fought terrorists who happened to be Sikh. Was Rao willing to apply strong-arm methods in Punjab only because Sikhs are not an important vote bank, outside the state?

The government needs to explain the distinction between terrorists and Muslims to Indians belonging to the Islamic faith. They are intelligent enough to understand.

Fourth, India needs to take the first step towards declaring Pakistan a terrorist State and limiting or cutting off diplomatic and economic relations till that country ceases all material support to terrorism. Simultaneously, we must continue to lobby with the US administration and Congress to stop Pakistan's promotion of international terrorism. (In fact, the Americans have better source material on Pakistan's involvement in the promotion of terrorism in Kashmir than us. Two Americans were also victims of terrorism in Karachi in February.)

It is for the Americans to decide if they would like to co-operate with Pakistan — described by the administration as a moderate Islamic republic — in tackling the problem of terrorism in Karachi or declare it a terrorist State.

In the long run, Pakistan will realise that it cannot promote terrorism in Kashmir and yet fight it in Karachi. This holds good for the Americans too; they cannot claim to fight international terrorism and co-operate with the promoters of terrorism at the same time.

Finally, the government has been on the defensive so far on its human rights record. Rao was very eloquent in rebutting India's alleged violation of human rights in his address on August 15, 1993. He said: 'While Pakistan is carrying out false propaganda about human rights violations in J&K, only two days ago terrorists from that country stopped a bus midway, pulled out 16 or 17 people and shot them dead. Do they mean that those who have been the victims of their bullets have no human rights? Have they no right to live? Only when the terrorists get killed in encounters, why do these people get perturbed, why do they campaign for upholding human rights? Do only terrorists have human rights?'

The prime minister's powerful words need to be translated into action. India should adopt an aggressive policy on human rights. It is necessary to highlight how by kidnapping and brutally killing tourists, the terrorists want to destroy any hope of revival of the Kashmiri economy. Is the chopping of a head a humane act? Is inscribing. Al-Faran on a dead body a humane way of communication?

It is also necessary to highlight the ethnic cleansing being practiced by the terrorists in Kashmir by drawing international attention to the plight of the Kashmiri Pandits who have become refugees in their own land. Unfortunately, the government is shy of doing so because the Pandits are Hindu, on the basis of a peculiar understanding of secularism which means protection of the minorities at the cost of the majority. But if the government does not speak for its citizens, of whichever community, who else is to do so?

3

US Doublespeak on Terrorism Must End

(The Blitz 7-12-1996)

Clinton had declared that "terrorism will not pay; terrorists will pay." Why not then make terrorists pay everywhere...?

In a recent address to the UN, US President Bill Clinton called upon all nations to show 'zero tolerance' against international terrorism.

Woefully, such professed American determination to curb terrorism suffers from a duality of attitude and double standards.

Pakistan, for instance, promotes international terrorism in J&K. But at the same time, Benazir Bhutto went to Washington and other world capitals to plead for assistance to tackle the menace of terrorism, particularly in Karachi.

With the US increasingly inclined to position itself as the world's sole Superpower, not only does such status begets responsibilities, the number one status begets number one responsibilities.

Nevertheless, during the days of the Second Cold War of 1980-1989, which were also the days of Ronald Reagan in the White House, the US had popularised the phrase that "your terrorists are our freedom-fighters."

This was particularly in context of the right-wing Contras who were fighting the leftist Sandinista government in Nicaragua and of the leftist guerrillas attacking the right-wing government in El Salvador.

The Contras were helped by the US "to keep their body and soul together" as they were "freedom-fighters." But at the same time, Reagan complained of the rightist El Salvadorian regime facing attacks of the leftist terrorists.

But then Reagan had at least an alibi of helping less dangerous authoritarian forces to keep at bay totalitarian forces who were, in his perception, working at the behest of the Communist Soviet Union.

But now, even despite the end of the Cold War within the US-conceived *new world order,* the White House continues to adopt double standards in its response to global terrorism. As the world's No. 1 power, it has arrogated to itself the right to declare any state a terrorist state solely from the point of view of its national interests.

Thus, Iran, Sudan and Libya are terrorist states, but Pakistan is not. President Bush had placed Pakistan on the watch-list for declaring it a terrorist state. But Clinton, his successor, found no hard evidence to declare it one. In fact, he certified that the Benazir regime had given up direct support to the terrorists!

In reality, Pakistan was found useful as a moderate Islamic state and as a bridge to Central Asian Islamic states. Hence, even though an American citizen has been held by Pakistan-based terrorists in Kashmir, Clinton remains unconvinced, although Islamabad's support to terrorists in J&K has been exhaustively catalogued by the Republican Party and Congressional sources.

Yossef Bodonisky, director of the Congressional task force on terrorism and unconventional warfare, has, for instance, confirmed the fact that Pakistan's ISI is not only "the sponsoring and guiding force behind the escalation" of Kashmiri terrorism, it has assumed direct control of the entire operation.

When it comes to terrorism against American targets on US soil, however, Clinton speaks a tough language and suggests stringent measures. These extend to curbing the human rights of Americans by legalising wire-tapping of suspected terrorists, imposing longer sentences and confiscating their properties.

However, when ISI-sponsored terrorists attacked the Republic Day function last year, India was lectured by Assistant Secretary of State for South Asian Affairs Robin Raphel on the lesson India should draw from such extremist onslaughts.

She theorised that the attack made "more painfully obvious the need to resolve the problem of the Kashmir conflict."

Clinton was similarly elated by the fact that just prior to Bhutto's visit to Washington, Pakistan handed over Ramzi Ahmed Yusuf, a terrorist suspect in New York's World Trade Centre bombing in February 1995.

Clinton had then declared that "terrorism will not pay; terrorists will pay." Now in the UN, Clinton said the international community should ensure that terrorists have "no place to run, no place to hide."

Why not then make terrorists pay everywhere in the world, irrespective of whether they attack the US, its friends or neutrals? Why not punish a state like Pakistan which shelters so many Punjabi and Kashmiri terrorists?

Owing to such inconsistency in US attitude, state and non-state organisations sponsoring terrorism have been emboldened to play the US at its own game. The US-created distinction between terrorists and freedom-fighters is being boldly insisted upon by others now.

Iran and Sudan, two terrorist states in the eyes of the US, insisted on this at the ninth UN Congress on Crime Prevention held last year in Cairo. They demanded distinction between "freedom-fighters and those who fight in the defence of their country and terrorists."

4

Never Say Die

(Mid-Day, 14-5-1997)

India should stop soft-pedalling on the Kashmir issue. It should insist on reciprocity from Pakistan and no longer behave like the considerate big brother.

India's relations with Pakistan has been an important preoccupation with our political leaders of all hues and colours as well as the Ministry of External Affairs.

However, dealing with Pakistan is always a thorny issue to policy-makers for two reasons.

First, because national priorities of the two nations differ so sharply that finding a degree of congruence is next to impossible.

Pakistan has taken the extreme position that the core issue in their relations with India is Kashmir and unless that issue is resolved, Pakistan cannot have normal bilateral relations with India.

Their representatives in Kashmir, the All Party Hurriyat Conference have also reiterated it.

They think that all other steps to deal with Pakistan are futile.

India, on the other hand, desires to improve bilateral trade, social and cultural relations and hold in back-burner contentious issues like Kashmir or Siachen.

India's mission

The purpose of India is to create necessary confidence and mutual trust between two nations because at present very little of it exists.

Thus, for instance, the Task Force report on A New US Policy Toward India and Pakistan (1997) sponsored by the Council on Foreign Relations, New York rightly observed: "Almost half a century after independence, Indo-Pakistani relations are less extensive than were those between the United States and the Soviet Union at the height of the Cold War."

Politicised

The second difficulty is the fact that India's relations with Pakistan become at once an extensive domestic political issue, unlike relations with any other country.

Any move by India will attract both favourable and critical responses from the informed public.

In this context, the Indian Government's decision of unilateral liberalisation of visa to the visiting Pakistanis has attracted both bouquets and brickbats.

Hawks have argued that it will only open the floodgates for Inter Services Intelligence agents to enter India to continue their nefarious activities.

While the liberals, who are willing to go to any extent to seek friendship with Pakistan, find the move of government as a welcome step.

They desire that the government take more such unilateral steps to improve relations with Pakistan.

What could be the right way of dealing with Pakistan?

Reciprocity

There are two important issues involved in doing so. First, an insistence of strict reciprocity.

Hans Morgenthau, well known realist thinker of the post-war period has characterised reciprocity as the heart of international relations.

When India and Pakistan have nothing but adversarial relations, it becomes important that two nations take reciprocal steps to improve relations and build mutual confidence.

In this particular case, the Indian announcement on March 20 of liberalised visa regulations, was followed by Pakistani President F. A. Leghari's statement on March 23.

The statement supported the Kashmiri separatist cause and asked all Muslim nations to help Pakistan to end "repression and human rights violations in Kashmir" at the meeting of the Organisations of Islamic Countries (OIC), specially convened by Pakistan to mark its golden jubilee.

The OIC then called for "right of self-determination" for the people of Kashmir.

Pakistani agents in Kashmir also responded by killing seven Kashmiri Pandits.

Even if we dismiss it as Pakistan's way of acting with strength and not toeing a soft line towards India, India having made the first move to encourage economic, social and cultural interactions between the peoples of two states, should now wait for Pakistan to announce similar liberalisation of visa for Indians before taking any further unilateral steps.

Time factor

Pakistan's foreign minister has said recently that they will reciprocate "slowly."

Let them take their own time.

Second, India is always advised by liberals that we are a big country in the region and therefore should always make concessions.

It is a fact that India is a big country. But while expecting big country to be generous, small nations should also not forget their obligations.

Why make concessions, when Pakistan is determined to create internal security problems for India by working for the disintegration of India?

Further, the experience of the South Asian Association for Regional Co-operation also shows that in more than one case, Pakistan has tried to enlist the support of smaller nations like Sri Lanka or Nepal against Indian positions.

If small countries can gang together against a big power, why should a big power be generous beyond the need? In such an event, India making unilateral concessions to Pakistan is likely to be interpreted as a sign of weakness.

On the other hand, it is necessary for a big power also not to appear as appeasing the demands of a small neighbour, particularly when all of India's neighbours are small.

Too condescending

India has today another handicap in dealing with Pakistan. Prime Minister I. K. Gujral, who spent his youth in Lahore before Partition, is perceived as sympathetic to Pakistan.

Whether accurate or not, this perception will not enable him to appear decisive in dealing with Pakistan.

His being able to speak to Nawaz Sharif in Punjabi is not necessarily an asset.

On the other hand, it is likely to be seen as condescending too much to an adversary.

Hence, India needs to pursue the policy of reciprocity while always taking the first initiative in a new direction.

5

The Burden of Refuge

(Mid-Day, 5-7-1997)

The international community must ensure that internally displaced persons are cared for.

The most tragic situation for a human being is to be displaced from his normal place of residence because of the fear of life, limb or physical assault.

During the height of Pakistan-promoted terrorism in Kashmir, over 2,50,000 people were forced to flee from the Kashmir Valley and settle in other parts of India.

There are over 23,000 pandits in Jammu and another 20,000 in Delhi. Many of them are also in Mumbai and elsewhere in India.

It is not merely Hindus - though their number is large - who have been displaced by terrorism in Kashmir. Muslims have also been forced to seek refuge elsewhere in India.

The United Nations High Commissioner for Refugees (UNHCR) calls such people who have been forced to flee their homes as Internally Displaced Persons (IDPs) and distinguishes them from 'refugees'.

Who is a refugee? The 1951 Convention relating to the status of refugees clearly defines a refugee as a person who, "owing to a well-founded fear of being persecuted for reasons of race, religion, nationality, membership of a particular social group, or political opinion, is outside the country of his nationality, and is unable to or, owing to such fear, is unwilling to avail himself of the protection of that country."

Those who cross international borders are termed 'refugees' while those who move internally are called IDPs.

Both the refugee and IDP fear for their life and feel that the authorities of their normal place of residence cannot protect them.

However, what separates them is the fact that a refugee has crossed his state's international borders, while an IDP has moved from his place of residence but still is within state boundaries.

There are over 26 million refugees in the world, according to the UNHCR. But the UNHCR also acknowledges that there are more IDPs than refugees, globally.

In the 1950s and the 1960s, refugees and IDPs were the offshoot of political and ideological persecution, in addition to military conflict.

However, in the 1990s, more refugees and IDPs have been created by ethnic and religious conflicts, wherein the protagonists of one or the other ethnic or religious group instigate the use of terrorism.

There are, in addition to the Pandits of Kashmir, millions of IDPs in various countries like Sri Lanka, Afghanistan, Bosnia, Croatia, the Russian Federation.

All are victims of race, religion and ethnicity-related conflicts. However, the UNHCR is extending assistance only to the IDPs.

The problems of dislocation, health, employment, life and physical security to the IDPs are as severe as those faced by refugees.

As a matter of fact, whether one becomes an IDP or a refugee is determined by the geo-political location of the territory in question and the nature of conflict.

In the case of Pandits, they had no option of crossing international borders to become refugees, as their persecution was caused by their being a Hindu minority in a Muslim majority state.

But in the case of the 1994 Rwandan conflict, since the country was small and the entire state was engulfed in ethnic conflict, millions were compelled to be refugees in neighbouring countries.

Hence, the distinction between the refugee and IDP is very tenuous. The fear of persecution is common to both the categories; the causes giving rise to this fear are also the same.

Yet, states may resist the international effort to assist IDPs on the ground of interference in their internal matters, while not doing much for alleviating the IDPs' problems. Nations, forgetting human values, may also seek diplomatic mileage in assisting refugees.

But IDPs are seen as a blot on a civil society. Thus, India would find it an embarrassment to acknowledge the Pandits' plight, but would speak up on Sri Lankan refugees or Chakma refugees from Bangladesh.

The international community has a twin task. First, to see that IDPs get the same assistance as do refugees. Second, and more importantly, focus attention on the factors which cause millions to be refugees and IDPs and prevent conflict.

The use of international terrorism to settle scores, or the persecution of people on religious, ethnic or racial grounds, needs to be prevented.

This can be achieved by cultivating the perception of equality among humans, and the need to live as a multi-ethnic, multi-religious or multi-racial society.

The international community should see to it that the number of refugees and IDPs is drastically reduced to an insignificant level before the beginning of the next millennium.

In the meantime, the Government of India and the state Government of Jammu and Kashmir need to see that all Kashmiri Pandits are rehabilitated with dignity.

6

Taking on Terrorism

(Mid-Day, 6-1-1998)

The crucial question is: are we really willing to fight terrorists, whether in Punjab or Kashmir or are we still trying to play politics with terrorism?

'Terrorism is now truly a global phenomenon. Its global nature is established last December when the United Nations General Assembly condemned all forms of terrorism and also approved a global convention for greater co-operation among nations to control terrorism. What is interesting is the fact that the resolution was introduced by the United States' delegate. For the first time in the UN's history, the General Assembly also defined terrorism comprehensively as "criminal acts intended to provoke terror in general public or a group of persons" and termed it "unjustifiable, whatever be the considerations — political, religious, ethnic or ideological."

India has been a victim of Pakistan-sponsored terrorism not only in Jammu and Kashmir, but in other parts of the country as well. Four American civilians working for an American oil company in Karachi were recently gunned down by terrorists, suspected to be in retaliation to a US court imposing the death penalty on a Pakistani national, Mir Aimal Kasi, for killing two CIA agents in 1993 just in front of the CIA headquarters in Langley, Virginia. Another Pakistani terrorist, Ramji Ahmed Yousef, was convicted around the same time for conspiracy in the 1993 bombing of the World Trade Centre in New York.

As such, two democracies — one the largest (India) and the other the most powerful (the US) — have increasingly developed a congruence in their perception of the menace of terrorism.

Being an old friend and ally, the Pakistan government does not encourage terrorism against the US. But Pakistani nationals, in their anxiety to promote specific or general grievances of Islam, target American civilians. But India for Pakistan is a historical enemy and in an attempt to found an Islamic state in Kashmir, it is covertly funding, training and arming Kashmiri terrorists.

Pakistan's complicity in running terrorist camps was earlier admitted by its late president Zia-ul-Haq to American scholar Selig Harrison. More recently, a secret report submitted to the then prime minister Benazir Bhutto admitted the existence of 38 terrorist training camps which train not only Kashmiri youths but nationals from Islamic countries like Bosnia, Sudan and others.

Strangely, one democracy is Pakistan's friend, another is an enemy, but both are targets for terrorist attacks by Pakistanis. Thus, in his second term, US President Bill Clinton has found some commonality in the terrorist problems faced by the two countries. He had said in September 1996 in his address to the UN General Assembly that the international community should ensure that terrorists have "no place to run, and no place to hide." And the Americans are capable of translating their words into action. Kasi was hiding somewhere on the Afghan-Pakistan border but US agents, with help from Pakistan, captured him and took him to the US to stand trial.

Americans also extended the hand of friendship to India, though Indian policymakers may grumble that it came a little late to combat terrorism. There were clear indications of a change in US policy last year, beginning with the handling over of Daya Singh Lahoria — wanted for the attack on former Youth Congress president Maninder Singh Bitta — even before the two countries had signed an extradition treaty. Then came the signing of the extradition treaty last June, followed by the US declaring the Pakistan-based Harkat-ul-Ansar a terrorist outfit. Soon after, US Undersecretary of State Thomas Pickering clearly offered his country's help in fighting terrorism "whether it is sponsored from moon or from any other corner."

The message is very clear: we face the problem of cross-border terrorism from Pakistan and the US is willing to help. Now the crucial question is: are we really willing to fight terrorists, whether in Punjab or Kashmir, or are we still trying to play politics with terrorism?

India's lack of willpower to fight terrorism in Kashmir is clear from at least four interrelated facts. First, since terrorism began in its present avatar in Kashmir in 1989, more than 32,000 people have been arrested for terrorist activities, but not a single one has been convicted. Is it because they are "misguided boys", Jammu and Kashmir Governor Lt. General Krishna Rao described them? If so, let us see how the US has handled their 'misguided boys'. One Timothy McVeigh has been awarded death penalty for the bombing of a federal building in Oklahoma in 1995 and another, Terry Nicholas is currently facing trial.

Second, look at our legal process and prosecution style. While the terrorists involved in the Oklahoma bombing have already come close to paying the price, those involved in Mumbai bomb blasts of 1993 are still facing trial. The contrast glaringly exposes our pathetic slowness in deciding cases.

In February 1995, when Pakistan handed over Ramji Yousef, Clinton had said that the case indicated that "terrorism will not pay; terrorists will pay." By making Yousef and Kasi pay the price so swiftly, the US has demonstrated that they mean business. Unless our policy makers also follow this example of pursuing stringent action against terrorists, our rhetoric will sound hollow and earn, not international respect, but ridicule.

Unless justice is delivered swiftly, terrorists will not feel the cost of the price they are made to pay.

7

Is India Serious about Curbing Terrorists?

(The Sunday Observer, 24-01-1998)

...UN resolutions on the Kashmir issue were no longer relevant and the matter should be resolved bilaterally. US Ambassador, Thomas Pickering.

Indian policy makers and foreign policy commentators are happy that India and the US have reached an identity of views on the phenomenon of global terrorism. Undersecretary of state Thomas Pickering said in October 1997 in New Delhi on the conclusion of

Troubled Kashmir: Terrorist make no distinction between Muslims and Hindus. The Mirwaiz of South Kashmir fell victim to their bullets.

his two-day strategic dialogue with Indians: "Both of us are committed to work together to enhance our capacity to fight terrorism, whether it is sponsored from the moon or from any other corner."

This congruence of views on terrorism was later rearmed by the visiting US Secretary of State, Madeline Albright, in November. Earlier, the same views were also expressed by Richard Frank Celeste, new US Ambassador to India, at his confirmation hearings on October 28, 1997.

We need to remember that all three had prior knowledge of India. Celeste was an assistant to pro-India US ambassador Chester Bowles in the 1960s. Albright's interest' was indirect. Her father had authored a book on the Kashmir dispute.

Pickering was the US envoy at the UN (1989-1992) before coming to India (1992-93) as ambassador. It was he who in clear terms for the first time in 1991 had said that UN resolutions on the Kashmir issue were no longer relevant and the matter should be resolved by the two countries bilaterally. Hence, Ambassador Pickering may not be in a position to help us to fight terrorists from the moon, but he can be of help to us in fighting the cross-border terrorism.

The Clinton administration has followed a step-by-step diplomacy to bridge conflicting Indian and US perceptions on terrorism. First, it was handing over Daya Singh Lahoria, required in the case of attacks on Maninderjit Singh Bitta. This was done even before the two countries had an extradition treaty. The second step was signing an extradition treaty with India which could go a long way in getting back terrorists taking shelter in the US. There are still some Punjabi terrorists in the US: for instance the killers of General A. S. Vaidya. The third step was declaring the Pakistan-based Harkat-ul-Ansar as a terrorist organisation despite Pakistani protests against the move.

Finally is the recent declaration that the US is willing to fight terrorism without any distinction about motives. In retrospect, Bill Clinton was gradually preparing to take this position. He had said in February 1995, when Pakistan handed over Ramzi Ahmed Yusuf, a terrorist suspected of the New York World Trade Centre bombing: "Terrorism will not pay: terrorists will pay." Later, in September 1996, in his UN address, he had stated that the international community should ensure that terrorists have "no place to run, no place to hide."

Hence, let us not minimise the significance of the US move towards viewing terrorism in whatever name as an unmixed evil by looking for the US motives. Many critics are willing to dismiss the US declaring the Harkut-ul-Ansar as a terrorist outfit as the result of two American tourists being taken hostage together with a German, two Britains and one Norwegian in July 1995 by the Pakistan-based terrorist outfit Al-Faran. The US suspects Al-Faran to be a front organisation of the Harkat-ul-Ansar. One of the two Americans escaped and the Norwegian was murdered, but the fate of four, inlcuding one American, is still unknown. Last year, two US consuls were gunned down in Karachi while four US businessmen were killed by a car bomb. The US stand on terrorism is also an outcome of its experience of terrorism in the Oklahoma bombing in 1995 where 168 people lost their lives and 850 were injured.

But sceptics need to remember that no nation makes a policy altogether to suit the interests of another nation. The US is acting in its national interest. But we need to co-operate when there is a congruence in the national interest of two nations.

However the question is: Is India ready to decisively act to handle terrorism effectively? The record since 1989, when the current phase of Kashmir terrorism began with the taking hostage of the then Home Minister, Mufti Mohamad's daughter Rubiya, whose liberty was restored by the release of hardcore terrorists in exchange, shows that has been strong on rhetoric and weak on action.

There are many cases to prove this point, though three should suffice. One indication of this is the fact that over 32,000 have been arrested in Kashmir for terrorist activities but not a single one has been convicted so far. In sharp contrast, in the US, McVeigh conspirator in the Oklahoma bombing, has been awarded the death penalty and another, Terry Nicholas, is currently facing trial. Same is the case with World Trade Centre bombing where the Pakistani terrorist Ramzi Ahmad Yusuf has been jailed along with a few others.

A second indication of the Indian attitude is that TADA has been revoked, but no substitute law has been passed to handle cases of domestic and international terrorism to provide quick justice. Hence, prosecution is afraid of terrorists and defence lawyers take advantages of built-in loopholes in law to protect terrorists charged with heinous crimes. But with one example of domestic terrorism in Oklahoma, the US took strong measures to curb terrorism. It passed a law to provide stringent punishments and another law to confiscate funds of organisations suspected of terrorist activities.

The third and the strongest indicator is a lack of will to take effective steps to curb terrorism. Terrorists are described as "misguided boys" by the Indian policy-makers though they not only commit crimes against humanity but also take pride in it. After his release, Yasin Malik, a Jammu and Kashmir Liberation Front leader, compared himself to Gandhi in a TV interview, though he has admitted to have cold-bloodedly asassinated six officials in Kashmir.

This lack of will arises because we make the mistake equating terrorism with religion. The Indian state is not fighting Muslims, nor has it any design to do ethnic clensing in Jammu and Kashmir, though Kashmiri terrorists have adopted this very path in the Kashmir valley by hounding out Pandits. What the Indian state is fighting is terrorists and terrorists have no religion, as is evident from the fact that often terrorists have also gunned down Muslims in Kashmir.

Unless we develop will-power to distinguish terrorism from religion and handle the situation in Kashmir, whatever help Americans extend is likely to go down the drain.

8

Division of Interest

(Mid-Day, 27-2-1999)

The solution to the Kashmir imbroglio is to turn the line of actual control into and international border.

The personal diplomacy initiated by Prime Minister Atal Behari Vajpayee in agreeing to symbolically ride in the Delhi-Lahore bus on February 20 aroused worldwide interest.

Pakistan Prime Minister Nawaz Sharif, who had suggested that Vajpayee make such a trip, had also announced that Kashmir will very much be on the agenda for their discussion. Vajpayee also got hints that every bilateral issue, including Kashmir, would be discussed. And after the historic Lahore meeting both prime ministers mentioned that they discussed all issues affecting relations between the two countries, including the Jammu and Kashmir (J&K) dispute.

The dispute which has existed for the last 51 years cannot be resolved in one meeting. What could be the solution to the Kashmir tangle? The question assumes significance in view of the possession of nuclear weapons by both parties. Hence, a war initiated by either of the parties to wrest control over Kashmir, can easily be ruled out.

Second, is a plebiscite, as envisaged by the United Nations Security Council resolutions of 1947-48, a probable way out? Under the terms of the original resolutions, Pakistan is required first, to pull out their troops from Pakistan-occupied Kashmir (PoK). By any stretch of imagination, Pakistan is unlikely to accept such a proposition.

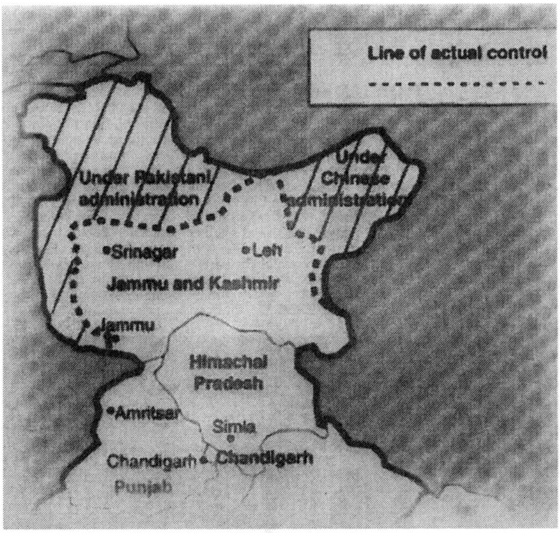

***A MAP DEPICTING CONTROL OF KASHMIR:* The dispute which has existed for the last 51 years cannot be resolved in one meeting**

India too is unlikely to take such a risk for the simple reason that it will cut at the very roots of her secular principle.

Then, what are the two leaders likely to negotiate? Unfortunately for a long time, India under various regimes at the Centre, has taken a defensive and guilty attitude, as if it doubted the legitimacy of their control of Kashmir.

However, after the nuclear tests, there has been a change in attitude. Vajpayee, after the two-day meeting of the Bharatiya Janata Party (BJP) national executive in the first week of January, said that what needs to be discussed is Pakistan's evacuation of one-third of J&K.

On the same day, Sharif also said that since the world has awakened to the Kashmir issue once again in 1998, 1999 will "be the year of solution."

Sharif seems to be sincere. During his first term in office he had suggested that after resolving the Kashmir dispute, the two countries should compete only to improve living conditions of their people.

In early 1993, I had written that the nuclear weapons status of India and Pakistan "could have an important effect. It is likely that the threat/fear of annihilation will have a great influence in promoting 'live and let live' policy in both countries. This will also de-emphasise rhetoric on Kashmir and could help to agree on a compromise in turning the line of actual control into an international border."

The only solution, that ultimately could work, is therefore, one of turning the actual line of control into an international border. This was discussed by former Indian President Zail Singh and Pakistan's military dictator Zia-ul-Haq. Zail Singh writes in his memoirs that following Zia's persistence in having a concrete suggestion on resolving the Kashmir problem, he gave his personal opinion to Zia, "If both the countries could accept the line of actual control as the international boundary, then there could be a possibility of ending the conflict giving rise to a new era of friendship and co-operation."

Unfortunately such a proposal cannot be made by Pakistan, because, their claim for J&K is based not on international law but on the basis of J&K being a Muslim majority state. Hence, by getting one third legally, they cannot religiously forego their claim for the remaining two-third. This attitude was well reflected by Zia when he told Zail Singh "that he would do everything possible to agree to this proposal, if the initiative came from India."

India on the other hand, has a strong legal basis for her claim in asking Pakistan to vacate PoK, because the whole of J&K has legally joined the Indian Union through an instrument of accession. Therefore, such a proposal cannot be expected from India. This is clear from the early comments of Jaswant Singh when the BJP led coalition government came to power last year though he was in favour of turning the line of actual control into an international border.

Now as external affairs minister, he said on the eve of his Lahore trip, "After 50 years, I feel the time for map-making in the region is over." However, he did not elaborate as in early 1998 when he had said clearly that such a proposal can be considered provided it came from the other side. Since both the sides want the proposal to come from the other, in practice, it will not come at all; particularly when India does not desire third party mediation.

One possible way out will be to hold a conference of intellectuals from all countries of the SAARC to evolve a solution and make both countries to accept it.

The BJP led government, having always taken a nationalist stand on the issue, is unlikely to suffer any adverse fall out. Any political accusation by the opposition of surrendering national territory, can be met with an accurate analysis of how the government decision has only helped in clearing a blunder created by Jawaharlal Nehru -founder of the Nehru-Gandhi dynasty.

For Sharif, as a member of Muslim League, it could mean getting one third more territory legally and peacefully as against his main opposition party of Benazir Bhutto which was responsible for the loss of East Pakistan in 1971. Thus both the countries can put the Kashmir dispute into the historic past and make a new beginning to live as good neighbours.

9

Kosovo now: Kashmir next?

(Mid-Day, 13-4-1999)

The period since the Gulf war of 1991 has been a period of 'Pax Americana', in which the US intervenes in the affairs of sovereign nations.

Since March 24, the North Atlantic Treaty Organisation (NATO) forces, under the leadership of the United States (US), have been bombarding the Federal Republic of Yugoslavia's (FRY) military and civilian areas, first in Kosovo and then in other cities including their capital Belgrade. Not satisfied with the destruction caused so far,

NATO bombings have increased the number of refugees fleeing Kosovo

American and European leaders are threatening Belgrade with more bombing.

This is the most brazen use of air-fire power by a regional organisation, under the dominance of a leading member against another member of the United Nations(UN). But the use of force has not been authorised by the UN, as was the case in the war against Iraq in 1991. On the other hand, two permanent members of the UN Security Council, Russia and China have vehemently opposed the attacks on a member of the UN as unwarranted and unjustified. The FRY has committed no aggression against any of its neighbours.

What is the American rationale for such brazen use of destructive air power? The Clinton administration has accused the government under president Milosevic of gross violation of human rights in Kosovo, a province of Yugoslavia, inhabited by ethnic Albanians who happen to be Muslims.

The Clinton administration has arrogated to itself the right to interfere in the internal affairs of another country. Addressing newspaper editors in Annapolis, Maryland Bill Clinton had, in early 1993, said "During the cold war, our foreign policies largely focused or relations *among nations.* Today, our policies must also focus on relations *within nations,* on a nation's form of governance, on its economic structure and on its ethnic tolerance."

This is not a justification of violation of human rights by the government in Belgrade. But was bombing the only option available to protect the human rights of ethnic Albanians? Today, NATO bombing in Kosovo has created more refugees than the Serbian military operations against the ethnic Albanian terrorist outfit, the Kosovo Liberation Army(KLA).

However, under the leadership of the US, the NATO was itching for the use of force. Madeline Albright is reported to have said: "In case the Serbs do not accept the agreement for K and M (Kosovo and Metohija), they will be bombed, while, if the Albanian side refuses, they will no longer have the help and support."

Appropriately, in pursuance of their prejudiced approach, the Americans embraced the KLA, which is an extremist force equipped with weapons looted from Albania, for fighting for an independent

Kosovo. An American journalist who travelled with Richard Holbrooke in his failed mission to resolve the Kosovo crisis, filed this report for the New Yorker, January 11,1999: "In early 1997, following the collapse of Albania, the people looted the government arsenals, making off with an estimated three million grenades and bombs, and seven hundred thousand rifles. These arms quickly found their way into the hands of the Kosovo guerrillas, who now gather in Albania, train there, and cross the border into their homeland."

Thus, the Americans, instead of assisting the moderate forces in Kosovo, who were willing to settle for genuine local autonomy within Yugoslavia, threw their weight on the side of the KLA. The Yugoslavian leadership, on its part, was willing to concede autonomy to Kosovo, and even accept NATO's aerial surveillance of the implementation of the agreement. But the US and NATO wanted Yugoslavia to accept NATO's ground troops in Kosovo to supervise implementation of the agreement. Yugoslavia, rightly, was not willing to accept the presence of NATO troops on their soil. It seems, as of now, that the American-led NATO troops intend to totally cripple the Yugoslavian armed forces and then land ground forces to liberate Kosovo and enable 400,000 ethnic Albanians to return.

This is a dangerous doctrine of violent interference in the internal affairs of another country, in the name of maintaining peace, security, and protection of human rights. What explains the behaviour of the US? Within Europe, unified Germany led the first strike to disintegrate the FRY by recognising Slovenia and Croatia as independent states. Then the US stepped in to seek the separation of Bosnia from the FRY. Now, the US is pursuing its predetermined policy of separating Kosovo from the FRY.

If the NATO plan is allowed to succeed, it will pose a severe threat to the national security and integrity of many multi-ethnic and multi-religious societies, big and small like Russia, China, India, Iraq, and even Sri Lanka.

Why does the US, which itself is a multi-ethnic, and multi-religious state, consciously follow the policy of breaking all such states? The US thereby hopes to maintain its preponderance of power. After the break up of the Soviet Union in December 1991, American scholars were not lagging behind in predicting similar disintegration of India and China.

Hence, India and other multi-ethnic states need to ponder over the policy implications for their highly pluralistic state structure. Professor Raju Thomas, an American of Indian origin teaching in the Marquette University in the US, recently wrote: "If the West can unilaterally draw up and dictate a settlement over Kosovo to the Serbs and follow it up with a massive NATO bombing campaign to enforce it, what will prevent NATO from doing the same over Kashmir (or Tibet, Tamil Eelam, Iraqi Kurdistan) ?Though India is not Yugoslavia, strong similarities of issues involved cannot be ignored. There are fringe groups in Kashmir demanding separation from the Indian Union, aided, trained, funded and armed externally, as in the case of Kosovo. What if the US, as a friend of Pakistan, decides in having an independent Kashmir so that there can be peace and promotion of human rights in South Asian region - particularly now that both India and Pakistan are armed with nuclear weapons?

India, of course, has strongly urged the Kosovo crisis to be peacefully resolved. Foreign Minister, Jaswant Singh had said that India is committed to preservation of the territorial integrity of Yugoslavia as a nation state. But it is not enough. India ought to have taken the initiative, together with Russia and China, to see that the issue is raised in the UN Security Council so as to highlight the sinister designs of the West in Yugoslavia.

When George Bush spoke of creating a new world order in the wake of the Gulf war of early 1991, no one thought of the American dream of creating a world order chiselled by American artisans. After the unilateral bombings of Iraq, now it is the turn of Yugoslavia to be ordered by the Americans to follow their dictates. Whose turn is it next?

10

Double Trouble

(Mid-Day, 4-6-1999)

The Americans totally forget the fact that once a person is trained as a terrorist, he remains one forever. Only his causes change.

The United States (US)-led bombing of Yugoslavia brings out vividly the double standards of the US government in dealing with international terrorism. To understand the nature of these double standards, we must begin with the very connotation of terrorism.

Terrorists rely on disproportionate violence to frighten the populace into pressuring its government to resolve the purported reason for the terrorist acts. The ongoing bombing of Belgrade by the US-led North Atlantic Treaty Organisation (NATO) forces, described as a "barbaric act" by the Chinese ambassador in the United Nations Security Council, is aimed exactly at coercing the innocent public in Yugoslavia. Six hundred bombing sorties a day to compel Slobodan Milosevic to surrender to NATO's dictates. Their warplanes and missiles have hit residential areas, market places, hospitals, power stations, the television centre and civilian convoys - killing scores of innocent civilians so far. It is nothing but state-sponsored international terrorism unleashed by the superpower.

All this is being done ostensibly to protect the ethnic Albanians in Kosovo from the brutality of Milosevic's armed forces. But can you really protect the rights of one minority group in a multi-ethnic society by punishing people of another community? Americans expect the Serbians to pressurise their government to resolve the cause of international terrorism unleashed by the NATO by accepting its terms.

The US has embraced the Kosovo Liberation Army (KLA), whom the Yugoslavian government has declared a terrorist organisation, in achieving their goal. That it is a terrorist organisation has been confirmed by independent observers; including those from the US. After 45 days of incessant bombing of Yugoslavia, American intelligence discovered that the KLA is involved in international drug trafficking. More shocking was the information that KLA was trained by Saudi billionaire-turned-terrorist, Osama bin Laden's 'terrorist training university'. But American policy-makers continue to deal only with the KLA.

This is not unusual behaviour for the US. Iran is one of the seven countries declared as a 'terrorist state' under US law. Yet in 1993-94, the US openly permitted it to supply weapons to the Bosnian Liberation Army. Now it is the turn of KLA to get weapons and training from Islamic countries. Of course, branding of a person or a group as terrorist changes according to the purpose the US intends to achieve at a given time. For them, one is a freedom fighter today; tomorrow, a terrorist. Bin Laden received training and funding from the Central Intelligence Agency (CIA) when the US was fighting a proxy war against the Soviet Union in Afghanistan through the CIA-trained Mujahidin. Sultan Ahmed, a senior member of Lashkar-i-Taiba (Soldiers of the Holy Places), reported to have said that soldiers of Lashkar and Bin Laden fought together against the Soviet Union. Bin Laden at that time was a freedom fighter for the US.

The Americans totally forget the fact that once a person is trained as a terrorist, he remains one forever. Only his causes change. Thus, once the Soviets were driven out of Afghanistan, terrorists either fought among themselves, as happened in Afghanistan, or fought against another country. Many Afghan and other Islamic terrorists have found their way into Pakistan and Pakistan-occupied Kashmir (PoK) by making liberation of Kashmir their new cause.

Bin Laden has found the cause of fighting against the US a worthy challenge. In an interview to *Time* magazine (January 11, 1999), he admitted: "If the instigation for *Jihad* (holy war) against the Jews and Americans constituted a crime, then let history be witness that I am a criminal." However, he considers that he is performing a "religious duty."

American double standards are not merely limited to the current issue of Yugoslavia. But it is a reflection of past behaviour patterns. When Bin Laden's supporters were suspected to have attacked the American embassy in Nairobi and Dar-es-Salaam, in which 14 Americans lost their lives on August 7 last year, the Americans swiftly retaliated on August 20 by bombing Bin Laden's hideouts in Afghanistan. Now the Americans want Bin Laden dead or alive. State Department spokesman Foley said: "The presence of Bin Laden anywhere but in the hands of justice is unacceptable to the US."

If that is so, what about others who face similar or much graver threats from international terrorism? American policy-makers had confirmed that in their attacks along the Pakistan-Afghanistan border, the persons killed were Pakistani trainee-terrorists. India has pointed out to the US several times that there are 21 terrorist camps in Afghanistan, 39 in PoK and 47 in Pakistan run by the Inter-Services Intelligence (ISI). But the American policy-makers have not even once publicly condemned Pakistan for promoting international terrorism. All this is being pursuad when US President Bill Clinton in his address to the UN General Assembly last September exhorted nations to their basic responsibility of denying refuge to terrorists. In the light of this, when an Indian correspondent asked the US Undersecretary of State Thomas Pickering whether it means India too can attack the terrorist training camps in Pakistan, his answer was an emphatic 'no'. That was the right reserved exclusively for the US as the global policeman. It is ironic that despite many lessons in recent history that terrorism, in the ultimate analysis, does not pay either terrorists or their sponsors, the US continues to patronise different terrorist groups and individual terrorists at different times. This only creates a chain reaction of brutal attacks in which politicians achieve their transitory political goals but on a long term basis it is ordinary citizens who suffer the most.

Take the case of Bin Laden. He was a hero for the promoters of terrorism in Afghanistan. But once his task was over, he applied his training in terrorism to his own promoters. His supporters attacked American targets because they were protesting against the US sanctions imposed against certain Muslim countries. Once he is suspected to have been the brain behind the Nairobi and Dar- Es-

Salaam attacks, he became a "most wanted" terrorist in the eyes of the Americans.

It's the same case with the KLA. American law enforcers in the Drug Enforcement Agency say that the KLA in its earlier *avatar*, known as Ushtria Clirimtare-e-Kosoves, was declared as an international terrorist organisation, but in its new garb it has become a patriotic body though in fact it continues to be a terrorist organisation. One drug enforcement official is quoted to have said: "They were terrorists in 1998 and now, because of politics, they're freedom fighters." This is the most damaging condemnation of Clinton. What a way to go down in history books!

11

Blame Game

(Mid-Day, 21-9-1999)

...if Opposition parties do not want the BJP-led national Democratic Alliance to take credit for the Kargil victory, then they should stop mudslinging.

A Few days before the end of the Kargil war. Bharatiya Janata Party (BJP) general secretary and spokesperson Venkaiah Naidu had promised that the diplomatic victory of the Atal Behari Vajpayee government would be turned into a military victory. The prime minister, as the political face of the country, said Operation Vijay has given the nation a grand *vijay* (victory). He mentioned it in his briefest Independence Day speech from the ramparts of the Red Fort.

The Congress has been asking the BJP not to make the Kargil victory an election issue. If it is really serious about this, it should also, in all fairness, not make it an issue for criticising the government. But Congress leaders, from its president Sonia Gandhi down, have blamed the crisis on the government's weaknesses, while praising the military for its bravery and sacrifice. In effect, it has tried to drive a wedge between the armed forces and the current political leaders in office.

For instance, the Congress manifesto vows to prevent "Kargil-type episodes" from recurring, blaming it on intelligence failure. Lawyer-turned-politician-turned-freelancer Kapil Sibal, a Congress MP, has already concluded that the loss of lives could have been avoided by a "more vigilant government and a more vigilant leadership."

Even during the conflict, the Congress foreign policy cell chief and former diplomat, Natwar Singh blamed the government for its immature, naive and unprofessional handling of the crisis. All India Congress Committee general secretary Madhavrao Scindia also attributed the crisis to "total negligence on the part of the government." The Congress decision to make the Kargil crisis an election issue is clear from the fact that its working committee accused the prime minister of "criminal negligence" leading to the loss of many lives.

Now that the crisis is behind us, it is fair and necessary to objectively assess the government's claims for bouquets and Opposition's over-willingness to offer brickbats. Such an assessment cannot be made without considering the management of past crises over Kashmir. The present performance of the BJP-led government has to be placed within the context of the past performance of the Congress government.

Take the decision of prime minister Rajiv Gandhi to send the Indian Peace Keeping Force (IPKF) to Sri Lanka in 1987. A non-partisan view of Rajiv's decision is that it was an unmitigated disaster because India lost her leverage with the Sri Lankan government as an honest broker of peace. We became a surrogate enforcer of law for Sri Lanka but could not disarm the Liberation Tigers of Tamil Eelam (LITE). We paid a heavy price, losing over 1,000 soldiers and the life of a youthful prime minister.

If the Congress does not disown the P. V. Narasimha Rao government, then it is stuck with two major failures in decision-making on the Kashmir dispute and international terrorism. First, in the case of terrorists taking control of Hazratbal Mosque in 1993, not only was the government forced to feed the intruders, but it was finally forced to provide a safe passage to the holed-up terrorists! If only the government had exposed them to the international media, the involvement of mercenaries would have come into the open then rather than now.

Second, in the occupation of the Charar-e-Sharif shrine by international terrorists in 1995, the government was not only unable to prevent the burning of the Sufi saint's temple, it could not prevent the escape of Mast Gull who became an instant hero in Pakistan. Then minister of state for home affairs Rajesh Pilot had spoken of war, but had to accept peace as dictated by the terrorists. In contrast to these past fiascos, the Vajpayee government handled the Kargil crisis well. After initial blunders and cacophony, the government was decisive in stating its goal of first forcing Pakistan to withdraw their forces - regular and international mercenaries -from the Indian side of the Line of Control (LoC) and then achieving it with the price tag attached to a 'war-like' but not a war-type conflict. It was able to secure an international understanding of Pakistan's treachery in the background of Vajpayee's efforts to initiate a new level of trust between the two governments following their newly acquired nuclear status. The Vajpayee government not only won international support - even if it was prompted by other nations' interests -but also won a decisive victory in the Kargil region.

Of course, India paid a price with 410 young army officers and soldiers killed and another 594 wounded. But in comparison to the IPKF experience, the Indian flag was honoured when it was hoisted again on Tiger Hill, unlike a forced withdrawal of Indian troops in 1989!

This does not mean that the Kargil crisis was managed flawlessly by the BJP-led government. The PM's national security adviser has admitted that the crisis was not anticipated by the government as it was complacent about the possibility of Pakistan crossing the LoC, as other governments have been since 1971. The policy-makers in the government also failed to anticipate that groups opposed to the Nawaz Sharif government's undeclared surrender to India, in the name of preventing a war, would attack soft targets in Jammu and Kashmir, as they did by attacking families of the Border Security Force (BSF) in Bandipora.

This was not the first time that the government failed to anticipate terrorist attacks. Innocent civilians were killed by terrorists on February 20, while Vajpayee was visiting the Minar-e-Pakistan in Lahore. Being prepared for the worst while hoping for the best is an elementary precaution of effective diplomacy when negotiating with an adversary like Pakistan, which has a record of treachery since 1947.

Again, it goes to the credit of the Vajpayee government that it took swift commando action to free the hostages at the BSF camp in Bandipora, rather than negotiate with the terrorists, as V. P. Singh's government did to secure the release of the daughter of then Home Minister Mufti Mohammad Sayeed in 1989. Similar swiftness was shown by the government when a Pakistani spy plane tried sneak into Indian territory on August 13.

These facts indicate that the Congress and other Opposition parties who have ruled so far have a greater share of the responsibility for bad decision-making on the Kashmir issue than the BJP-led government. The lessons of the Kargil crisis, therefore, are that if the Opposition parties do not desire the BJP-led National Democratic Alliance to take credit for the Kargil victory, then they should stop mudslinging.

12

Save Children from Terrorists

(The week End Observer 4-9-1999)

There are very disturbing reports of teenagers being trained in mosques and Madarasas in Pakistan in the name of Jihad.

Last year on 27 January, Pakistan sponsored mercenaries brutally massacred 25 Kashmiri Pandits of two families. The only survivor, 14 year young Vinod Dhar, loudly cried: "Where should I go now?" This cry must have been repeated by several young victims of terrorist attacks on buses, trains, temples and mosques in Jammu and Kashmir during the last ten years. Similar cries from child-victims from several countries had helped to arouse conscience of nations in the United Nations (UN).

Recently, there was an interesting debate in the UN Security Council (SC) on the issue of 'Children in armed conflict'. The debate was interesting at least for three reasons which are highly relevant to Indian society at the present moment. First the enormity of sufferings imposed on innocent children all over the world. Second, the extent to which nations exhibit a duality of approach to this problem and their ability to live with it. Third, the time has come for the UN to discuss and decide: Is terrorism a legitimate instrument to achieve a nation's foreign policy goal?

According to the UN, in the last decade, two million children were killed, one million were orphaned, six million were seriously injured or disabled and 12 million were made homeless because of International conflicts and acts of terrorism. Obviously, these figures do not include latest victims of Kargil.

There are two broad categories of conflicts under which the 'children in armed conflict' fall. One is induction of children to do fighting in regular or guerrilla warfare by the nations or armed groups aspiring to be a nation. During the Iran-Iraq war (1980-1989), Iran used thousands of children to fight in the war against Iraq. In Sri Lanka, the LTTE has indiscriminately inducted very young, even teenagers to fight against Sri Lankan forces for their separatist cause.

Second and of particular concern to us in India is the use of children to promote international terrorism in the name of *Jihad* (holy war). Under the same UN SC report, some 300,000 children under 18 are known to be under arms, obviously a large number of them are trained and armed for *Jihad.*

A recent report suggested that ISI recruits young uyghur Muslims from Xinjiang province of China on a contract for six months on a sum of $20,000. These are being used to fight in Kargil and Afghanistan.

Recently, when the Northern Alliance fighting against the Taliban regime threatened to try mercenaries from Pakistan captured by them as criminals, and not as prisoners of war, Nawaz Sharif admitted that though young Pakistanis receive religious education, denied their being sent to Afghanistan.

But in reality, there are very disturbing reports of teenagers being trained in mosques and Madarasas in Pakistan in the name of *Jihad.* In the first week of August, Indian armed forces captured a group of armed teenager-militants, sneaking into Kashmir. Earlier, in the last week of July, police in Kashmir, rescued two boys — Arshad Amir and Nasser Ahmed, only ten and nine years, respectively, from Mujhideen training camp, two months after their parents lodged a complaint.

The fact that Pakistan-based terrorist outfits use mosques to train terrorists is borne by the photographs released by the supporters of terrorist organisations, depicting two mosques pulverised by American cruise missiles fired by them last year August at alleged camps of Osama Bin Laden on Afghan-Pakistan borders. Recently, the organisers of the *Lashkar-e-Toiba,* the new incarnation of old *Lashkar-e-Ansar,* banned by the Americans as a terrorist organisation, also claimed that

they are training around 80,000 young men — some are too young — in religious studies and warfare.

The SC passed for the first time a resolution, 'Children in armed conflict' asking nations and warring groups to protect children and stop turning them into soldiers. The resolution obviously lacked any teeth to prevent its violation.

The earnest pleas made by the Indian representative, Kamalesh Sharma, to add teeth to the resolution at least as a first step, by banning the use of educational institutions and mosques as recruitment grounds, to begin with, which could help save children, fell on deaf ears. So was his pleas to increase global co-operation in fighting terrorism.

This brings out my second area of concern: Continued dual approach of big powers, particularly the United States, towards the menace of international terrorism on the one hand and saving the children on the other. Last year in mid-August, Americans fired cruise missiles at the terrorist camps on Pakistan-Afghanistan borders as Bin Laden was suspected to be the mastermind behind bombings of the American embassies in Nairobi and Dar-es-Salaam.

Commenting on the US action, George Fernandes had rhetorically asked: "Why is it that Americans keep quiet when other countries are afflicted by terrorism, but apply a different set of rules when they are at the receiving end?" To be fair to the American government, it has changed its attitude quite a bit since last August when, for the first time, secretary of state Madeline Albright condemned the killing of 15 civilians in Doda district in July this year. But that is too little and so late after several hundreds of children were massacred in Kashmir by the militants.

The duality of the approach is also evident in another area of protecting children. The US while supporting the UN resolution to save children from armed conflicts, indirectly adds to their misery in Iraq. There is a growing rate of children dying in Iraq because of economic sanctions imposed by the US-led UNSC. A survey by the Unicef showed that under-five mortality in Iraq went up from 56 deaths per thousand during 1984-1989 to 131 per thousand live births in 1994-1999. The UN Secretary General, Kofi Annan, supported the conclusion that sanctions are responsible for the increase in the death rate of children in Iraq.

The Clinton administration have rejected the findings; but the linkage between the rise in the death rate of under-five children and economic sanctions becomes indirectly evident in the fact that the State Department denied the permission to the aides of four Congressmen to visit Iraq to do an on the spot study of the impact of economic sanctions.

The US deputy ambassador in the UN, Nancy Soderberg, while participating in the debate over the children under the armed conflict resolution, very rightly said: "Today's children are tomorrows hope. We must all work to ensure that hope is not extinguished by the blight of armed conflict." This needs to be an universal concern, irrespective of whether children involved are Iraqis or Indians or Americans.

That can be achieved by answering my final concern: Is terrorism a legitimate instrument of a nation's foreign policy? If, not this is the time, for major powers to come together and act consistently against global terrorism. The lead obviously has to be taken by the US. Once the US takes the lead today, other members of the UN will fall in line. Terrorism *per se* is an evil. Terrorists can no longer be freedom fighters. And those who support financially, terrorist movements like Saudis ought to remember that Osama Bin Laden is waiting to strike at them, too.

13

Spare the Child

(Mid-Day, 7-9-1999)

The Security Council has for the first time passed a resolution asking nations and warring groups to protect children and stop turning them into soldiers.

The United Nations Security Council recently saw a debate over the important issue of 'children in armed conflict'. The debate was interesting for at least two reasons relevant to Indian society at present— one, the enormity of suffering imposed on innocent children all over the world and second, the extent to which nations exhibita duality of approach to this problem and their ability to live with it.

The Security Council estimated that in the last decade, two million children were killed, one million were orphaned, six million were seriously injured or disabled and 12 million were made homeless because of international conflicts and acts of terrorism. One has to only recall recent memories of children orphaned and displaced because of the Kargil conflict as an example.

There are two broad areas in armed conflicts which affect children. One is the induction of children to fight in regular or guerrilla warfare by nations or armed groups. During the Iran-Iraq war (1980-1989), Iran used thousands of children to fight against Iraq. In Sri Lanka, the Liberation Tigers of Tamil Eelam (LTTE) has inducted even teenagers to fight for their separatist cause. These youngsters are brainwashed into even killing themselves in the form of human bombs to achieve a separate state for Tamils.

LEGACY OF WAR- A child with an assault rifle in Afghanistan

Second, and of particular concern to us in India, is the use of children to promote international terrorism in the name of Islamic jehad (holy war). According to the Security Council report, some 300,000 children under 18, some as young as seven, are known to be under arms, obviously a large number of them are trained and armed for jehad. It is now a well-known fact that Pakistan has emerged as a major nation for training young children in extremist religious education and training them in the skills of using weapons of destruction.

This is how the Taliban was created by the Pakistani army and Inter-Services Intelligence (ISI), which now holds around 90 per cent of Afghanistan's territory. Recently, when the Northern Alliance, comprised of forces opposed to the Taliban regime, threatened to try mercenaries from Pakistan captured by them as criminals, and not as prisoners of war, Pakistani Prime Minister Nawaz Sharif admitted that young Pakistanis receive religious education but denied their being sent to Afghanistan.

In reality, there are very disturbing reports of teenagers being trained in mosques and madrasas in Pakistan in the name of jehad. In the first week of August, Indian armed forces captured a group of armed teenager militants sneaking into Kashmir. Earlier, in the last week of July, police in Kashmir rescued two boys - 10-year-old Arshad Amir and nine-year-old Nasser Ahmed - from a mujahideen training camp two months after their parents lodged a complaint.

The fact that Pakistan-based terrorist outfits use mosques to train terrorists is borne out by the photographs released by supporters of terrorist organisations. The photos show two mosques pulverised by American cruise missiles in August last year, fired at alleged camps of Saudi terrorist Osama bin Laden on the Afghanistan-Pakistan border.

Recently, the organisers of the Lashkar-e-Toiba, the new incarnation of Lashkar-e-Ansar, listed by the US as a terrorist organisation, also claimed that they are training around 80,000 young men - some too young - in religious studies and warfare.

After a marathon debate in which representatives of more than 50 nations participated, the Security Council, for the first time passed a resolution, 'Children in Armed Conflict', asking nations and warring groups to protect children and stop turning them into soldiers.

The resolution obviously lacked any teeth for action against its violators. Pleas by Indian representative Kamalesh Sharma to add teeth to the resolution by at least banning the use of educational institutions and mosques as recruitment grounds, fell on deaf ears. The same happened to his pleas to increase global co-operation in fighting terrorism.

This brings out a second area of concern: the continued dual approach of big powers, particularly the US, towards the menace of international terrorism on the one hand and saving the children on the other. The US fired cruise missiles at terrorist camps on the Afghanistan-Pakistan border in mid-August last year, as Laden was suspected to be the mastermind behind bombings of the US embassies in Nairobi and Dar-es-Salaam. Over 500 locals and 14 American lives were lost in these attacks.

Commenting on the US action then, Defence Minister George Fernandes had asked rhetorically, "Why is it that they (the Americans) keep quiet when other countries are afflicted by terrorism, but apply a different set of rules when they are at the receiving end?"

To be fair to the US government, its attitude has changed quite a bit since then. For the first time, US Secretary of State Madeleine Albright condemned the killing of 15 innocent civilians by militants in Doda district on July 20 this year. But that is too little, and much after several hundred children were massacred in Kashmir by militants. The duality of the US's approach is also evident in the area of protecting children.

While supporting the UN resolution to save children from armed conflicts, the US indirectly adds to the miseries of children in Iraq, where they are dying at an increasing rate because of economic sanctions imposed by the US-led Security Council.

A survey by UNICEF showed that mortality rate of children in Iraq below five years went up from 56 deaths per 1,000 during 1984-1989 to 131 per 1,000 live births in 1994-1999.

UN Secretary General Kofi Annan had supported the conclusion that the sanctions were responsible for the increase in deaths. The Clinton administration rejected the findings; but the linkage between the rise in the death rate and economic sanctions becomes indirectly evident from the fact that the US State Department denied permission to the aides of four Congressmen to visit Iraq for an on the spot study of the impact of economic sanctions.

The US deputy ambassador to the UN, Nancy Soderberg, while participating in the debate on children in armed conflict, very rightly said: "Today's children are tomorrow's hope. We must all work to ensure that hope is not extinguished by the blight of armed conflict"

This needs to be a universal concern, irrespective of whether the children involved are Iraqis or Indians or Americans.

When mercenaries brutally assassinated 25 Kashmiri Pandits on January 27 last year, the only survivor - 14-year-old Vinod Dhar - loudly cried: "Where should I go now?" This cry should be the cry of the universal child, irrespective of colour, creed or nationality.

14

Pakistan as a Terrorist State

(The Free Press Journal, 12-1-2000)

Despite evidence, the US is unlikely to declare Pakistan as a terrorist state....

Hijacking of Indian Airlines (IA) aircraft IC 814 on Christmas eve by Pakistani terrorists has moved Indian policy of fighting terrorism backward by a decade. India has suffered a serious setback in her fight against Pakistan-promoted international terrorism. This sense of loss was evident when Prime Minister Atal Behari Vajpayee appealed to the US to proclaim Pakistan as a terrorist state.

What is the possibility of such a determination forthcoming from the US? What are the implications? What needs to be done? These are the questions which need to be examined.

The US has a domestic law that empowers the secretary of state to make a determination that a nation is a terrorist state when it consistently promotes international terrorism. Today for instance, the US has on its list, countries like Iran, Sudan and Libya among others, as terrorist states.

Pakistan has had close and friendly relations with the US for the last fifty years. Yet, the Bush administration had in the early 1990s placed Pakistan on the watch list, one step away from it being declared a terrorist state. But, in January 1993 Bill Clinton replaced Bush as President and his observation of Pakistan was coloured by his own political perceptions and compulsions.

In short, these compulsions were: Clinton's desire to retain close relations with Pakistan as a so-called 'moderate Islamic state', and use it as a counterweight to pressurise the Narasimha Rao government (1991-1996) to yield economic and security related concessions in return for reducing US pressure on India to protect human rights and accede to the non-proliferation regime.

Hence, instead of taking the issue of declaring Pakistan as a terrorist state to its logical conclusion, the Clinton administration dropped Pakistan from its watch-list in December 1993. But this did not result in any improvement in Pakistan's behaviour in handling international terrorism. On the other hand, Pakistan's direct and indirect involvement in terrorist activities against US personnel and interests only increased.

It is not necessary to give a catalogue of such activities to prove the above point. Suffice if I provide here a few globally well known examples.

Pakistanis were involved in World Trade Centre bombing in 1993. Later one of the terrorist, Ramji Ahmed Yousef was arrested in Pakistan. Another, Mir Aimal Kanshi was involved in assassination of two agents of the Central Intelligence Agency (CIA) in front of the agency's headquarters in Langley, Virginia.

Four American businessmen were assassinated in a car bomb attack in Karachi and two American Consuls were also killed in this city in 1997.

More recently, Osama bin Laden has emerged as the terrorist most wanted by the US. He was accused of masterminding the bombing of US embassies in Nairobi and Dar-e-salaam in August 1998 in which 14 Americans and scores of native Africans working in the embassy were killed.

The US was prompt in bombing the terrorist training camps of Harkat-Ul-mujahideen (HUM) on the Pakistan - Afghanistan border. But that was only a warning shot fired against Bin Laden's forces; US has vowed to bring him to justice.

The assistant secretary of state, Karl Inderfurth has asked Pakistan and the Taliban regime in Afghanistan to hand over Bin Laden who has taken shelter in Afghanistan to the US. Bin Laden instead, has issued a fatwa asking his followers to kill Americans. The fatwa is co-signed by the leader of HUM.

Under General Musharraf, Pakistan has encouraged and given a free hand to various terrorist groups to operate in Pakistan. At a congregation of fundamentalist and terrorist groups held in Lahore on November 5 last year, terrorists vowed to attack American interests and see that Bin Laden is never handed over to the US.

These terrorist groups have clubbed India with the US. This is because of an increased co-operation between India and the US in recent years in combating terrorism. In October last year, an US expert on counter terrorism, Michael Sheehan visited New Delhi. Ever since, the anti-Indian rhetoric by the Pakistan based terrorist groups clubbing India with the US has gained momentum.

Michael Sheehan in his testimony before the Senate Foreign Relations Committee in November last, has also categorically said that Pakistan has given a free hand to HUM and other terrorist organisation in its land and also given "material" assistance to terrorists operating in Kashmir against India.

Despite such evidence, the US is unlikely to declare Pakistan as a terrorist state as the US would like to retain its leverage in that country. What at the most will happen is that Madeline Albright, US secretary of state, after the November 2000 presidential elections might decide to place Pakistan on the terrorist watch list. This will mean that Pakistan will be where it began at the commencement of the Clinton presidency - on the watch-list.

However, it does not mean India need not carry on its co-operation with the US. The US has provided India certain intelligence inputs during the Kargil crisis as well as during the hijack crisis. However, Indian efforts to create international opinion against Pakistan's promotion of terrorism has to be broad based. While creating world opinion, India need not appeal only to the US to declare Pakistan as a terrorist state.

This is undesirable, despite our co-operation with the US in combating terrorism, because it will amount to giving legitimacy to the US domestic law of authorising its officials to declare a country as a terrorist state.

If we accept that instrumentality, we cannot reject the US claim to oversee human rights or religious freedom globally and threaten to declare a state, in their perspective, as a violator of human rights or religious freedom.

Hence, India needs to take its campaign against Pakistan sponsored terrorism to the United Nations (UN). The US itself had mobilised the UN Security Council (SC) to impose economic sanctions against Libya for its alleged role in bombing of a Pan Am flight 103 in 1988 by two Libyans which recently forced Libya to agree to hand over two of its citizens to stand trial in Britain.

India may not be able to get the Security Council to impose economic sanctions against Pakistan. But the campaign will at least expose those who pay lip sympathy to the cause of fighting terrorism and those who really mean business.

15

Pledge to Commit

(Mid-Day, 18-1-2000)

As a nation we need to do things with a greater commitment and concern than we are normally accustomed to.

The Terror created by terrorists of Harkat-Ul-Mujahideen (HUM) by hijacking Indian Airlines' plane from Kathmandu last month refuses to die out. Though it ended when India agreed to release three hardcore terrorists - Maulana Masood Azhar, general secretary of HUM, Mushtaq Ahmed Zagar (HUM), both Pakistani nationals and Omar Sayeed Sheikh, a British national in return of 159 passengers and crew.

Releasing hard-core terrorists, arrested at the cost of numerous lives, is not the best way to handle terrorism. But under the circumstances created in this particular case, by the omissions and commissions of various persons involved in the crisis, the government might have been left with no other alternative. This was neither the first time government of India was forced to release the terrorists in return for hijacked or kidnapped civilians nor probably is it the last time.

But we need to ensure that this is the last time the government is forced to bow to the demands of Pak-promoted terrorists. It is therefore, necessary, to introspect over the factors which enabled terrorists to hijack the IA plane. So that, as President K.R. Narayanan, very rightly said, we could "be further alert to prevent such events from occurring in the future."

STAND AT EASE- the security officials at the Sahara International airport

I propose to focus on two important domestic lapses which enabled the hijacking. First, a telling failure on part of the Indian Airlines (IA). What strikes most as a keen student of terrorism and security, is the utter lack of concern and alertness by the IA. After the hijack episode, every one who was even remotely connected with the airlines and security arrangements at the Tribhuvan International Airport, expressed their profound knowledge about security being lax there. If it was a part of knowledge of recently-retired personnel, it must be part of the knowledge of those who manage airlines and passenger safety.

Second, there is a total failure of intelligence machinery. It must be said here that intelligence is not dependent only on secret information. Often, intelligence is a shrewd task of purposeful analysis of openly available information and warning agencies and government institutions likely to be affected by it. If so, the information that Islamic terrorists were likely to strike during the Christmas and millennium celebrations was there on the intelligence screen, at least one week before the day the hijacking occurred.

The US State Department had issued an advisory around December 17 stating that the forces associated with the most wanted terrorist of America, Bin Laden, are going to strike against some US interests; hence the Americans were warned to be most careful. The tenor and tempo of this warning was gradually increased by the US government, first by informing that the Jordan government has arrested a person involved in such a plot. Then came the information that an Algerian has been arrested in Seattle while trying to smuggle in bomb-making material into the US from Canada. Then there was another incident involving an Islamic terrorist.

The CNN relayed the information replete with minute details. The level of warning was also gradually raised - from the State official to the Secretary of State, Madeline Albright; then National Security Advisor, Sandy Berger and finally to the President himself.

You may wonder about its relevance to India as it was a warning to the Americans. But one should know that after the visit of Michael Sheehan, US counter-terrorism expert to New Delhi in October last year, Bin Laden forces had openly warned that they would next target India, alongwith the US. The latest was the one issued on November 5 at Lahore at the congregation of Islamic fundamentalist and terrorist groups. The congregation specifically thanked General Musharaff for taking over power in Pakistan. Otherwise, Nawaz Sharif would have physically crushed them they felt. Thus, they were obliged to do something to boost the morale of the -Pakistani Army that was badly bruised post-Kargil.

Now, I am sure the Research and Analysis Wing (RAW) has at least one person who watches CNN, unless of course, we are totally raw in intelligence-gathering. If one had watched CNN, the gut reaction ought to have been to alert Indian agencies prone to terrorist attacks.

If these two observations are seen in a co-ordinated manner, the IA should have imposed extra security at the Kathmandu Airport at our cost. This is not something uncommon for airlines to do. Sri Lanka and Israel are doing it in Indian airports. But Indians do it only after an experience like the hijack and even then in an ad hoc manner. This is borne out by my personal experience.

I boarded Air India(AI) flight 128 from Chicago on the same day as the hijack. After the usual security check by the Chicago airport authorities, AI officials announced at 8 pm that they will conduct another check at the gate and asked passengers to bear with them. They did conduct physical check of about 20 to 30 people. However, the plane was to depart at 8.40 pm and any delay would have involved paying a huge sum as additional tax to the airport authorities. As a result, abruptly the gate-security was suspended and every one was asked to board.

If additional security check was deemed necessary, it should have been started much earlier as passengers were expected to be at the airport at least two hours before the departure and no one would have grudged little extra inconvenience in the interest of their own safety. AI could have also avoided ad hocism of security concern which was mocked at by passengers because of the manner in which it was done. Henceforth at least, as a nation we need to do things with a greater commitment and concern than we are normally accustomed to.

16

Divide and Rule

(Mid-Day, 29-4-2000)

It is believed in informed circles in the US that the Clinton administration is backing or at least favourably inclined to the division of J & K on religious lines as proposed by the Kashmir Study Group (KSG) led by one Farooq Kathwari.

Newspapers in Mumbai carried a brief item on April 11, saying that the Chief Minister of Jammu and Kashmir (J & K), Dr Farooq Abdullah has threatened to resign if the Bharatiya Janata Party (BJP)-led government made an attempt to reopen "settled issues" of Kashmir. Who is attempting to reopen the settled issue? Who is behind this move? What is the BJP doing on it? What are the implications for the Indian nation?

It is apparent that the behind-the-scenes activities began to unfold just before the President of the United States (US) Bill Clinton visited India. These activities continue after his return. One indication of unfolding activities in the federal government is the release of some leaders of All Party Hurriyat Conference (APHC) from Jodhpur jail on April 3. Home minister L. K. Advani described Hurriyat as a dissident Indian group. He ignored the fact that Indian dissidents do not campaign in Pakistan and other Islamic countries by questioning validity of accession of J&K to the Indian nation. These leaders have all along demanded separation of J&K from India or its integration with Pakistan.

However, having won their freedom from confinement, separatist leaders have begun to raise their expectations from the government.

MOOT ISSUE: Dr Farooq Abdullah making a point

These include release of all jailed separatists, a formal invitation for talks without any pre-conditions, while home minister has stipulated talks within the framework of Indian Constitution.

What is at the back of these developments? It is believed in informed circles in the US that the Clinton administration is backing or at least favourably inclined to the division of J&K on religious lines as proposed by the Kashmir Study Group (KSG) led by one Farooq Kathwari. Kathwari is owner of Ethan Allen Furniture, which is incidentally used in the White House. He is, according to Panun Kashmir sources, mentor and major financier of Dr Ghulam Nabi Fai, a Kashmiri separatist lobbyist in Washington. It is to him that Clinton had written in 1993 expressing his desire to work with, to establish peace in Kashmir.

The KSG plan envisages division of J&K on religious lines for the creation of "sovereign Muslim-majority entity with its own constitution, citizenship, flag and legislature." The new state will have its own currency and police to maintain internal security. India and Pakistan would be responsible for defence and foreign affairs and they would also workout financial arrangements for the new state.

The new state to be carved out on the Indian side of the Line of Control would include the entire Kashmir valley, the districts of Kargil and Doda, three northern tehsils of Rajouri and one tehsil of Udhampur, according to reports. Kathwari had visited India in March 1999 and met some of the leaders of APHC and Chief Minister Farooq Abdullah. He again visited India as a member of Bill Clinton's entourage.

The KSG plan does not speak about Pandits in the Kashmir valley. However, the attacks on Sikhs on March 20 in Chattisinghpora during the Clinton visit to Delhi, fits into the plan to get rid of non-Muslims from Kashmir valley. Of the 35,000 Sikhs in the valley, around 8,000 had already migrated to other places in the wake of the beginning of the crisis. The terrorists have already thrown out Pandits from the region. Nearly 3.5 lakh Pandits live as refugees in their own country.

If at all, the BJP is not averse to the formula put forward by Kathwari it would be very disturbing for the following reasons. The BJP has taken so far very rightly a strong nationalist approach to the so-called dispute over J&K. PM Vajpayee publicly said in January 1999 that the only thing to be negotiated with Pakistan is the vacation of Pakistan Occupied Kashmir (POK).

As he put it, "Now India will ask Pakistan to give up POK prior to any negotiations." Jaswant Singh, Foreign Minister, just before PM's Lahore visit, had called for an end to all efforts in mapmaking.

Apart from the BJP's stand, the division of J&K on religious lines is a deathblow to the very foundation of secular Indian democracy. Of the many effective observations made by President Clinton during his visit to India, what appealed to many, was his observation in Nayla village where the people "are proving that democracy... can be used to bring people of different tribes and castes together;" After his return, he again mentioned his Nayla visit where " all the different tribes and castes have an opportunity to be represented...."

What he was basically referring to was the mosaic character of Indian society where all cultures, castes and religions live and work together. Should we disturb this mosaic because of the pressure created by Pakistani-sponsored cross border terrorism? What will then happen to 120 million Muslims in India? Pakistan has not reconciled to the accession of Junagadh and Hyderabad to India as well. Are we going to permit formation of Muslim-majority states in these states as well?

This is an invitation to the disintegration of the Indian nation. It is in this context, Dr Abdullah's statement that "Any such move (opening settled issue) will not only create one Bosnia but many Bosnias in J & K" has to be seen. He is right. The plan must be opposed tooth and nail.

17

War on Terrorism: Impact on India

(The Free Press Journal 19-10-2001)

But there could be long-term negative security implications for India. Pakistan's public cooperation with the US, spells dangers for Musharraf personally and for Pakistan collectively.

Though India was first to have offered help to the US, it is in the fitness of things that the US should use Pakistan rather than India in its immediate aim of bringing to books terrorists involved in the attacks against them. Geopolitical location, access to Taliban and ability to share intelligence on Osama Bin Laden- all favour Pakistan rather than India.

But these attacks started on Sunday (October 7) have their immediate and long-term effects on India's problems with Pakistan-promoted cross-border terrorism. Even after the bombings started, Pakistan President, Musharraf tried to insulate his terrorism in Kashmir as having nothing to do with Afghanistan. As a matter of fact, he has set up terrorist training camps in Afghanistan. This gives him the benefit of plausible deniability.

Some of the immediate positive effects on India's terrorism-related security threats could be anticipated. First, the US attacks might lead to a replacement of Taliban government in Afghanistan. A broad-based government in Afghanistan would result in closing down all Pakistan-promoted terrorist camps in that country. This should help India in choking down the foreign sources of terrorism; in turn, helping to control disgruntled elements in Kashmir valley and bringing them into mainstream.

Second, if India still thinks that Pakistan has continued their training camps in Pakistan-Occupied Kashmir (POK) territory, India will be justified in conducting surgical strikes at those camps. The US strikes have created much-needed international environment to support India. It must be made clear to the world opinion that an attack against POK territory is not a violation of Pakistan's territorial integrity as the area belongs to Jammu and Kashmir, which had joined India.

Third, the crisis should help India to inject some vital strength into its spine. If Musharraf could place a staunch supporter of Taliban in Islamic Pakistan, secular India can also discipline Shahi Imam of Jamma Masjid in Delhi for his advocacy of support to Taliban in India. There are enough provisions in Indian law permitting such action.

However, there are also possibilities of immediate negative effects on the security of Indian polity and society. As a result of Indian extension of unsolicited public support to the US and Taliban's threat to attack any one who supports the US, the Jihadi forces still might attack targets in India. One should remember that attack on the Legislative Assembly building of Jammu and Kashmir (J & K) cannot merely be considered as an act by desperate forces against democracy, but it is a warning shot against India for its support to the US. This calls for extra vigilance by the Indian external security forces as well as forces dealing with internal security.

What are the long-term effects of the US attack on Afghanistan on India? Going by the proclamations of intentions of the US policy makers and analysis of their perceptions, it can be reasonably surmised that the US and the West will take steps to curb finances of the terrorist outfits operating in J & K. It is a fact that all these terrorist outfits are interconnected and grow like amoeba. In their current thinking regarding long-term threat from China and perception of building closer linkages with India, the US cannot ignore security concerns of India. Their economic approach to India as a growing market for the US goods also makes them to side with India.

But there could be long-term negative security implications for India. Pakistan's public co-operation with the US, spells dangers for Musharraf personally and for Pakistan collectively. While some of the prominent Islamic states like Saudi Arabia, UAE and Egypt have joined the global efforts to combat terrorism, it is only Pakistan that is directly and actively involved in the US war.

Pakistan by all accounts, has joined in it under duress. The US has worries about Pakistani nuclear weapons eventually falling in the hands of Islamic terrorists. It is reported that President Bush did not even give time for Musharraf to think. If he had demurred, it would have been construed as that he is not joining against the global war on terrorism. Bush had any way made it clear that those who are not with them are with the terrorists. Was there a US threat to Pakistan's nuclear assets?

But now that he has joined the US-led coalition against terrorism, as the war lingers on, he is bound to face a threat to his regime from Islamic extremists, who according to him are only 15 percent of the population. But he has already called for a quick end of the military attack. How are the forty percent extremely religious minded personnel within the armed forces going to react? The report is that he has already reshuffled some officers in his pack. Yet threat is real for Musharraf's regime. The pro-Taliban forces have already come on the streets.

If he goes, India will not shed tears. But India will find either a Talibanised Pakistan or a Pakistan in civil strife. Both these options pose an extremely dangerous situation on our border.

The US and Pakistan share a fifty-fifty percent responsibility for the birth of Taliban and for the entire Afghan situation of today. If Pakistan also goes the same way, the US alone will be responsible for it, unless the US also works simultaneously to secularise Pakistani polity and society.

18

What is Central? Kashmir or American Interest?

(The Free Press Journal, 30-10-2001)

The clear message of General Powell was that even if you consider Kashmir as the heart of the problem, Pakistan cannot resolve it through cross border terrorism.

During his visit to Islamabad according to press reports, Secretary Colin Powell said that Kashmir is at the heart of the tensions between the neighbours; Kashmir is the central issue between Pakistan and India. Indians were unhappy. It was said that Powell's visit was Pakistan-centred. In India there were comments to dispute the Powell's statement.

However, a careful reading of transcripts of Secretary Powell's press conference in Islamabad on October 16 and his subsequent press conference in New Delhi on 17th indicate things in a different form. In Islamabad, as a matter of fact it was Pakistani President, General Musharraf who first said "Kashmir remains at the heart of Pakistan-India tension." He also emphasised that "normalisation of relations would require that the Kashmir dispute is resolved in accordance with the wishes of the Kashmiri people."

Then when Powell spoke he-talked of "stability" in South Asia and he "praised" General Musharraf's "phone call to Prime Minister Vajpayee..." In this background Secretary Powell echoing Musharraf's concerns said: "we, too, believe that the Kashmir issue is central to the relationship...." But he was categorical in stating, "Issues must be resolved through peaceful, political and diplomatic means and not through violence and force...."

Naturally, for General Musharraf, Kashmir is the issue, that can prolong his military rule in Pakistan. Though he remembers to take into consideration wishes of the Kashmiri people, he forgets that he did not take wishes of Pakistani people into account either while usurping power or while continuing in power.

But the clear message of General Powell was that even if you consider Kashmir as the heart of the problem, Pakistan can not resolve it through cross border terrorism. He repeated again "That terrorism has no place in the civilised world...." In diplomatic parlance he also expressed thanks to Musharraf "for his condemnation of terrorism" that the world saw on October 1, in Srinagar. Now Powell would know as much as General Musharraf that terrorism of October 1 is condemnable, so is the terrorism of earlier days as well as later days like the one world saw at the air force.

In New Delhi next day, it was again Indian minister for external Affairs, Jaswant Singh who defined what constituted central to Indian polity. Thereby he was also disabusing Powell's thought process of what occupies central place. He said that the "question of the state of Jammu and Kashmir is an example of secular traditions of the Indian nation. In that sense, we really cannot move towards reinventing two nations and we have shared these views with the secretary of state..." Colin Powell agreed "totally" with the formulation of Jaswant Singh. But then, it will be inaccurate for us to attribute it to Colin Powell. However, it did not mean that the US is only giving lip sympathy to the Indian concerns. He also mentioned the fact that the "United States and India have responsibility as the world's largest, multi-ethnic democracies to work in close partnership with each other."

The. Secretary of State must have read formulation within his own department of state articulated by former Director of Policy Planning Council, Dr James Steinberg. After almost six years study of Kashmir question he had come to the conclusion:

That what was going on in Kashmir is a procces to "Create a mono-ethnic and mono-religious society in Kashmir."

Yet, Indian secularism, or multi-ethnic democracy is not the central issue now in US-India bilateral relations.

Then what is the central to American policy makers? What is the purpose behind Secretary Powell's visit? As of now, their single aim and by extension, that of the international coalition against terrorism is to bring Osama bin Laden to justice and eradication of Al Queda terrorist network from Afghanistan. Of course, Secretary Powell agrees that "efforts" must be "directed against all terrorism." But it could wait. It is this centrality of the US concern with its own national interest that made Secretary Powell to speak on some issues in agreement with Pakistan, while in Islamabad while touching on Indian concerns peripherally. Hence, one may even say the US policy makers are playing politics with Indian concerns. Because in the unipolar world, the US as the only surviving super power is concerned only with its immediate national interest of retribution to Osama Bin Laden's sins. But once Al Queda bases are destroyed in Afghanistan with the capture of Bin Laden, India will have to tell bluntly the Americans that if global war against terrorism is not continued, Al Queda bases elsewhere in the world-including those in Pakistan and Pak Occupied Kashmir, will rise from the ashes to continue their war against the US.

19

Why do Our Politicians Lack will to Fight Terrorism?

(The Free Press Journal, 21-12-2001)

So long as we have this parliamentary system of government, every party, including the BJP is bound to follow vote bank politics.

December 13 Fidayeen attacks on the Indian Parliament, after their attacks on the Assembly building in Srinagar on October 1, is an expression of sheer contempt by these terrorists towards democratic process. However, those journalists who wrote on animal husbandry or cricket till yesterday, will now write on how these were carried out, who covertly collaborated with them, what were our security failures etc.

But here I would like to focus on two larger issues, which are unlikely to be the subject of comments by the journalists. First is that of India's national will to decisively tackle the scourge of cross-border terrorism. Do our policy-makers possess the required national willpower to handle the crisis? Unfortunately, at the moment, it appears that the national will is miserably missing.

National will is a part of national character and that, which boosts national morale in times of national crisis. This enables policy-makers to take decisive actions demanded by the national crisis irrespective cost involved. The post September 11 scenario has not altered our weak willpower. A crisis of October 1 magnitude should have resulted in India striking at the terrorist camps, particularly those of Jaish-e-Mohammad in Pakistan Occupied Kashmir (POK). Instead, we sent a protest letter to George Bush!

I am writing this with a sense of responsibility. Such an action would have been justified on several grounds. First, international environment was and even today is favourable for such action. If the Americans can hit the Al Quaida bases in Afghanistan and dethrone a repressive Taliban regime in Afghanistan for sheltering Osama Bin Laden, we could have easily justified our action. Second, POK is for Pakistan a part of disputed territory. For India eradication of terrorist camps in its own territory or even in a disputed territory is not a violation of international morality. After all, one of the grounds on which Pakistan has been justifying its promotion of cross-border terrorism is its being disputed territory.

There was a legitimate concern amongst the security experts on the possibility of Pakistan escalating the crisis into a nuclear war. I also had expressed this possibility prior to September 11. But American 9/11 experience and declaration of war on global terrorism has changed the international environment. Of course, if you ask the Americans their views they would not say:

"Go ahead, and do it." But if you do it, world community will understand it.

Of course, India will have to be prepared for such an eventuality. As Lt. General N. S. Malik recently wrote: "Pakistan's nuclear umbrella for 'jihad' need to be breached through the national resolve to fight a nuclear war if necessary, because to desist from use or threat of nuclear weapons, would be akin to behaving like a virgin in a brothel. However, that decision, India has to make only after the first strike by Pakistan because of our commitment to no-first strike with nuclear weapons. But the question is: will Pakistan sacrifice Karachi or Islamabad for the sake of Srinagar? If our nuclear doctrine is in right mould, answer is 'no.'

The second issue is relating to the first, of lack of national will to fight terrorism. Why politicians lack this will? Answer is simple misplaced unwillingness to hurt sensitivities of Muslim voters in pursuit of vote bank politics. Even on the same day after terrorist attacks on Parliament, our politicians are willing to find fault with security measures rather than speak with one voice in combating terrorism.

Kamal Nath, Congress MP appearing on the Star TV on the very day of attack found fault with security slackness. Undoubtedly, government will have to explain what additional security measures did they take after they had the intelligence on a likely attack on the Parliament. But was it the right time and occasion for Kamal Nath to raise this issue? If the security performs its job irrespective whether the person crossing a barrier is an MP or a Minister, our MPs and Ministers are first to object.

Some years ago when Kamal Nath was a Minister of State, he is said to have brought a video camera for his personal use. When the custom official imposed a duty as per the government rules, he was instantly transferred! Imagine what will happen, if security personnel insist on checking every MP's car before he is admitted into the Parliament House!

Former Chief Minister of Punjab, Beant Singh once said rightly that earlier, "people had mistaken terrorism for some religious movement. But now it has been established that terrorism has nothing to do with religion." He, with the help of K. P. S. Gill, was able to bring under control terrorism in Punjab that was going on in the name of an independent Khalistan.

He was able to do so as Sikhs constitute an important vote bank mainly in Punjab and any way it was lost already by the Congress to the Akali Dal. Even then Beant Singh paid his life to bring terrorism under control. But it is a different story with Muslims, who are an important vote bank to every party and in every state. Hence, every one soft-pedals terrorism in Kashmir because it is perpetrated by Islamists though from across the border in the name of religion.

So long as we have this parliamentary system of government, every party, including the BJP is bound to follow vote bank politics. On the other hand, look at the decisiveness with George Bush handled the post 9/11' global terrorism. He did not worry about Muslim votes. Nor did the American politicians speak in cacophony to drown government measures to combat terrorism because of their vote bank politics.

20

Pakistan-sponsored Terrorism and China

(The Free Press Journal, 1-1-2002)

China may not actively support Pakistan; it will not also bring any pressure on Pakistan to stop its use of terrorism against India.

General Musharraf visited China in the third week of December for high-level discussions with Chinese leaders and ended with a summit meeting with President, Jiang Zemin on December 20. Musharraf mission was to plead for Chinese support on Kashmir. Since the visit came after the December 13 terrorist attack on Indian Parliament, obviously it must also have figured in his talks.

It is now a tradition that whenever Pakistan faces a security crisis with India, its leaders go to China for series of consultations. During the Kargil crisis while Nawaz Sharif was still holding Prime Minister's office, Musharraf was in Beijing just when the Kargil crisis was developing. Musharraf's involvement in initiating the Kargil War is clear from his famous dialogue with the then corps commander of Pakistan, which became public. Later Sharif also had visited China when going on the Kargil War became extremely hot for his chair.

India has been a victim of Pakistan sponsored terrorism for the last almost two decades. What has been the general attitude of China towards Pakistan? What has been its approach to terrorism? How has it viewed India's predicament in the recent period? Answers to these questions should help us to determine future course of Indian response to terrorism in the region.

China seems to be playing a double game as far as the current problems of global terrorism as well as regional terrorism. On the global terrorism, China is in favour of the UN as a fount of all decisions — a proposition with which India also agrees. On South Asian regional terrorism, China sees Pakistan as an easily manoeuvrable pawn in their hands, which can be used as and when required. Jiang Zemin has said that Chinese friendship with Pakistan is time tested one and not a fair weather one. What does it then mean to India?

In the current crisis, China has only extended financial assistance to Pakistan. It seems to be a part of ancient adage 'money now, blood later.' According to media reports, China has committed financial help of $1.5 billion but is unlikely to help Pakistan publicly on its current problems over Kashmir and their promotion of terrorism in India. China is also unlikely to give up the opportunity to use India's current predicament over terrorist attack on Parliament for its own advantage.

So, China has given the financial assistance but withheld open support to Pakistan on Kashmir. On the other hand, China has strongly condemned terrorist attacks on Indian Parliament. Obviously, China does not wish to completely to alienate India. For the first time China and India has set up a consultation mechanism on terrorism. After the first meeting, Indian foreign minister-and his counterpart in mid-October had expressed their determination to eliminate scourge of terrorism.

Later China held its first-ever official level dialogue on terrorism with India in the last week of November. Chinese Spokesman then had said, "Chinese side is firmly opposed to all forms of terrorism." Now in absolute terms, there is no dispute on that. Every nation is committed to absolute principles. No nation says that it supports terrorism not even Pakistan.

But when terrorism is cloaked in some emotional justification, like freedom movement or liberation of occupied territories, terrorism looks differently to interested parties. Thus during the latest visit to China, Musharraf linked Pakistan promoted terrorism to what he calls "core issue" of Kashmiri Liberation that is the "root cause" of the current problem of "high degree of tension" between two nations. At the same time, he is said to have advised Muslims in Xinjiang province of China (only province in China which has a large population of Muslims), he appears as a statesman-secular and not interested in using religious differences for national gains.

However, China's use of phrase "core issue" in relation to Kashmir in its public statement brought instant adverse reaction from India. But China, just because of its commitment to eliminate the scourge of terrorism, could not be expected to oblige India by asking Pakistan to stop its promotion of terrorism. Though even China does not believe in Pakistan's claim that it is not involved in the promotion of terrorism.

After all, it helps China when India is bleeding in fighting terrorism. That weakens India and takes pressure away from China, giving it more time to settle its border problem with India. Thus, Jiang Zemin have advised Pakistan bilaterally and peacefully resolve its problem with India. But India has refused to hold talks till Pakistan stops its support to terrorism. That puts Musharraf in a bind.

What this means to India is that while China may not actively support Pakistan, China will not also bring any pressure on Pakistan to stop its use of terrorism against India. The same thing is true of the US. In its so-called global war on terrorism, may ban terrorist groups operating on Pakistani soil as they have done with Jaish-e-Mohammad or Lashker-e-Toiba, it will not ask Musharraf to stop the use of terrorism as an instrument of its foreign policy. Thus India is left with the only option of self-help in putting off the threat of terrorism.

21

American Moment of Decision on Terrorism

(The Free Press Journal, 25-02-2002)

"All nations will head our call and eliminate the terrorists...But some governments will be timid in the face of terror. And make no mistake about it, if they do not act, America will" —*George W. Bush.*

During his three-day visit to Washington, DC that concluded on February 15, General Musharraf appeared to be desperate and under pressure. Watching him speak on camera I felt that he was wearing only the General's suit and his statesman's Sherwani was missing. Though while using the strong language against India, he remembers to remind that he holds two positions together, as was the case in his speech on January 12.

His desperation was evident practically in his every utterance. Thus, he alleged that India might have conducted a nuclear test. He was forewarning his American audience, that India plans to explode a nuclear device if she had not done it already. He also was thereby trying to alert US to be careful in entering into military relationship with India. He knew that the chairman of the US Joint Chiefs of Staff, General Richard Myers was to visit India on February 18. He had to face the embarrassing situation created by kidnappers of Daniel Pearl, the Wall Street Journal's South Asia correspondent. Pakistan had earlier tried to implicate India in it to show that India masterminds terrorist acts against the US only to blame Pakistan. The US media and the government did not buy that logic. Hence he told them that Pearl is probably alive. But also tried to win their sympathy by stating that his kidnapping was by forces opposed to his domestic reforms.

But then main suspect in kidnapping, Sheikh Omar Saeed, one of the three terrorists released by India in return for passengers of hijacked Indian Airlines flight at Kandhar in December 1999, owned up his involvement in the kidnapping of Pearl and informed the court in Karachi that Pearl is dead. Musharraf, however, discounted the news. He said despite their intensive search they did not even get his body! He took it as a proof of his being alive. Now it is evident that Sheikh Omar is also involved in Srinagar Assembly bombing on October 1 and Indian Parliament attack on December 13 last year.

Compounding his frustration by an attitude of defiance he reversed his earlier admission that December 13 attack on Indian Parliament as an act of terrorism. He probably knew in advance, that Sheikh Omar is likely to spill beans. Therefore, in his address to National Press Club, in Washington, he also reiterated his earlier refusal to hand over 20 criminals and terrorists wanted in India. The list as everyone knows included Sheikh Omar as well. On one breath he denied having them but on the second, he linked the question of their being handed over to India to beginning of negotiations on their bilateral disputes, including Kashmir.

The US silence over Pakistan's outbursts creates a doubt in Indian listeners, since the Bush administration simultaneously is trying to improve its relations with India. This of course goes far beyond fighting against global terrorism. Bush himself in his state of the union message to the Congress not only equated India with Russia and China but also had described new relations with India as unparallel in history of Indo-US relations so far.

This is evident in the US clearing General Electric Engine for Light Combat Aircraft. During Myers visit to Delhi he also indicated that military to military relations would be intensified. But asked about India Pakistan mobilisation of troops on the borders he categorically said: "Indo-Pak issues will have to be worked out by India and Pakistan."

Then what would be the US position on India's immediate problems of cross border terrorism? Does the US recognise Pakistan as the source of many of India's problems of terrorism? Publicly the US president as well as the officials has maintained a stance of praising Pakistan's co-operation in the global fight against terrorism.

But quietly the US is said to be pressurising Pakistan to act and act fast. During Musharraf's visit to Washington DC President Bush only agreed to retire $ 1 billion of more than $ 3 billion debt. Any further writing off of debt would be conditional to Pakistan retiring their army of Jihadi terrorists and carrying out domestic reforms as laid out by Musharraf in his January 12 speech.

There are other cues in the air as to what the US expects from Pakistan. Thus, for instance, during their joint media conference on January 18, Pakistan's Foreign Minister Sattar proclaimed that their dream is "to build Pakistan as a modern Islamic state." But later US secretary of State Colin Powell stated that Musharraf's, decision to confront extremism would transform Pakistan "into a modern, moderate state, as the minister just noted." Powell's substituting 'Islamic' by the 'moderate' can be interpreted only as a deliberate and not accidental. But India recognises the fact that the task before General Musharraf is extremely difficult and his path is full of thorns. Yet it is serious that Musharraf should reverse his public stand on terrorist attacks in India. In the light of it, the US public praise of General Musharraf is disturbing, if not surprising.

It ought to be disturbing to the Americans as well. The western media is full of stories regarding Al Quida and Taliban leadership regrouping in Pakistan-particularly in Baluchistan and Pakistani security authorities are not very effective. Once the severity of winter becomes less, the terrorists could be a threat to American interests globally in addition to continue to stir trouble in Kashmir.

But what if the US signals are not read clearly understood by General Musharraf or his advisers? Then there is the only one option. The US has already termed India as a "frontline state" in war against terrorism. In the current usage of the term, it means that the threat of global terrorism has touched Indian borders. It is recognition of India facing cross border terrorism.

Hence, using Indian facilities, the US should once for all, clear Pakistan of terrorist training bases, camps and schools, as they did it in Afghanistan. Remember, Bush had expressed in the state of union address his hope that “all nations will head our call and eliminate the terrorist parasites.... But some governments will be timid in the face of terror. And make no mistake about it, if they do not act, America will.”

More or less identical ideas were repeated by President Bush during his Joint media conference with Musharraf in Washington DC. He Said: “I think one of the worst things that can happen in the world is terrorist organisations mating up with nations which have had a bad history and nations which develop weapons of mass destruction. It would be devastating for those of us who fight for freedom.

And therefore, we, the free world are going to, must make it clear to these nations they have a choice to make. And I will keep all options available, if they don’t make the choice. The time for decision has come now.

22

Evolving a Strategy against Cross-border Terrorism

(The Free Press Journal, 19-03-2002)

India has to retain the option of use of coercive power in case the US fails to end the scourge of terrorism in South Asia.

Now that the Indian problem of cross-border terrorism has become an inseparable part of international terrorism, India needs to pursue a very constructive strategy to eradicate the scourge of terrorism through international co-operation. What could be the main directions in this regard?

India has mobilised troops on the borders of Pakistan. Defence authorities seem to be not in a hurry to withdraw the troops from the borders. The US also is not in the mood to ask India to withdraw her troops to barracks.

On the other hand, the US unnamed official on a background basis while speaking to correspondents from India and Pakistan, reportedly said that "President Bush has personally told General Musharraf and the US ambassador in Pakistan also keep telling him to stop cross-border terrorism before there can be a meaningful dialogue."

Then, so long as the US is in the fore-front of the war against terrorism, India ought to follow the strategy of using all diplomatic levers to achieve the goal of eradicating terrorism without fighting a war.

At the same time, India has to retain the option of use of coercive power in case the US fails to end the scourge of terrorism in South Asia. After all the US considers that the epicentre of global terrorism is located in this region.

Second, Indian policy-makers need to accept the dominant role played by the US in the fight against international terrorism. We have suffered at the hands of Pakistan-sponsored terrorists for such a long time — over two decades and have been accustomed to the US application of double standards for almost the same period.

Hence, it is extremely difficult for us to admit that since September 11 there has been a qualitative difference in the US approach to the Indian problems of cross-border terrorism. Of course one must remember the presence of fully mobilised Indian army on India-Pakistan borders as a major factor.

Yet the US-led war against global terrorism has its greater impact than Indian war against terrorism in the last two decades.

Third, India needs to overlook the fact that the US has in public totally ignored all evidence of Pakistani complicity in perpetuating terrorism against India. On the other hand, President Bush does not miss a single opportunity to praise Musharraf's contribution to the war, against terrorism. The US accepts possibly General Musharraf's claims as a reformed reformer of Pakistan. Let us publicly go along with the US while diplomatically pointing out Pakistan's involvement in various terrorist acts.

Does the US really need any more evidence to be convinced? Sheikh Omar was earlier secretly indicted for the kidnapping and murder of an American tourist to Kashmir in 1994. Now it has publicly indicted him for Daniel Pearl's kidnapping and brutal murder. Musharraf is now saying that Pearl was "over intrusive" in his investigations and "got over involved." Was he getting so close to nail the ISI involvement in cross-border terrorism or was so close getting too close to reveal the full story about the whereabouts of Dawood?

Another person wanted in India is Maulana Masood Azhar released by India in exchange of passengers of hijacked Indian plane in December 1999.

Investigating agencies are now saying that he is the long suspected link between Osama Bin Laden and killing of 18 American soldiers in Somalia in 1993.

Fourth, India should avoid any public pronouncements against General Musharraf, as it will affect his strength in carrying out reforms at the American bidding. His own people in Pakistan, which India cannot prevent, are undermining him. Jihadis desire to get rid of him.

Riyaz Durrani, Secretary General of the Jamaat Ulema Islam said that under US pressure, Musharraf has put Kashmir issue under backburner but they "will not allow this to happen." Musharraf also had attributed Pearl kidnapping to Jihadis anger against various measures taken by him to control terrorism.

Fifth, India has to sharpen not only their intelligence gathering but cultivate a willingness to share sensitive information. Despite technological sophistication in gathering of intelligence, it is surprising that even the US failed to take adequate measures to prevent the occurrence of 9/11. A report had appeared from Islamabad based TV correspondent, Bakr Atiani of Middle East Broadcasting Centre to the effect that he was called to meet Osama Bin Laden.

Though Bin Laden was present, his close aides did much of talking. Laden smiling, these aides said "there would be attacks against American and Israeli facilities within next several weeks." Yet human intellect was unable to discern or detect the plot of terrorists.

This calls for greater co-operation and intelligence co-ordination between India and the US. The terrorists might attack nuclear power plants or even the conventional power plants to create the impacts of social chaos according to some international experts. India needs to arrange to get full information from the US on the developing terrorists' schemes.

Sixth, India has a very poor rating in their ability to try the offenders under domestic laws to control terrorist activities.

For instance, if India had expeditiously tried terrorists like Maulana Masood Azhar or Saeed Omar Sheikh instead of allowing them to languish in jails for four to five years international image of India could have been better than it is now. It could be worth exploring the possibility of trying these terrorists by the US.

But if the diplomacy through Super Power fails to achieve the goal of eradication of terrorism, Bush has already committed himself to do the job.

In his joint media conference in mid-February in Washington, DC with General Musharraf he had said: "I think one of the worst things that can happen in the world is terrorist organisations mating up with nations which develop weapons of mass destruction. It would be devastating for those of us who fight for freedom.

And therefore, we, the free world going to, must make it clear to those nations they have a choice to make. And "I will keep all the option available, if they don't make the choice."

Since these words were put in general terms, Musharraf may think that these are addressed to Saddam Hussein of Iraq. But the words are equally applicable to Musharraf of Pakistan. He repeated the same thought on March 11 in the White House while remembering the incident of September 11 in its sixth month.

However, if the US wavers in its war against Pakistan-sponsored terrorism, India has the option of doing it. The first lesson of international relations is that self-help is the only help a nation gets in the community of nations.

23

Godhra Terrorism: Is it Political or Communal?

(The Free Press Journal, 6-04-2002)

Intelligence failure has not only caused loss of life and property but has brought bad reputation to the country.

The attack on Sabarmati Express at Godhra station by which Kar Sevaks were returning from Ayodhya on February 27 is a shocking incident. Sixty innocent lives were lost. These Ram bhaktas never ever must have imagined that they will never return to see their family members. Who could be behind the incident? What could be their motives? Till investigating agencies complete their tasks, it could be only guess work of the people however experienced they are.

There are three probable theories of conspiracies. My own initial reaction was to see the Congress hand behind these developments. The reasoning is very simple. Soon after the February elections in the states, the BJP as a party had lost power in the UP, Punjab and Uttaranchal. In Uttaranchal and Punjab the Congress gained power though no one has emerged a clear winner in UP. If one looks at the political map of India, the Congress is the dominant party today being in power in Maharashtra, Karnataka, MP, Chattisgarh, Rajasthan, Uttaranchal and Punjab. But the BJP is in power only in Gujarat, Himachal Pradesh and Jharkhand if you discount Goa.

Under these circumstances, if the BJP's stronghold in Gujarat is destabilised and discredited then it will not be too long for the political forces to realign at the Federal level as barring the Shiv Sena, others in the NDA have no ideological or political affinity with the BJP other than that of sharing power. Thus, on the very first day of the beginning of Gujarat Assembly session on February 26, the Congress members were vehement in demanding the resignation of the BJP government. If the government failed to comply, the Congress wanted the governor to dismiss the government.

The theory of the Congress hand would make the Godhra inferno a political affair. This approach is based on the past use of engineered communal violence for political gain for the Congress Party. The Congress has used the communal violence or pure violence to get rid of an inconvenient Chief Minister (CM) even if he belonged to its own ranks. Thus for instance, Rajiv Gandhi got Veerendra Patil ousted as the CM in Karnataka after party functionaries engineered communal riots in Davangere and elsewhere. Real reason was that he refused to collect huge amounts for the use of party functionaries in Delhi.

Mrs. Gandhi also used secular violence in contrast to communal violence, to destabilise the CMs during her tenure at the centre. Thus for instance, she used central control of food grains to starve Gujarat and engineer "food crisis" in 1974 to get rid of Chimanbhai Patel as the CM.

In the present Godhra case, based on reports now available, it is clear that the Congress leaders of Godhra took the lead in the attack on Kar Sevaks. Among those arrested for their alleged involvement are Mohammed Hussein Kalota, President of the Godhra. Municipality and two councillors-Abdul Dhamita and Salim Sheikh— all belong to the Congress Party. Another councillor, Haji Bilal Ismail Sujela who was absconding was arrested on March 16.

However, presence of the foreign hand cannot be ruled out. Vipul Vijoy, Deputy Inspector General of Police, Anti-Terrorist Squad, investigating the crime has said that involvement of Pakistan's Inter Services Intelligence (ISI) cannot be ruled out. When their own game of promoting terrorism in India is coming out more and more in Pakistan as in the involvement of two former ISI agents in the kidnapping of Daniel Pearl, it is a good tactic to divert the attention from international terrorism to domestic terrorism within India. Those arrested like Bilal are said to have travelled to Pakistan and were linked to the ISI.

Third, as we are on conspiracy theories behind the Godhra incident, the theory of BJP's own hand cannot be ruled out. Though it takes long to learn the art of governance, it does not take much time for politicians to pick up tricks of trade from long ruling Congressmen. Then why not investigate the possibilities of Chief minister Modi's rivals within the BJP instigating an incident of this magnitude to discredit him? It is reported that former CM of Gujarat, Keshubhai Patel stated during the February elections that he would campaign for the BJP but not for Shri Modi in Rajkot.

During the election campaign, CM, Modi had emphasised that there were very few instances of communal violence in Gujarat unlike during the Congress regimes of the past. But now that over 600 lives are lost in the post-Godhra riots in Gujarat, only Keshubhai can claim that and not Narendra Modi.

The communal riots, after the Godhra shock, which took place in many parts of Gujarat, are shameful events even as a reaction to the initial shocking acts. Whether aims of perpetrators were political or communal, the BJP government has played into the hands of either domestic criminals or their international masters.

There are obvious lessons-both political and administrative for the BJP. Politically, the BJP need to prevail upon its various front organisations or sympathetic organisation. I hate to use the phrase Sangh Parivar, because the feeling of community does not exist amongst the players — like the Viswa Hindu Parishad and Bajrang Dal etc. These have to accept the fact that politically it is in their interest as well as the, nation that the BJP completes the five-year term.

Second, the way in which Chief Minister Modi has run the state so far, shows that he has a long way to go in learning that politics is different from governance. If a CM has to enrich the party fortunes by retaining the voter support, he has to treat all citizens with the same standard even if some of them have not voted for him or his party. The way he proposed to offer ₹ two lakhs as compensation to the kith and kin of those killed in the Godhra while offering only ₹ one lakh to the relatives of those who were killed in the-post Godhra riots, is really bad governance. His theory that Godhra is 'action' and riots are 'reaction' is good politics but bad administration.

In this the Congress has not set a good precedent either. Mrs. Sonia Gandhi is reported to have visited to console the widow of former Congress Member of Parliament, Ahsan Jaffrey. But I have not seen any reports of her or any other Congress leaders visiting the homes of the victims of Godhra carnage. Are these families so dispensable, as the constituents of vote bank politics?

Administratively, it is a commentary on failure of our intelligence apparatus. A former, Intelligence Bureau director, once complained that they only get blamed for intelligence failure. But never get any praise, for good work. It is worth reminding that they are employed and paid to do good job. Hence failure attracts criticism while good work goes on. Their failure has not only caused loss of life and property but has brought bad reputation to the country.

24

Criminals in India are Favoured Guests of Musharraf

(The Free Press Journal, 19-04-2002)

India can offer to transfer to Musharraf all our criminals to the safe custody of Pakistan.

Pervez Musharraf, Military dictator and self-styled President of Pakistan goes to any extent to protect his own and Pakistan's interests irrespective any principles of law, constitution or equity. He can, because any law does not bind him. All laws, including constitutional law, are under him. He is, in Austinian sense the supreme lawgiver.

In the domestic sphere, he wants to hold a referendum to perpetuate his personal rule for next five years, before he can introduce new democracy in Pakistan. Even if democracy is brought back, it cannot be above his presidential power. If such an arrangement is not provided in the law, so what? It is he, who is provider of democracy to Pakistan. But while India is interested in a stable, democratic, modern Pakistan, what he does within his own country ultimately is a matter for the people of Pakistan to comment.

But what interests India is what affects her interests. And here, look at the way in which he has dealt with the question of handing over India's most wanted terrorists, like Dawood Ibrahim and his henchmen. Pakistan's Interior Minister, Moinuddin Haidar, during the recently concluded Organisation of Islamic Countries meeting in Kula

Lumpur said that Dawood Ibrahim is not in Pakistan. He complained that India had merely given list of persons whose extradition is being sought.

However, it is reported by the Indian intelligence that Pakistan has conferred its citizenship on Dawood, Tiger Memon and Chota Shakeel. Then it should be possible for India to give his residential and office address, Passport number and his new name/names to Pakistan's Interior Minister and Musharraf as well!

Now that Pakistan has acknowledged, albeit indirectly, their existence by making them Pakistanis, two issues become worth pondering. First, Pakistan was created as an independent nation according to its founder, Mohammad Ali Jinnah, where the Indian Muslims can live in peace and dignity. However, after 1957, Pakistan effectively closed the door to Indian Muslims making legally impossible for Indian Muslims to immigrate to Pakistan.

This is most unlike Israel another nation-state created to accommodate political aspirations of Jewish people. True to its founding philosophy, it continues to welcome Jewish people from anywhere in the world.

Be that as it may, but more importantly, it suggests that despite closing doors to Indian Muslims, a special category of them are still welcome to make Pakistan their home. These are of course, those who commit criminal and terrorist attacks against India and Indians.

This reminds me of a pre-civil war interstate incident in American history. A southern slave had fled to Massachusetts where there was no slavery. When the governor of the southern state asked the governor of Massachusetts to return the slave — as running away of a slave from his master was a crime — governor of Massachusetts refused to hand him over, as there was no slavery. Enraged at this, the governor of Southern state concerned offered to transfer all criminals from his state to Massachusetts! In the like manner, but without getting enraged, India can offer to Musharraf to transfer all our criminals to the safe custody of Pakistan!

Pakistan's action in making those who have committed heinous crimes against Indians, their citizens and property is extremely surprising as well as intriguing. It is surprising, as it has still left thousands of Pakistanis who migrated to East Pakistan from Bihar after partition, still languishing in Bangladesh, though they were very loyal to Pakistani cause of butchering Bangladeshis in 1971.

It is also intriguing; hence naturally questions arise as to what is so special about these Indian criminals who merited Pakistani citizenship. Though answers are obvious, some times they have to be narrated for greater clarity. The obvious inference is their involvement in organising terrorist attacks in India including those of Mumbai Bomb blasts of March 1993 by Pakistan's Inter-Services Intelligence (ISI) as a guiding force.

There is a larger perspective on it. Now it is well documented that Daniel Pearl, the Wall Street Journal's correspondent was trailing on the linkage between the ISI and Dawood. It is this that made Musharraf to say that Pearl had been "over intrusive in areas he shouldn't have been." As a result he "got over involved." Now Musharraf had not laid down for foreign journalists in Pakistan, guidelines on intrusive and non-intrusive areas!

It is the links of ISI to terrorism in the region that made Musharraf to blow hot and cold. Initially he was willing to consider extradition of Sheikh Omar Saeed after he was first tried in Pakistan. But as Sheikh's involvement not only in Pearl's kidnapping but terrorist bombing of Indian Parliament came out that made Musharraf to say that he would rather hang him himself rather than extradite him to the US.

So the dictator is not in a mood to oblige the US by extraditing Sheikh, there is no question of his buckling before the US. If so, there is no question of his obliging India by handing over twenty terrorists demanded by her. Obviously, all these terrorists in question whether it is Bin Laden of Al Quaida or Omar Sheikh or Maulana Azhar Masood of Jaish-e-Mohammad or Dawood and company — all are linked in their goals and targets.

All of them are linked, individually and collectively, inseparably to Pakistan's ISI and armed forces. Hence, handing over one could stir hornet's nest spilling lot of dirt. Two fires — one in Army's head quarters and another in ISI head quarters — have destroyed numerous papers detailing their links with terrorists. However, those papers cannot speak, but even one human being can do enough damage to Pakistan's active involvement in training, financing, arming aiding, sheltering and protecting terrorists in the last two decades. Musharraf is protecting Pakistan's national interests. Is America going to challenge it? If not, what is holding them?

25

Ramifications of Violence on Indo-Pak Relations

(The Free Press Journal, 23-04-2002)

It argues that internal domestic violence between Hindus and Muslims affects bilateral relations between two nations, causing distortions abroad about interfaith relations. Need is to emphasize unity of India.

Stimson Centre in Washington conducts an Internet dialogue on various subjects. The latest one states "communal and sectarian violence continues in Pakistan and has again flared menacingly in India. The latest tragedies have come at a time when the military forces of both countries remain in a very high state of readiness to fight another war." Then raises the question: "What are the likely ramifications of internal tensions on India-Pakistan relations?" Our readers may not always have time to go through the dialogue on the Internet. Hence, I propose here to delineate briefly two examples of how Muslims abroad see internal violence in India. I will conclude by suggesting a way out to check internal violence so as to improve India Pakistan relations.

The comments by some Muslim participants in this dialogue are illustrative of their mindset. It is necessary to correct some of the impressionistic stereotypes presented by these scholars. Thus for instance one Brigadier (Retired) Usman Khalid, President of Ansar Muslim League, UK recalls that as an aftermath of so called Babri Masjid demolition in December 1992, Muslims were massacred in India.

He conveniently forgets that in the post-demolition riots, a large number of Hindus were also killed. Of course, this kind of amnesia is not merely on the part of Muslims but is also exhibited by Marxists in India. In a seminar in Calcutta in 1997, I was surprised when a Marxist historian lamented killing of Muslims in Mumbai during communal riots of 1992. He didn't know, at least he pretended not to know, that Hindus were also killed. In Mumbai communal riots for instance, 1500 were killed of which at least one third were Hindus.

To revert to the views of Brigadier Khalid, as a military man, he knows that in external relations damage to the side starting the war is irreparable. In the like manner, being a minority, Muslims suffer greater casualties than Hindus in most of the communal riots. It is a well-known fact that many of Hindu-Muslim riots in India are Muslim-initiated.

The brigadier also exhibits this kind of selective amnesia on another unfortunate fact in the context of Gujarat riots. He refers to "kerosene can terrorism" in Ahmedabad. He ought to know that a premeditated attack in the wee hours of February 27th at Godhra by Muslim hooligans with kerosene can terrorism of Hindus travelling in Sabarmati Express coach S6 that in reality set in motion the retaliatory attacks in Ahmedabad.

What is really surprising is Brigadier Usman Khalid refers to Muslims in India as "children of Babar" in contrast to Hindus as "children of Ram" as though Indian Muslims are direct descendants of Babar. He overlooks the fact that majority of Indian Muslims are descendants of original Hindus who were converted to Islam. Pakistan traces its history to Mohenjodaro and Harappan culture. Then, why do they love nation's invaders? Is it just because they have embraced invaders' religion?

However, one fact has to be admitted here and that is on both sides, it is innocents who get killed. Sons of Ram who were returning from Ayodhya, who allegedly picked up a quarrel with the Muslim Vendors on Godhra Railway station did not cause deaths of any. But along with few teasers many more innocent passengers were burnt alive in the train coach. Even teasers do not deserve to be punished with death. In retaliation those who were killed in Gujarat had apparently no role in original sin.

This has an international parallel. The victims of terrorist attacks on the World Trade Centre (WTC) had no role at all even if the terrorists were attacking the US for its alleged crimes against Islamic world. It is equally true that the victims of the US bombing on Afghanistan were not, by and large, involved in the terrorist attacks on the WTC. However, at least these innocents could have been saved from death and destruction, if only the Taliban government in Afghanistan had agreed to hand over alleged brain behind international terrorism, Osama Bin Laden to the US.

Another Muslim scholar, Nazir Hussain of Quaid-I-Azam University in Islamabad says that Hindutva wants no other minority tolerated. They are killing Muslims in Gujarat, burning churches and Sikhs are not safe in India! Yes, all these things happen in India. But if Hindus were so cruel, Muslim population would not have grown from a seven per cent in 1947 to around 12 per cent in the 1990s. On the other hand, non-Muslims constituted 14.1 per cent of Pakistan's population in 1951. Now, they hardly constitute 2 per cent.

He also refers to Hindutva forces destructing Golden Temple, Babri Mosque and churches. Alas! For one mosque in disuse destroyed, hundreds of temples were destroyed in Pakistan. Pakistan sponsored terrorists attacked Raghunath Temple in Jammu very recently. For all this Muslim extremism in Pakistan, he blames "western inspired Jihad" of the 1980s!

Who are responsible for the original sin? Though it is too early to predict with confidence, it is clear that the riots were political in nature and not communal. And the basis for the conflict lies in the Congress promoted peculiar secular political culture. Under this secularism, seeking votes of minorities by reminding them they are Muslims is a symbol of secularism but seeking votes of Hindus is communalism. They shed lot of tears when a Muslim is hurt, but blame Hindus, even if Muslims kill them.

What India needs as the largest country in the subcontinent is to promote religion-blind civic culture. There is only one majority and that is Indians. All the others are minorities including Hindus. They have been divided into hundreds of castes. And our most secular leaders like of V. P. Singh and Mulayam Singh keep trying to further divide Hindus on caste lines. If there are not enough castes, they will divide them on their Gothras. When a Yadav from another party contests against him; Mulayam will differentiate the other Yadav on the strength of Gothra!

However, for the development of that kind of secularism, co-operation of our extremely important neighbour—Pakistan is essential. If Pakistan harps on Jihad and Islam India alone would find it difficult to maintain religion-blind civic culture.

26

Will the US Fight India's War against Terrorism?

(The Free Press Journal, 01-06-2002)

Post 9/11, though US under George Bush was promoting better relations with India, while having Pakistan as a partner in the fight against global terrorism! The contradictions in national interests of three nations are obvious since admittedly Pakistan promoting terror against India!

The May 4 massacres of innocent civilians that included women and children in Jammu has once again raised the war clouds in India - Pakistan relations. Ironically, India is a victim of international terrorism promoted by Pakistan while Pakistan is the epicentre of international terrorism. But both are valued allies of the US in its war against global terrorism! As Frank Pallone said Pakistan globally fights terrorism while locally promoting it.

George Bush, US President has a different goal when he fights terrorism aimed at the US interests. While he equates it with international terrorism, his immediate aim is to capture 'dead or alive' the brain behind 9/11 terrorist attacks-Osama Bin Laden. In this direction, he needs complete co-operation from military dictator of Pakistan-General Pervez Musharraf. After all Al Qaida Islamic terrorists and their sympathisers in Pakistan can destabilise his regime as well.

That President Bush is not interested in finding an end to cross-border terrorism affecting India and India is not a priority in his mental screen is evident during his visit to Europe on May 23. He said in Berlin: "Even though we had some initial successes, there is still (terrorist) danger for countries such as ours or Germany, France, Russia or Italy." Getting Bin Laden has acquired added urgency. Domestic leaks indicate that there was ample evidence within the intelligence agencies to conclude that Al Qaida terrorists were planning to use hijacking as a part of their attack on the US. Though Bush administration admits it they argue that hijacking was expected in 'the traditional sense" and not as a missile to hit the targets like the Pentagon or the World Trade Centre (WTC).

The opposition controlled Senate is proceeding to hold public enquiries to establish the truth. The truth could be politically blurred to some extent if Pakistan is able to help the US in tracking Bin Laden. And Bush knows it well that Musharraf is ready to betray Bin Laden as he betrayed Taliban if only that can get some economic benefit to Pakistan and help him to survive in office for the time being.

It does not mean that Indian troop mobilisation since the December 13 attack on Indian Parliament has been of no consequence. The US has come round to accept terrorism anywhere— and not merely against it— is an evil. It is US pressure that made some say that it was the US Secretary of State Colin Powell who wrote the main skeleton Musharraf to deliver January 12 speech.

Now again with India informing the world community that her patience is running out for the first time, the US has publicly accepted that Pakistan is involved in promotion of cross-border terrorism. In his media briefing, on May 23 state department spokesman, Joseph Reeker repeated often-stated US plea for "all sides in Kashmir to exercise restraint" and called for a "productive dialogue." But what is new is his admission that an important component in "dialogue process is an end to infiltration into Kashmir."

But Reeker repeated Musharraf's proforma statement that Pakistan will not allow its territory to be used by terrorists for attacks anywhere. Musharraf is trying to fool the world. Is the territory of Pakistan Occupied Kashmir (POK) Pak teritory or disputed territory? Since Pakistanis can move freely into POK, does Musharraf promise to prevent movement of Pakistani persons into POK and from there to Jammu and Kashmir (J&K)?

Many of the present problems in relation to Kashmir are of the US origin as a part of Cold War in the 1940s and 1950s. The US considers entire territory of J & K as a disputed territory. If the US is unwilling to accept the accession J&K as legal, why should India accept creation of Pakistan as legal, since both the processes were laid down by the same Act of British Parliament. Even today American newspapers refer to J&K as "Indian administered Kashmir." It is necessary for the US to give up its Cold War reasoning and rhetoric in favour of historic reality.

Thus India is in a dilemma. Moment she talks of a decisive war against Pakistan-sponsored terrorism, the leader of the international coalition—the US, asks India to exercise "restraint." Though US is itching to fight another war against Iraq. What explains this? After all Saddam Hussain poses no threat to regional powers like Saudi Arabia or Iran. These two are also against, the US fighting another war against Iraq in the name of a fight against international terrorism. The only explanation that can figure is: Father Bush had promised to dethrone Saddam Hussain. But he left the task unfinished. So Son Bush wants to complete it.

But the US cannot be expected to do anything other than pursue its own national interest. India cannot expect the US to fight her war against international terrorism. India has to decide to fight her own war in her own way. Now Prime Minister Vajpayee says that India should have fought it soon after the December 13 attack on Indian Parliament. One can ask: What prevented him to do so? Wars however, are not fought by public announcement.

India has lost over 70 thousand innocent lives in Pakistan-sponsored terrorism in Punjab and J & K in contrast to 3 thousand lives lost in the Al Qaida attacks of 9/11. But then, the US announced its intention to punish the perpetrators of crime. Afghanistan had no role in sending the suicide bombers to attack WTC and the Pentagon. Their only crime was that of harbouring Al Qaida leaders including Bin Laden.

Pakistan's Musharraf harbours not only well-known Indian criminals wanted in Bombay Bomb blast cases of March 1993 but Pakistani terrorists involved in hijacking IA flight from Kathmandu in December 1999, like Maulana Masood Azhar. India says infiltration from across the border from POK continues unabated. But the perpetrator of international terrorism is armed with nuclear weapons. But this should not affect an attack on terrorist bases in POK-disputed territory for Pakistan and Pakistan-occupied territory for India.

However, the government must decide and act. In case it thinks even an attack on terrorist bases in POK would backfire — a risk not worth taking — the government should continue to bring pressure on major powers of the world to see that Musharraf cannot be a promoter and fighter of terrorism at the same time.

27

Different Options to End Pak-sponsored Terrorism

(The Free Press Journal, 07-06-2002)

Pakistan uses cross border terrorism under the cover of its nuclear weapons while discussing various options to end Pak-sponsored terrorism; author favours the US to try an Afghanistan on Pakistan to make it a modern state.

Pakistan's new envoy to the United Nations (UN), Munir Akram in his very second day in the office has held out a threat of Pakistan using its nuclear weapons against India if it tries to cross the border or takes any aerial action against terrorist camps or any of its assets or tries to squeeze Pakistan economically. He has made it clear that Pakistan suffers from a low threshold of nuclear tolerance. There is no ambiguity on Pakistan's thinking on the utility of nuclear weapons.

Is the fact that Ambassador Akram is not the ultimate decision maker in the use of nuclear weapons, a saving grace? Not really, not withstanding General's late realisation of consequences of nuclear insanity! Because, General Musharraf himself had in an interview with the German weekly, Der Speigel in the first week of April had said that Kashmiri blood runs in Pakistani hearts as well. If the pressure on Pakistan became too great, he said, use of nuclear weapons could be possible as the weapon of last resort.

What is the difference between the statements of two? The weapon of last resort has become the weapon of the first resort if India dare attack even the terrorist Camps in Pakistan occupied Kashmir

(POK). However, international opinion was aroused so much over Akram's tantrum, that Musharraf was forced to backtrack on Pakistan's threat to use nuclear weapons. Thanks to Colin Powell's advice that it is foolish on the part of Pakistan to threaten the use of nuclear weapons when Indian stated policy is not to use them in first strike.

As a result, Musharraf told CNN "I don't think either side is that irresponsible to go to that limit." He added: "One shouldn't even be discussing these things, because any sane individual cannot even think of going into this unconventional war whatever the pressures."

Now, as a result of present confrontation, what India has been saying all these years since 1989, Pakistan's best friend in international relations — the US, is also stating — that infiltration continues to occur even after General Musharraf promised to be a good boy by controlling domestic groups of terrorists whose singular purpose of existence is to attack Indians and their assets.

Why is Pakistan holding this threat against India? India is after all not at war with Pakistan nor India desires even an inch of Pakistani territory. Even after General Musharraf's German interview; Indian Prime Minister, Atal Behari Vajpayee had said even after knowing Musharraf's views that India rules out a nuclear war. He reiterated that India's declared policy that "it will not be the first to use nuclear weapons." What India wants is that she be left to live in peace without Pakistan ever sending terrorists to infiltrate into India.

Then answer to the above question lies in the fact that Pakistan is at war with India. It is a multi-layered war. And this war is fought by the armed forces and its objectives are shared by a fairly large section of political leadership. One layer of war is motivated by an intense urge for revenge for its defeat by India in 1971 Bangladesh war. Another layer is religious war or Jihad for completion of what Ms Bhutto said process of partition of India on religious grounds. Then there is the third layer aimed at disintegration of India. Fourth, there is a desire to economically weaken India which otherwise is set to emerge as a regional power. All these layers are interconnected and pursued simultaneously.

In this pursuit of multi-layered war, its low-key, low-cost instrument is terrorism. Pakistan is the first country to have developed and used terrorism as an instrument of state policy. It is a low-key instrument as terrorists, sneak into Indian society, and until they are detected they operate as part of civil society. It is a low cost instrument as maintenance cost of a terrorist is negligible compared to a soldier since highly motivated, religiously brainwashed foreign and Pakistani mercenaries are never in short supply.

While terrorists are instruments of first use in the offensive wars, they are also a first line of defence for Pakistan. This was nowhere as clear as during the Kargil conflict. It was Northern Light Infantry men who fought along with a sprinkling of foreign terrorists.

With Pakistan holding out a threat of use of nuclear option and India raising the ante, there is a remarkable change in the US understanding of the role of Pakistan in promoting cross-border terrorism. US Secretary of State Colin Powell now says that Musharraf has not been true to his words. Infiltration continues and he confirmed Indian evidence that Pakistan has moved its terrorist training camps to Pakistan-occupied Kashmir. It is also reported that former Taliban and Al Qaida operatives freely move in Pakistan.

Under these circumstances world community led by the US has three options. First, India attacks terrorist training camps in POK in self-defence to punish terrorists and to eliminate them. It has to be a quick surgical attack. General Musharraf actually should welcome this, while making noise, as it will guarantee safety and security his life and presidency, little longer than the present juncture. It will also help him partially achieve what he set himself achieve in his January 12 speech to become a modern and moderate state.

So long as the US presence is felt in Indian Ocean and in Pakistan, the latter dare not use nuclear weapons against India. Any such adventure by Pakistan could be nipped in bud in the larger interest of humanity. However, there is one danger in this option. It will not eliminate the feeling of revenge felt by Pakistanis. On the other hand Pakistani army would nurse their revenge longer.

Second and more lasting and sensible option is for the US and European Union (EU) to threaten to impose an economic squeeze on Pakistan, to make it to see the darkness at the end of tunnel unless it ends playing with terrorist fire. Pakistan since September 11 has been encashing its past loyal service to the US to embrace it as a fighter against terrorism, by getting cash doles from the US and other western powers. A threat with firmness to withdraw goodies could bring Pakistan to see the light to escape from its creation.

Third, if the US finds that Pakistan fails to end cross-border terrorism even after economic squeeze, the only option left is to try an Afghanistan on Pakistan. The US need to bomb out terrorist bases in Pakistan and POK, impose a modern secular, democratic and Republican constitution with a built-in clause against military in civilian roles on Pakistan. Vast majority of Pakistanis, I am sure would welcome the change. The US bombing out terrorist camps will be in the larger interest of peace in South Asia.

28

Time to Pursue Uniform Policy Against International Terrorism

(The Free Press Journal, 05-07-2002)

Under the continued practice of use of double yardsticks against international terrorism by the US, it can airlift Musharraf to stand trial in Washington DC if he fails to control cross border terror.

President George Bush unveiled his policy to resolve Palestinian crisis in the last week of June. He has bluntly asked Palestinian people to elect new leaders "not compromised by terror" if they want their state in the next 18 months. Thereby Bush has effectively ruled out any negotiations with present leader, Yasser Arafat who after all began his career as a guerrilla leader fighting against Israel.

The message was so blunt, that even his closest ally Tony Blair of Britain felt it needed to be blunted somewhat. Hence, he tried to soften the bluntness of the message by stating that it "is for Palestinians to elect their leaders but what President Bush said was it is easier to negotiate a settlement if we negotiate with the people who are preferred to take action necessary to secure a settlement." But President Bush is firm that Arafat must go as has been demanded also by Israeli Prime Minister, Ariel Sharon.

But is it ever possible today to get such leaders in Palestine who are "not compromised by terrorism?" Can a society that grew up in a climate of using terrorism to achieve their political goals, produce such leadership all of a sudden? We need to look at the Indian history. Soon after independence; for at least forty years, we had satyagraha to resolve every socio-political problem. Often it appeared, in a democratic context, as duragraha.

I am pointing out the above dilemma to discuss the situation nearer home in Jammu and Kashmir (J & K) and the American double standards. Pakistanis have been also using terrorism as an instrument of their foreign policy ever since early 1980s on an experimental basis in Punjab and later since the, 1990s in J & K on a determined basis to achieve the goal of acquiring the territories of that state.

By now two generations in J & K have been brainwashed to believing in Islamic terrorism as a means to achieve their goal of self-determination or becoming a part of Pakistan, Senior political leaders supporting terrorists, like Geelani of Jamaat-e-Islami have even so to say as registered themselves, as Pakistani citizens by proclaiming that he is a "proud Pakistani." They are unlikely to achieve these goals.

But for the sake of argument, let us say J & K is liberated. An independent Kashmir is bound to face the same problem of terrorism in an intensified way from the people of Ladakh, Jammu and various other ethnic minorities demanding a separate state for them. Even Kashmiris would freely use terrorism as an instrument of domestic policy determination!

Or let us assume that Kashmir becomes a part of Pakistan. It will then inherit millions of terrorists from that state. But Pakistan as a society, which has supported or tolerated terrorists for the last two decades or more is soft to terrorism; possessing divine tolerance to terrorism. With another 12 million population from J & K it will be a formidable ungovernable state with Islamic terrorists roaming freely in the daylight with their kalashinokovs hanging on the shoulders.

This will have a positive effect on ethnic separatism now dormant as one ethnic group can provide support to another to gain independence from dominant Punjabi population of Pakistan. Mohajirs and Sindhis will be the first ones to go.

Now, in international relations, the US is the best friend of Pakistan. President Bush has to ponder over the effect of terrorism that is widespread in that country. Pakistan's General Musharraf having achieved his goal of easing tensions of war with India has tried to deny that he ever gave a promise to Under secretary of State, Richard Armitage on permanently and visibly ending terrorist infiltrations into J & K.

This is what he said to American readers in his interviews to the *Washington Post* and *Newsweek*. "I have told President Bush nothing is happening across the Line of Control. This is the assurance I've given. I am not going to give you an assurance that for years nothing will happen." It is necessary therefore, for India to get a written commitment from Musharraf counter guaranteed by Armitage as to their exact commitment to end permanently cross-border terrorism.

But Musharraf's track record is such even if he gives in writing his commitment; there is no guarantee that it will be visible and verifiable on the ground. It is here that the US plays a major role. Taking into consideration past record of Musharraf in the Kargil incursion, his double standards in Afghanistan in permitting his troops to fight with Taliban against the international forces, his reluctance to fight Al Quida terrorists in Pakistan until driven to wall etc. shows that he is no way less compromised by terrorism than Arafat.

Hence, the US has the option of bluntly telling Musharraf that unless he implements his promises of permanently and visibly ending cross border terrorism, US would prefer him to step down in favour of a leader not compromised by terrorism. President Bush would have many such Pakistanis settled in the US who could provide a modern, democratic and republican administration to terrorism-torn Pakistan. Bush might have a similar plan to export Palestinians settled in the US, as he did in the case of Afghanistan.

Bush has also held out a threat of financial squeeze to Arafat. As he said: "We won't be putting money into a society which is not transparent and (is) corrupt and I suspect other countries won't either." If he fails to listen, the US can airlift him to the US as the Bush senior did to General Noriega of Panama to stand trial for a lesser offence of drug trafficking.

Options are hard. But alternatives are harder as Armitage himself admitted in a frank interview with the *Financial Times* (London) that

Al Qaida network is active and operating in Pakistan and "Kashmir" and "would like nothing better than a splendid war between India and Pakistan. If a war breaks out, and escalates into a nuclear one, casualty could be anywhere between 13 million to 30 million innocent lives according to international estimates of Pandits specialising in MAD (mutually assured destruction) in a nuclear conflict. Is sacrifice of one Musharraf, too great a price to pay?

29

Post-election Kashmir Scenario: Implications for Indian Foreign Relations

(The Free Press Journal, 30-10-2002)

Post-election scenario would have been ideal for the leaders to make Mehabooba Mufti the CM who had a better equation with youth in Kashmir.

The much publicised elections for 87-member Jammu and Kashmir (J&K) Legislative Assembly are over. These elections provided some ammunition to military dictator of Pakistan and Indian Prime Minister to test their skills in public diplomacy in the United Nations (UN) General Assembly (GA) in September. Addressing UNGA first, General Musharraf characterised elections in J&K as a farce. A theme he had used in his Independence Day speech in August.

Taking the podium after him Atal Behari Vajpayee returned compliments to Musharraf by hitting him personally when he said that those who had to adjust voting and counting procedures to win a referendum were ill-placed to lecture others on freedom and democracy. After all the purpose of UNGA is to influence the world opinion and they have done their role well in influencing their hard-core supporters.

The elections were not without their dose of violence. The major brunt was borne by the National Conference (NC) supporters. While many workers of the party were attacked and killed by terrorists, Farooq Abdullah's brother and Industries Minister in J & K government was gunned down. The terrorists also made two unsuccessful bids on the life of Tourism Minister, Ms Saleema Ittoo. But as Girish Chandra

Saxena, governor of J & K said during the entire election process from the time of announcing the elections to its completion 129 men from the army and paramilitary were killed.

Elections are unique in many ways in the background of infection of terrorism, global attention; neighbourly efforts to disrupt the elections and the nature outcome are all of more than transitory significance. First, there was a grave threat to life of individual voters. This emanated from two adverse sources-call for boycotting of elections from All Party Hurriyat Conference (APHC) and terrorists' violence based on gun culture. These were in addition to general voter apathy. Yet voter turnout of 44 percent was an evidence to confirm the faith of ordinary voters in J & K in democratic electoral process.

Second, the electoral aftermath brought out an important fact that APHC, a 23 party conglomeration world wide known as political face of terrorist groups based in J & K and outside and operating in the state is a big loser. Barring a few constituencies in Srinagar, elections show that their influence is negligible. Efforts to disrupt the elections were not spared by the APHC trying to enforce their boycott call. There were similar efforts by their terrorist groups as well. But on the whole will of the people emerged supreme.

Third, the elections were free and fair and successful in preventing any fraud and totally transparent. The fact is confirmed by the loss of power by NC. Part of the problem in public perception was the hold of Abdullah family on the government and administration and a public sense of lack of an alternative party to the NC. Irrespective community to which they belonged, a wide section of voters shared this feeling. The fairness of elections is doubly confirmed by the loss suffered by Omar Abdullah in a constituency nurtured by the family for years.

Fourth, the election at the same time confirms the fact that NC is still the main party in the J & K with 28 seats. Their percentage of vote has come down only by 4 percent from 34 to 30 as a result of incumbency factor and anti-NC campaign by all parties including the BJP with which it shares power at the centre! It is somewhat similar to the Congress Party under Rajiv emerging as the single largest party but without a working majority in 1989 Lok Sabha elections. Yet it did not form the government as anti-Congress Parties had gained a majority.

Of course, before we move to discuss the foreign policy implications, we need to know whether politicians in J & K can rise above their narrow individual, and party interest to protect the larger national interest? Since it was a denial of power to the NC by the voters, it is logical that the non-NC parties should form the next government. It is best in the national interest, that the Congress and People's Democratic Party (PDP) form the government with the help of the rest. However, it is unfortunate that senior leaders like Mufti Mohammad Sayeed and Ghulam Nabi Azad squabbled for the Chief Minister's (CM) post.

Looking at the post-election scenario, it would have been ideal for these leaders to make Ms. Mehaboba Mufti the next CM instead of Mufti trying to go down, as the CM. Youth would have responded more favourably to Mehaboba than they are likely to her father. There is a precedent in the UP. Though the BJP is the larger party, it has entered into a coalition with Bahujan Samaj Party and permitted the BSP to hold CM's office. There can be change of CM every six months or once a year or once in two years. If the parties coalescing have a common programme for the next five years, it should not matter if the' CM's post alternates.

Now turning to India's foreign policy in relation to long pending Kashmir problem, first, General Musharraf will have to accept the election results as the people's verdict in J & K. One needs to look at the results in Pakistan elections in October. Though the observers from European Union were very critical of these, the United States has endorsed them as fairly free and fair. Musharraf will be in a bind to accept the electoral verdict in J & K.

Second, the Hurriyat leaders will be left with no alternative other than the one of dropping their demand for independence or merger of J & K with Pakistan if not to be totally irrelevant. Their refusal to participate in the elections and inability to enforce, boycott call has negated their claims to represent dominant aspirations of the people in the state. Already Mirwaiz Umar Farooq has said in an interview with Washington Times that alternate solution through negotiated settlement could be possible. This is in the face of his earlier statement that their participation in the elections would have meant their acceptance of Indian constitution. Chairman of the Hurriyat Abdul Ghani Bhat has also admitted to be under pressure from the US on the subject.

Third, both India and the US would be required to take into consideration in different ways the likely consequences of the possibilities of an extreme Islamic right coalition called the Muttahidda Majilis-e-Amal forming the government in Pakistan. For the US this would negate the entire rationale so far for their support of Musharraf regime as the best bet to fight against terrorism, as the latter is committed to promote moderate and modern Islamic state in Pakistan. Alternative to Musharraf, they used to say is religious right. But that is exactly what has emerged. For India it holds a direct threat of further radicalising movement in Kashmir and escalating terrorism unless the problem is resolved early.

Hence, fourth, India and Musharraf might find time opportune to settle the problem with turning the Line of Control (LoC) as international border in Kashmir. This has been in discussion between India and Pakistan since Ayub Khan's time but was taken up more seriously during Shimla talks in 1972. Former Indian President Zail Singh mentions it in his memoirs as a topic Zia having discussed with him. The fact is: with all probability it was discussed between Vajpayee and Nawaz Sharif. Recently, during his visit to New York, right-wingers in his team leaked it to press that Musharraf is going to discuss this very topic with India. That effectively scuttled the issue. But, as an usurper of power in Pakistan seeking an honourable way out, Musharraf should consider the proposal seriously. This could provide him a home in US and or in Delhi.

30

UN Must Make all Nations Pursue Secularism

(The Free Press Journal, 22-11-2002)

Pakistan promoted terrorism is aimed at creating a wedge between "Hindus and Muslims" within India. U.N. "must make all nation pursue secularism"

India is a multi-ethnic and multi-religious state. That character of the state is under threat from ethno-religious terrorism and separatism promoted from across the state and ugly reactionary forces from within. The latest is the attack on innocent pilgrims at Akshardham temple in Gandhinagar. Often scholars and journalists commenting on communalisim only see the domestic roots of communalism. But they do not see any linkage between domestic problem of communalism and its international roots, encouragement and promotion.

On the other hand, it is a very simple truth for any one to say that secularism can thrive nationally in an international environment that is conducive and supportive of secularism. In the long drawn Cold War since 1945, the US as the most powerful super power used religious identity in its fight against its rival and the second super power the Soviet Union. It is nowhere so abundantly clear as in its last phase in its war against the Soviet military intervention in Afghanistan in the neighbourhood of South Asia.

The Soviets intervened militarily in Afghanistan in December 1979. The US converted it into an opportunity to pay back to the Soviet Union for its role in the ignoble and forced withdrawal from

Vietnam. In this attempt the US directly trained Afghans in their war against non-believers in the Soviet Union. It was a war against godless communism led by the Mujahiddins-freedom fighters where Arabs and Pakistanis joined Afghans in big numbers. They too were trained and equipped by the US in making it a religious Jihad.

Though the US was able to drive away the communists from Afghanistan and end communism in the Soviet Union, the costs in terms of disturbance of global peace are quite heavy. The present ethno-religious strife is the direct outcome of these developments. If the Soviet's were suspected of spreading communism in different parts of the world, the US can be directly held to account for the growing religious strife and Jihad in the world.

In Pakistan thus for instance, Zia-ul Haq had already initiated Islamisation of Pakistani society by dismantling last vestiges of Jinnah's dream of secular Pakistan. Zia used Islamisation to make his military rule more palatable to Pakistanis and consolidate his hold over power. Pakistan became an ally, a frontline state in the US war against the Soviets in Afghanistan.

The Pakistan since its birth had for the first time gained a foothold in Afghanistan as a conduit to supply weapons to Mujahiddins. Pakistan's borders with Afghanistan becoming open. Pakistan with US connivance became instrumental in training, brainwashing and equipping Taliban as a force to fight for political power. After the Soviet withdrawal from Afghanistan, Pakistan and Afghanistan became torchbearers of religious war in the region.

This phenomenon has given rise to overt linkages between global ethno-religious identity and tensions on the one hand and domestic communal disharmony on the other. External forces have and are indulging in encouraging communal strife in India.

For instance, Indian Sikhs in Britain are fighting to get the government recognition as a separate ethno-religious community. Campaign is led by Sikhs associated with a group, which calls itself as "Civil Service of the Sikh Nations." Though the leaders of the organisation claim that it has nothing to do with Sikh separatists in India, its implications cannot be ignored. In the event British government obliging the group by recognising its demand it can provide impetus to separatist movement in India on the strength of religious identity.

Hence, a simple fact is that longer the strife goes on in J & K under the directions of Pakistan, deeper will get the communal divide between Hindus and Muslims within the country.

Pakistan's sponsorship of cross-border terrorism has to be seen from this perspective. The terrorists are attacking Hindus and even those who do not subscribe to communal agenda amongst Muslims. Here what Bill Clinton said about Indian democracy can also be rightly said about Indian secularism.

During his sojourn to India in March 2000 he had said while addressing the joint session of the Parliament: "it is difficult to be a democracy bordered by nations whose governments' reject democracy." In the like manner, isn't it true that it's difficult to be a secular society and polity when surrounded by anti-secular nations?

It is not that only Pakistan is a challenge to secularism in South Asia. In Bangladesh during the October 2001 elections, Al Qaida terrorist attacks on the US and consequent reaction of President George Bush created a chain of developments, which helped fundamentalism to grow in Bangladesh. India's joining hands with the US in its war against global terrorism directly influenced the electoral process in Bangladesh.

As it is, in the normal times it is unavoidable for the Bangladesh to make India as an issue in their elections. The then ruling party - Sheikh Hasina's Awami League, is generally perceived as closer to India as it was that Party which made Bangladesh emerge as an independent country. On the other hand, the Bangladesh Nationalist Party (BNP) capitalises itself by playing the card of anti-Indian sentiments.

The Indian support to the US was explained as Hindu support against Muslim cause and that helped the BNP to whip up anti-India feelings to win a few more seats. As it is it had entered into an alliance with Jamaat-e-Islam Party. The result has been growing Islamisation in Bangladesh.

Pakistan has been prompt in encashing the development. In July this year during his visit to Bangladesh, General Musharraf offered an apology for Pak atrocities of 1971. Since then there is a growing anti-Indian and anti-secular collaboration between Pakistan and Bangladesh.

The latest example is Bangladesh support in the Commonwealth in favour of withdrawal of suspension of that country imposed after its military coup in October 1999.

India is thus pressurised from north-west and north-east by anti-secular forces led by Islamic states. Others in South Asia are not far behind. Smaller countries like Bhutan and Sri Lanka adhere to Buddhism as a state religion while Nepal is the only country in the world, which is a Hindu state.

What is therefore necessary is that secularism like the human rights needs to be adopted as a global value to be promoted through international co-operation, understanding and collaboration.

One cannot promote human rights without committing to secularism, pluralism and democracy. It is time for the United Nations to develop a charter on secularism and make all countries in the world to pursue secularism in their internal as well as external relations. Then only the world society can become truly religion-blind.

31

Islamic Pakistan Posing a Greater Threat to the World

(The Free Press Journal, 14-12-2002)

Musharraf promised to build a "modern and moderate" Islamic State article anticipated at the end of 2002 that "International Islamic terrorists will have free play in Pakistan politics"

The New York Times on Sunday the 24 November carried an elaborated piece on marriage of convenience between Pakistan American Ally Number One in their war against global terrorism and North Korea—one of the trinity of evil states (other two being Iraq and Iran) in the eyes of George Bush. David E. Sanger, correspondent writing from South Korea details as to how as recent as in July this year, Pakistan dispatched nuclear weapons technology to North Korea in return for its missile technology. General Musharraf, trusted ally of George Bush, "needs to build a nuclear arsenal capable of teaching every strategic site in India."

Sanger adds that Musharraf used C-130 transport plane to ferry nuclear weapons technology to North Korea and bring missiles system. C-130 is specifically given to Pakistan by the US for use in its war against terrorism. Though US intelligence knew of this misuse of the plane, US winked at it in return for Pakistan's co-operation in its war against Taliban and Al Qaida.

The present developments in the US-India relations with Pakistan as a factor remind one of the post-Soviet military interventions in Afghanistan in 1979. "History doesn't repeat itself," Mark Twain once observed, "but it rhymes?' How true it is in the case of India-US relations in the context of ghastly terrorist attacks on the World Trade Centre (WTC), New York and Pentagon in Washington, DC! History seems to repeat itself with different tunes now some times actors reversing their roles.

What I have in mind is relevance of history of India US relations soon after the Soviet military invasion of Afghanistan in December 1979 to certain developments in our relations with the US in the event since the WTC attack. Until the invasion then during the Carter presidency, as until the attack now during the Bush presidency, India-US relations were on an upward swing.

The US relations with Pakistan, in contrast, were then at their lowest ebb. There were anti-American riots as late as in November 1979, in which two Americans were killed. Carter had imposed military and economic sanctions against Pakistan. In the like manner, just prior to the 9/11 attacks, Pakistan was isolated from the western states, US policy makers were considering it as a rogue state. Pakistan was desperate in seeking US lifting of economic sanctions imposed after its nuclear tests of 1998 and against Musharraf's military coup of October 1999. Pakistan had conducted a campaign to educate American policy makers that lifting of sanctions against India alone without lifting them against Pakistan would further create anti-American feelings in Pakistan.

Once the Soviet Army entered into Afghanistan, first thing President Carter did then was to send his personal envoy, Clark Clifford to New Delhi to seek India's co-operation to see the Russians out of Afghanistan. Mrs. Gandhi declined though during her election campaign in December 1979, she had categorically stated that Soviet presence in Afghanistan "was a danger to India." However, in the present case, soon after the WTC attack, Atal Behari Vajpayee went out of the way to offer India's co-operation in fighting the war against terrorism. There was apparently no solicitation of such support by President Bush.

Again, in 1979-80 the US approach to Pakistan changed overnight, after India declining to help US in getting Russians out of Afghanistan. President Carter then turned to Pakistan, offered an aid of $400 million, which Zia rejected as peanuts. Then Reagan turned peanuts into walnuts by raising the size of aid package to $3.2 billion! Pakistan became a frontline state as a conduit to pump arms and assistance to an army of Afghan Mujahiddins to fight against Russians. First seeds of terrorism in the region were sown in 1980s one of the products of it is Osama Bin Laden and as a result of which the Taliban also was born. Now again, a Pakistan, which had felt isolated until the attack, has emerged as an ally in US efforts to get Osama Bin Laden Dead or alive!' The logistics of terrorism in the region and inseparable linkages between Pakistan-Afghanistan as two sides of the same coin have made Pakistan an important ally.

The US was very prompt in extending economic aid, write off part of past debts and reschedule another part on the assurance of General Musharraf that he is turning Pakistan into a modern Islamic Republic. Americans have constantly tried to convince themselves if not the world that there is no alternative to General as the only alternative was one of growing Islamisation!

This has left many wondering whether US is playing the old game of trying to remove one thorn with the help of another! Because, Pakistan's alliance with the US has only resulted in making Islamic forces very strong. This is evident in the results of the October 2002 elections in Pakistan, where religious parties have won not only the second largest number of seats in the federal assembly but have also captured power in the North West Frontier Province (NWFP). Some of these parties have close links with Taliban.

The intelligence reports say that defeated Taliban and Al Qaida forces are very much in Afghan-Pak borders. With pro-Taliban forces winning power in NWFP international Islamic terrorists will have a free play in Pakistani politics and society. In another five years it is logical to think that fundamentalist forces will only further expand their hold over Pakistan's government, making it as faithfully Islamic as Taliban was. But the Islamic Pakistan of 2002 will be totally different from the Islamic Pakistan of the 1980s under Zia.

32

What can Indian Kashmiris Learn from Sri Lankan Tamils?

(The Free Press Journal, 17-12-2002)

Irish Republican Army that waged a war for secession of Catholic Ulster from England to join with Ireland sued for peace as their funds from the US were cut off, so was the case with the LTTE. Is there any lesson for Indian Kashmir?"

At last there is a hope of light at the end of tunnel in 19 years Tamil problem in Sri Lanka. After four days of talks in Oslo, Norwegian deputy foreign minister, Vidar Helgesen announced that plans envisage turning Sri Lanka into a federal state with Tamil areas constituting a federating unit in the federation. The joint statement issued after the negotiations said that the "parties have decided to explore a political solution founded on internal self-determination based on a federal structure within a united Sri Lanka."

The Liberation Tigers of Tamil Ealam (LTTE), chief negotiator, Anton Balasingham described it as a "historic decision." This development was possible because earlier LTTE chief, V. Prabhakaran for the first time had announced his intention to accept "substantial regional autonomy" in place of self-determination by seceding from Sri Lanka. There is a radical change in the approach of both sides. Some years ago when the then Sri Lankan ambassador visited the Mumbai University, I had suggested to him federal structure as a possible solution to the political crisis in his country. The Sri Lankan ambassador then had agreed that it could be considered, but had expressed general fear of Sri Lankan people that federal status could be the first step in the ultimate secession.

The LTTE had indicated a gradual change in their attitude. During the first round of negotiations in September this year, chief negotiator, Balasingham had said that the "LTTE does not operate with the concept of a separate state. We operate with the concept of a homeland and self-determination. A homeland does not mean a separate state." Later in November they also dropped the demand for an interim administration in North and East. They have also agreed to allow other parties to operate in their area. The LTTE has come around the present position after sacrificing the precious lives of more than 64 thousand people. People want peace to carry on with their livelihood without any hindrance. But more important is the effect of September 11. Irish Republican Army (IRA) that waged a war for secession of catholic Ulster from England to join with Ireland sued for peace as their funds from the US were cut off, so was the case with the LTTE. Is there any lesson for Indian Kashmiris? Obviously there are many lessons for Indian Kashmiris. Indian Kashmiris have to seek as in the case of Tamils a non-secessionist solution for their problem as well. Some Kashmiris have been clamouring for Azadi. Azadi is freedom. Regional autonomy that the Tamils in Sri Lanka have now settled to accept is similar to Kashmiri claim for Azadi, which means internal self-determination.

In Tamil dominated areas there are Muslims. If Tamils were to press for independence, it would not prevent Muslims from demanding similar independence or an option to remain with the Sinhalese people. Hence wisely, Tamils have agreed to include a Muslim delegation in their next round of talks in Japan with Sri Lanka. Kashmiris have to realise that any demand for independence by Kashmiris will provoke not only Dogra Hindus in Jammu but others like Ladakhis to demand similar independence. Kashmiris in India are in a better position than Tamils in Sri Lanka. The Jammu and Kashmir (J & K) already has a status of being a state in the Indian Union. As a unit in the Indian federal state, they have already exercising constitutionally derived powers. These powers are quite substantial though the federal government controls the money that is required to implement the powers enjoyed by the state. But that position is not unique to J & K. Practically every state in the Indian union would clamour for more powers. Demand for regional autonomy thus often is a political question. So long the Congress Party had a sway over the federal government as well as states, no one raised the question of autonomy. But once for the first time the Congress lost power at the Centre, of all the states, then Chief Minister of Maharashtra, Vasantdada Patil said that states have been reduced to the status of municipalities. The real problem is one of more resources. The federal government need to devolve more financial powers to the states.

Now that J & K has a new government, the federal government need to , discuss with it mechanism to evolve a conceptual understanding of regional autonomy as internal self-determination or Azadi. If the new leaders of J & K are able to clearly understand this concept and the Centre is able to devolve more financial powers to it, half the battle for the minds of Indian Kashmiris can be said to be over.

33

US Must Act Against Pak, The Real Epicentre of Global Terrorism

(The Free Press Journal, 11-03-2003)

The US allowed Pakistan to become the Jihadi University for the entire world. But now if the US fails to get at the real epicentre of terrorism, Pakistan might replace Afghanistan as its main concern.

India has been telling the US authorities that Pakistan is the epicentre of International terrorism. By implication, unless one fights against Pakistan's involvement in promotion, protection, funding, sheltering and arming of international terrorist, the global war against it will never see an end. The US has been dismissing so it appeared -Indian pleadings as it continued to co-operate and collaborate with it in their so-called global war against terrorism. The latest is the fact that number III man in Al Qaeda terrorist organisation, Khalid Sheikh Mohammad next only to Osama Bin Laden and Ayman al-Zawahiri, has been arrested in Pakistan.

Who is this Khalid Mohammad? He is a Kuwaiti by birth but has been a citizen of Pakistan as his father was a Pakistani. He has been in charge of military operations of Al Qaeda and supposed to have been the mastermind who planned the World Trade Centre (WTC) bombing. The US sources believe him as connected to the 1993 efforts to blow up the WTC, 1998 embassy bombings in Nairobi and Dar-e-Salaam as well as the attack on USS Cole in Yemen in October 2000.

Deputy Prime Minister; L. K. Advani has been repeatedly saying in India and abroad that Pakistan has been the epicentre of global terrorism. Anything that is talked about or stated by Indian leaders is not given due credence by the US. The Prime Minister expressed this feeling of frustration recently when he said in the Lok Sabha that the US administration has its own priorities. Bush must have been hurt by PM's utterances and he was quick in calling Vajpayee to assure him that pressure is being applied on Islamabad to end cross-border infiltration from across the borders, particularly after the snow melts.

The international opinion to some extent is shaped by the domestic response to such utterances by the plethora of political parties. These parties only see how to enlarge their Muslim vote banks. For that goal, they condemned the previous stringent law to control terrorism, popularly called TADA and its newer version Prevention of Terrorism Act (POTA).

Be that as it may, it is not the first time that either a Pakistani terrorist or an international terrorist has been arrested or captured in Pakistan with most reluctant co-operation of authorities. Their co-operation has always been so to say only through the gun point. The list is never ending but suffice if I give some important ones to illustrate my point. Take the case of Ramzi Ahmad Youssuf who supervised the WTC bombing in 1993. This man was responsible for a failed assassination attempt against Bill Clinton during his visit to Manila in 1994 and against Pope in early 1995. Pakistanis in Islamabad finally captured Ramzi in May 1995. In the present case Pakistanis claim to have alone arrested Khalid Mohammad. So they said in the case of Ramzi. But if the past behaviour of Pakistan is any guide, Ramzi's case should help every one to understand what it must have been in the case of Khalid Mohammad. Yossef Bodonsky, author of 'Bin Laden: The Man Who Declared War on America' says that the "US government confronted Islamabad with precise information about Youssuf's hiding place-an apartment complex sponsored by a Bin Laden-related company."

Islamabad had no alternative other than co-operate with the US. The US of course had held out a threat to impose stiff sanctions against Pakistan and also put it on the US list of terrorist states. It is only then that Benazir government put up a face of co-operating with the US. However, Pakistan's ISI saw to it that all other Al Qaeda terrorists escape from the hideout before the arrival of the search party.

In the case of Khalid Mohammad US claims that it was a joint FBI-ISI operation that led to his arrest. Even when Khalid was flown out of Pakistan for interrogation at the US controlled Air Force base at Bargram in Afghanistan, Pakistani authorities maintained that he is still in Pakistan! General Musharraf went to the extent of characterising the charge as "nonsense."

It is obvious that it is not a case of a foreign national infiltrating into Pakistan and Pakistani authorities from top to bottom co-operating with the US law enforcing agencies to nab the culprit to nip in bud his terrorist atrocities. Pakistani authorities, on the other hand, are hand in glove with the international terrorist groups based in Pakistan and abroad.

In the case of Khalid Sheikh a Pakistani woman political activist belonging to Jammat-I-Islami in Rawalpindi had sheltered him in her home. Her son Ahmad Qudoos has been detained and another of her family member, Major Adil Qudoos has also been arrested. It has to be taken note that Jamaat-I-Islami is a partner in MMA a coalition of six religion-based political parties, which emerged as a force to be reckoned with after last October national elections in Pakistan. The coalition is open supporter of Taliban of Afghanistan. Interestingly, the Foreign Minister of Pakistan, Kasuri says that the coalition cannot be equated to Taliban of Afghanistan, which is a tribal party. On the other hand, MMA is a democratic coalition! He accused countries inimical to Pakistan like India of spreading the canard.

But Khalid is reported to have told American interrogators that he met Osama Bin Laden in February 2003 and he thanked Allah for keeping him alive. This confirms at least three points. First, Bin Laden is alive, second he is most probably in Pakistan and third, their meeting might be related to a major plan of action. Unfortunately for the US President, George Bush, who is neither serious about bringing Bin Laden to justice "dead or alive" as he proclaimed on September 17, 2001 nor he is interested in ending terrorism permanently. But he is serious of only winning 2004 Presidential elections.

For that when he realised that he is unlikely to succeed in getting Bin Laden captured he began to divert the global attention to another of America's friend-turned enemy Saddam Hussein by painting him as a terrorist. Musharraf recently said that after Iraq, next target could be Pakistan! Looking at the goal of President Bush and the war against terrorism, Musharraf could be right. If Bush fails to get the UN resolution for a war against Iraq, he might turn against Pakistan! That may be the right thing to do, however.

In this connection what Jessica Stein, Harvard Professor, author of the book, 'The Ultimate Terrorist' said seems to be very accurate. Earlier by withdrawing from Afghanistan after the end of Cold War and by leaving them in a civil war as a failed state, the US allowed it to become "the Jihadi University for the entire world." But now, if the Bush administration fails to act against the real epicentre of terrorism, Pakistan might replace Afghanistan. Better, US goes after the epicentre rather than periphery.

34

Terrorism at Our Doors - How Do We Counter the Threat?

(The Free Press Journal, 19-03-2003)

Anyone who uses terror to create fear amongst civilians ceases to be a militant and becomes a terrorist.

For the majority of Mumbaikars terrorism has been a distant experience despite the serial bomb blasts of March 12, 1993 in which 270 innocent people lost their lives. The thought of Mumbai being a terror free city was expressed by a group of Kashmiri youth on March 13 who were brought to Mumbai and Pune by the Indian army to expose them to life outside Kashmir. Ironically, on the same day there was a bomb blast in Central Railway's Karjat local at Mulund Station. After similar bomb blasts in Vile Parle, Mumbai Central and Ghatkopar and now in the suburb where I live, make me to feel that terrorism literally has come to our doors.

Initial reports indicate that it is the handiwork of Muslim terrorists coming after tenth anniversary of the Mumbai , serial bomb blasts. It is time for every Indian to reflect now why the terrorism has prospered in the country ever since it began in a big way in the 1980s and also discuss steps needed to minimise terrorism and build a civil society.

First and the foremost is the compulsive urge for the politicians to use terrorism for their own narrow, immediate and self-serving interests totally ignoring public good. Public memory is too short and hence it has to be stated that the Congress Party under Mrs Indira

Gandhi initiated the trend. She had in the 1980s created the monster of Bhindranwale to divide Akali Dal in Punjab. Ultimately she paid by her life for encouraging terrorism in Punjab.

Second, it is the vote bank politics that has harmed Indian society. If terrorism is per say bad, it needs to be nipped in bud in the initial stage itself. But the Congress followed soft option of giving kid-glove treatment to terrorists in Jammu and Kashmir.

This is best illustrated during the five years (1991-96) of the Congress rule under Narasimha Rao. Then Home Minister S. B. Chavan used to call the terrorists as "misguided boys." The same lines were repeated by the then Governor of Jammu and Kashmir, General Krishna Rao. On the other hand, stern action right in the beginning would have helped to curb Islamic terrorism.

The best example of stern action helping to end terrorism comes from the US. In the late 1960s, Black Panthers, a group of blacks who had converted to Islam were indulging in arson, kidnapping, looting and terrorising attacks on civilian targets to highlight their demands, which among others, included a demand for their own state. Nixon as President disregarding civil liberties used the state power to end the movement completely.

It was not as though our leaders were unawares of this. The Congress did use strong-arm tactics to curb terrorism, as was the case with Sikh terrorism in Punjab. But the Congress Party was reluctant to use force to curb Islamic terrorism as Muslims constituted the most important segment of party's vote bank.

In this background, it is strange for Sonia Gandhi to suggest that the present NDA government has followed a weak-kneed policy against terrorism and hence, failed to tackle the problem

Third, terrorism has been nurtured by pro-terrorist approach of media. By taking a sympathetic view on the issues raised by the terrorists, journalists can get interviews of terrorist leaders. Who gets first at which terrorist leader, becomes a matter of journalistic competition. Media thus follows a pro-terrorist viewpoint always showering sympathies for their cause.

They call terrorists as militants. The militants are those who agitate or militate for a cause. In a democracy, militants have to adopt a difficult path of creating a favourable view for their cause and not use awe-inspiring terror. Any one who uses terror to create fear amongst civilians ceases to be a militant and becomes a terrorist.

Fourth, it is necessary to understand and accept the reality that at present main terrorist threat emanates from Islamic terrorists. While not all Muslims are terrorists, all terrorists are Muslims. The government and the Muslim community need to examine why the community members are turning to terrorism.

Unfortunately, there are intellectuals and commentators who adopt a double standard on terrorists. They criticise Sri Lankan Tamil terrorists as Hindu terrorists, while explaining with alibis Muslim terrorism. They will oppose stern action against Muslim terrorists, but will be too ready to attack others for terrorist activities.

What is to be done under these circumstances? First, we have to educate Muslims in India that terrorists have no religion; only deity they worship is indiscriminate violence. The Muslims themselves can do this better than others. Those who advocate communal harmony and are in forefront in combating communalism should do introspection as to their role in the growth of terrorism. Their taking a lenient view of the actions by their own community members on a communal feeling really may be unintentionally, contribute to strengthen terrorism.

Second, we need to know that there is inseparable link between terrorism on the border and inside the nation. The bomb blasts in Mulund are said to be handiwork of Students' Islamic Movement of India (SIMI) at the behest of Pakistan's Inter-Services Intelligence (ISI) promoted Lashkar-e-Taiba. Recent reports to the effect that Godhra train tragedy of February last year was again a foreign inspired act puts so much responsibility on the shoulders of Muslim leaders in India to protect their youth as well as the community from being exploited by a foreign power.

Third, media has to bear a great responsibility. It is necessary to investigate and critically examine every action of the government But to do armchair criticism from air-conditioned cubicles and always find fault with the government steps only can do great harm. One newspaper renders free advice to policy makers. Thus, for instance, the Times of India, on the arrest of Godhra Muslim cleric advised Gujarat government: "proceed with caution in the matter." If the sage behind the advice divulges his name the government could at least convey it's thanks to the person. But anonymity only helps terrorists to pursue their cause with impunity. Should media men wait till terrorism comes to their doors?

35

Pakistan Must Learn to Dictate to Terrorists: Sooner the Better

(The Free Press Journal, 20-05-2003)

Terrorism is like ballistic missile, it can be directed against any target.

Prime Minister's principal secretary and part time national security adviser, Brajesh Mishra during his discussions in Washington, DC with his counterpart, Condoleeza Rice had the occasion to address American Jewish Community's annual dinner meeting. Mishra, at this meeting, publicly advocated a trilateral effort-by India, US and Israel to fight the scourge of international terrorism.

There has been active co-operation between India and Israel ever since former Prime Minister Narasimha Rao upgraded relations between the two countries to ambassadorial level. But this is the first time any government official publicly favouring such an alliance. There could be many reasons for India taking such a stance. First, obviously it was a congregation of Jews who are after all very powerful as a community in the US. Their lobbying power is proverbialy so strong that many presidents have found it very difficult to overrule them especially as an election year approaches.

Second, it could be a signal to the US that India is running out of patience on the US promises to make Pakistan see the futility of supporting cross-border terrorism. It is particularly disgusting to know those double standards are applied to terrorism by the US. Latest in the series is the fact that Powell says in the Middle East that unless

Palestinians take steps to disarm militants, peace in the region is not possible. Is it not the case in South Asia? Unless Pakistan dismantles terrorist training camps and disarms them, peace in the region is impossible. Hence, in frustration, if India increases Indo-Israeli co-operation in political, diplomatic and security relations, US should not view it with alarm.

Third, it could be a message to Pakistan that unless it improves its ways in conducting bilateral relations with India, we will be left with the only alternative of intensified fight against terrorism on the borders, with any other means. In that India will be free to take help from any country it deems appropriate. Incidentally, an important technique developed by Israel is to penetrate into terrorist groups to foil their designs by taking counter-terrorist steps. India needs to learn it from Israelis.

Whatever may be the purpose behind the Mishra move, reactions from Pakistan and even within our country, are interesting and surprising. First let us look at the Pakistani reactions. Pakistan says it is already a member of international coalition floated by the US to fight against global terrorism. Pakistan's Foreign Office Spokesman, Aziz Ahmed Khan informed the media that many countries including the US have praised its role in the war against terrorism.

Indeed, Pakistan performs its role as a fighter by right hand against international terrorism in the west while promoting it by its left hand against India, so well that no one can really match it that easily. Beyond praise, the US has also waived off Pakistan's debts in billions. The US has even lifted sanctions economic and on sale of dual use technology to Pakistan while retaining the latter against India. Recently Prime Minister Vajpayee referred to the double standards adopted by the US in this regard while christening Light Combat Aircraft as Tejas in Bangalore.

The US is a promoter of democracy globally. But Pakistan is an exception. General Musharraf wants to hold dual positions and play a dual role-as a civilian President of incipient democracy and the chief of army at the same time.

Musharraf might even convince George Bush at his ensuing meeting in Camp David that he is in fact embodiment of American concept of civilian supremacy over armed forces! After all Pakistanis are now into democracy and they need his guidance!

Now turning to reactions within the country, Indian Muslims are upset over Mishra's proposal of fighting terrorism with the help of Israel and the US. Interestingly Raza Academy has said, according to a press report, that involving Israel in any process will not be acceptable to Muslim community. "To tackle the threat of terrorism, India cannot risk taking the help of terrorists themselves." The academy forgets the fact that the US is taking the help of Pakistan, which is the promoter of terrorism against India in its fight against Al Qaida terrorism.

The Academy also holds that visit by Ariel Sharon to India could lead to law and order problems. If India plays host to a foreign dignitary it is not that India approves all its policies. India had hosted Chinese leaders who were responsible for massacre of 2200 students in Beijing in 1989 pro-democracy movement. India does not condone massacre.

Hence the point is that if a country can provide us know-how for tackling the menace of cross-border terrorism, as Indians we should welcome it. Muslim intellectuals in India need to look to Indian national interest first rather than illusive interests of others. This reminds me of the behaviour of Communists in India and elsewhere. They irrespective of where they lived always spoke for the interests of the Communists in the Soviet Union. The nationalism for them was internationalism.

Since Raza Academy does not want India to have any connections with Israel, why not they promote a new mindset in Pakistan, to educate them, that terrorism is an unmitigated evil? Hence, that is against Islam so that they too join India in the fight against terrorism in Jammu and Kashmir. Already Al Qaida has engineered suicidal terrorist attacks in Riyadh, Casablanca and Pakistan killing innocents in hundreds.

Only other day, Pakistan's Foreign Minister, Khurshid Mohammad Kasuri has given us a quotable quote. He said: "When a suicide bomber goes on a martyrdom mission, he does not take permission from anyone." He admitted that Pakistan did have influence over the people of Kashmir-implying that terrorists crossing Pakistani borders are Kashmiris, which is incorrect by 99 percent. But, he added "we cannot dictate to them, they don't take dictation from us."

Pakistan should be made by its friends like the US to learn to dictate the terrorists. Sooner they learn, better it will be for them. Terrorism is like a ballistic missile; it can be directed against any target.

36

What do People in Islamabad Speak about Kashmir Issue?

(The Free Press Journal, 18-06-2003)

...Kashmir is an obsession of Punjabis in Pakistan. People elsewhere whether in North West Frontier province or in Sindh do not bother about Kashmiri issue.

During my recent visit to Islamabad to attend a seminar held by the Institute of Regional Studies Kashmir did figure though that was not the main subject of the seminar for which I travelled to Pakistan. In my presentation I made a point that for the success of secularism in India there is the need for regional environment favourable to the success of secularism in the largest country in South Asia-India.

One of the effects of the United States encouraging anti-Soviet movement in Afghanistan in the 1980s by making it a religious war, I argued, is the rise to religious identity on the one hand and terrorism on the other as manifested in Jammu and Kashmir (J & K). In the late 1990s there is an inseparable marriage between religion and terrorism when Muslims call it Jehad. This has driven a wedge between Hindus and Muslims despite best efforts by the nationalist forces. Longer terrorism continues greater will be the damage done to secularism. Hence I pleaded for the people in the region to shun terrorism and pursue secularism.

Then a questioner tried to provoke me by asking which terrorism was I referring to-state terrorism or the? Basically his tone and tenor was to say that there is only 'state terrorism' in Kashmir-what

Pakistanis call, "Indian Held Kashmir (IHK)'. As a matter of fact, majority of Pakistanis are aware of only 'state terrorism' as the media informs them only of it. My reply to him was that Terrorism per se is to be shunned. There are no 'good' terrorists and "bad' terrorists. Such an approach alone could lead to greater credibility in the global fight against terrorism.

Kashmir dominates the minds of Pakistanis much more than the Indians. One index of this dominance is the space devoted by the Pakistani newspapers to the issue of 'IHK'. Take one newspaper *The Nation.* The issues of May 26 and 27 have one full page devoted to news and views on Kashmir. But other pages would also have quite a bit of space devoted to Kashmir.

Going through the news items what emerges is that Pakistanis have only the information on Indian "evil deeds' in Kashmir. There is only problem of "state terrorism'. At popular level, the fact that Pakistan is actively involved in fanning terrorism is not known. The confessional boast of former Law Minister under Ms Bhutto, S. M. Zafar who said to a pro-Pakistani congregation in London in 1996: "Everything is done by Pakistan in Kashmir. Kashmiri movement is the official jargon for armed violence and terrorism in the state." Such statements are outside the knowledge of Pakistanis.

However, not every one belongs to that category. Now some like former President and Millat Party chief, Farooq Ahmad Khan Leghari, are blaming the militant groups for misleading Pakistani government about liberation of Kashmir and making tall claims for their imminent victory "over the occupied Indian forces." He blamed these groups for providing "India a chance to show the world that Kashmiri freedom fighters have no respect for human rights and democracy" by their "kidnapping and murder of foreign tourists, attack on Srinagar Assembly and Indian Parliament."

Mark it; even those who know about the terrorists' misdeeds in India do not know or pretend not to know that perpetrators of those acts are Pakistanis and not the Kashmiris. The terrorist movement has gone into the hands of mercenaries.

Pakistanis like Indians have a plurality of proposals for resolving the Kashmiri question. These include "UN mandated self-determination," "third option," "plebiscite." Again Pakistanis need to know that the major condition for plebiscite was withdrawal of their troops from Pakistan-occupied Kashmir. At the same time all Pakistanis, probably with the exception of army, want the issue to be settled peacefully, through dialogue. Both the nations are nuclear weapons states.

And when I say Kashmiri question, they are mostly referring to Kashmir valley and not to Jammu or Ladakh. From this it is clear that their claim for Kashmir is based on the fact that Valley is predominantly Muslim. There are two parts of Kashmir. What is Pakistan-occupied Kashmir (POK) for Indians is Azad (free) Kashmir for the Pakistanis and what is free Kashmir for us is 'IHK' or Indian occupied Kashmir for Pakistanis!

I met only one Kashmiri in the Sunday Market in Islamabad. This ordinary Kashmiri had come to Islamabad in search of better economic status. But when we met him, on his own admission, he is a disappointed man as even after two decades, he continues to make a living by hawking a few items of household on the street.

I was also invited while in Islamabad by a group of intellectuals-writers, poets, journalists, academics etc. Most of them had immigrated to Pakistan after partition. There was freelance exchange between this group of Pakistanis and visiting Indians. One question that was asked by a few to me was: What could be the solution to Kashmir dispute?

I highlighted the fact that the only feasible solution to the question seems to be one of making the present Line of Control (LoC) the international boundary between the two countries. Former military ruler of Pakistan Zia ul Haq, while on a visit to New Delhi had asked then Indian President, Zail Singh to suggest some ways to resolve the long pending Kashmir issue. Then Zail Singh gave Zia, according to his Memoirs, his personal opinion: "If both the countries could accept the line of control as the international boundary, then there could be a possibility of ending the conflict giving rise to a new era of friendship and co-operation." Zia had then told Zail Singh "that he would do everything possible to agree to the proposal, if the initiative came from India."

Interestingly, on May 26 there was a seminar in Peshawar on Pakistan-India relations. A galaxy of eminent speakers addressed this seminar. The report in the Nation says though the theme was Pakistan-India relations every speaker practically restricted himself to Kashmir. The report says that some of the speakers (it does not identify them) had made the suggestion that LoC should be declared as the permanent boundary. But Provincial Minister, Sirajul Haq is reported to have opposed the proposal of turning the LoC into international boundary.

While Kashmir continues to dominate the psyche of people in Islamabad a poetess told me that Kashmir is an obsession of Punjabis in Pakistan. People elsewhere whether in North West Frontier Province or in Sindh, do not bother about Kashmiri issue. What therefore both the countries need to do is to encourage people to discuss turning the LoC as the permanent boundary between the two nations to put the past in the burners of history and look forward to economic development of their nations.

37

Weed Out Anti-national Elements: Muslims Must Help

(The Free Press Journal, 30-08-2003)

Musharraf keeps on harping on the bigness of India that is an obstacle for the success of his scheme of disintegration of India.

The latest terrorist strikes in Mumbai (Zaveri Bazar and Gateway of India) may force the authorities to take a new approach to the problem. They killed 52 (number will keep rising as injured ones turn victims) and injured 178. All these years all terrorist attacks were the result of Pakistan-promoted cross-border terrorism. Those terrorist attacks mostly took place in North Indian cities either in Punjab or in Jammu and Kashmir.

Now terrorists have begun to target vital locations in Mumbai. After Bus-bombing and train bombing now it is the turn of taxi bombing. Thus there is a difference in the mode of madness. Earlier in suicide bombings cars were used and terrorists also died with it. Now it is Taxi-bombing. While the culprits survived, it is the taxi-drivers who were targeted to die. This may not be the last time we see such bombings in Mumbai.

What does this new phenomenon indicate? We can draw two interesting inferences from the new trend. First and foremost is the fact that Pakistan, having agreed under pressure from the US to stop permanently and visibly all cross-border terrorism against India, has determined to use their terrorists-in-reserve elsewhere in India-away from Jammu and Kashmir (J & K).

Of course when I say Pakistan, I must clarify. It is not the political face of Pakistan that apparently is responsible but its intelligence-ISI that is making terrorism-related decisions. So that civilian President and military General Musharraf-two in one, Prime minister Jamali and Foreign Minister Kasuri have face saving doctrine of 'plausible deniability' to fall back upon if India protests.

This is obvious from Musharraf-Kasuri simile of cross-border birds flying. As they cannot control birds flying from across the border into India, they cannot and do not control every terrorist entering into India. General Musharraf as recently as on August 12 alluded to "freelance elements [are] operating" in the realm of terrorism beyond their control. Pakistan's Foreign Minister has admitted that they do have some influence over them. But they can justifiably use it, if India agrees to talk. Musharraf also said to the visiting MPs that his government could facilitate their giving up the "gun." But India must talk. He was willing to "talk yesterday."

If Pakistan is keen to talk, Vajpayee too has for the third time after Lahore and Agra has gambled to initiate peace moves from Srinagar on April 18. He and NDA government do not wish to sacrifice a possibility of talks for peace on the altar of terrorism in Mumbai. This has brought about a conscious decision not to blame Pakistan again meaning political face but groups within Pakistan as bent on disturbing peace between two neighbours. George Fernandes did it best when terrorists recently had attacked military base in J & K.

Second, that does not mean Pakistan has given up the goal of internally bleeding literally and economically India to weaken it under the stress of communal strife. This is possible, as Islamic nature of terrorism promoted during the last two decades has already created a band of native Indian Muslim Jehadis to fight for the causes expounded by Pakistan. Politically Hurriyat was doing it by echoing Musharraf musings. Thus, for instance, Geelani used India sending troops to East Pakistan in 1971 to justify Musharrafs men coming in Mufti in Kashmir. Earlier, operationally Kashmiri youth were going to Pakistan for getting trained in Islamic terrorism, but now Gujarati Muslim youth is lured to Pakistan for the purpose.

So the Musharraf's single goal of avenging India's role in disintegration of Pakistan in 1971-he keeps harping on it continues.

During Indian MPs' visit to Islamabad he described how his close friend died in his arm during the 1971 war. He keeps on harping on the bigness of India; that is an obstacle for the success of his schemes to disintegrate India. It is a disadvantage in South Asian Association for Regional Cooperation (SAARC). Until India is reduced in size by secession, he wants SAARC to permit discussion of bilateral issues like Kashmir by agreeing to amend its charter prohibiting such discussion.

Thus cross-border terrorism has been internalised or domesticated by prevailing international circumstances. The local terrorists whether they belong to local branches of international amoeba like outfits, Lashkar-e-Toiba or Jaish-e-Mohammad or our own home-grown Students Islamic Movement of India (SIMI), Pakistan's promotion of terrorism has not ceased but has only transformed its location of operations.

Mumbai is extremely big in human size to absorb initial shock and blood on the streets. May be even for a longer period than Jammu and Kashmir. But there is a lesson in this madness to our politicians. When terrorism began in J & K it was handled by the governments in late 1980s and early 1990s as a problem created by "our misguided boys" by veteran politicians of the Congress, Janata Dal and the United Front as they were mainly concerned with deriving political advantages from terrorism.

A strong streak of that mentality reappears now when Chief Minister (CM), Shinde and Deputy CM, Bhujbal in Maharashtra allude to the fact that terrorism surfaced in Mumbai only after the Gujarat riots. This is not the first time that CM was making that kind of statement. He had made it in connection with bus bombing in Ghatkopar in July this year. Thereby CM was obviously pointing an accusing finger at the BJP. Can we ask then why not those elements operate in Gujarat? Why select targets in Mumbai? Is it because the Congress is soft to Muslim terrorists who carry out attacks against Gujarati community?

The local bred terrorists work so freely in Mumbai as possibly they know that the government is politically going to bail them out. Of course Maharashtra government took the initiative to ban the SIMI.

But if the governments in Maharashtra in the past had been alert and had adopted a stern approach to SIMI, the organisation would not have led the Muslim youth astray in the country. The fact that it was working to create communal problems for the government should have been clear to it long ago. During the agitation of Ambedkar followers to rename Marathwada University after Dr Ambedkar, Mumbai walls, railway stations and buses etc were all painted with slogans asking scheduled castes to quit Hinduism and join Islam, as it is a casteless religion! Even now it is not too late for the government to weed out anti-national elements amongst the Muslim community. But initiative ought to come from the community itself.

38

A strategic Triangle in the Offing: War Against Terrorism

(The Free Press Journal, 19-09-2003)

...cooperation against terrorism between US, India and Israel should also help the US to reduce its reliance over Pakistan in its war against terrorism.

Prime Minister of Israel Ariel Sharon came on his first-ever state visit to India and had to go back without visiting Mumbai. The visit had aroused considerable interest amongst Indian commentators. It used to be said about Franklin D. Roosevelt that no one could ignore him; you either like him or hate him. The same thing can be said about the Israeli PM. Some peculiar secularists have already begun to spit venom and condemn Indian government for having invited him. They of course do not fail to mention similarities between Sharon and Modi of Gujarat. While accusing him for massacre of Palestinians, Modi is targeted for executing "genocide" of Muslims.

And they allege that it is this likeness that made Indian government to welcome him. But Indian government has demonstrated that while it would like to firm up friendship with Israel, it will not sacrifice basic principles. Unfortunately, terrorism has so much disturbed social fabric in Israel that it makes them to go to extremes. One such extreme is Israel proposal to expel Arafat from West Bank and their loud support to kill him. Indian government has rightly opposed such bizarre ideas and reminded that Arafat is a democratically elected head of the Palestinian people. Though one cannot support under any circumstances such acts it only brings out sense of desperation experienced by Israeli people. If the US President could reinvent the need for the Central Intelligence Agency to be restored with power to kill foreign leaders in the aftermath of 9/11 one can understand the predicament in which Israeli government finds itself as it has been facing terrorism since its birth in 1948.

Indian Muslims have taken upon themselves to oppose Sharon's visit. Raza Academy has called upon the people to boycott the visit. The academy in May gave its advice that "to tackle the threat of terrorism India cannot risk taking the help of terrorists themselves." But these people who are advising the government against taking any help from Israel because they consider Sharon is a terrorist as his hands are reddened by Palestinian blood, do not label Pakistan's Musharraf as a terrorist or oppose the government trying to talk peace with him while he continues to promote terrorism against India! They did not raise their voice also against Vajpayee shaking hands with him in Agra.

Opponents of Sharon visit had given a communal colour to the visit and the reason for their opposition. Those people opposed the visit because their heart bleeds at the fact that Israel is responsible for violence in Palestinian territory. These people forget the fact that Israel is led to use force, as Palestinians are equally guilty of killing hundreds and thousands of Israelis. It is as though that Palestinians have a right to kill Israelis and it is a duty of Israelis to die. Situation is similar to that of Pakistani terrorists killing Indians— now throughout the country. But when a few terrorists are killed our liberals raise a hue and cry. Those who opposed Sharon's visit because of his tough policy against Palestinians however would demand that India talk to Musharraf though his hands are also reddened by blood of thousands of innocent Indians killed in cross-border terrorism in addition to his misadventure in Kargil.

Then what is the significance of the visit? Since the relations were upgraded by India in 1992 there has been steady co-operation in all fields between India and Israel. But it is the defence and strategic co-operation that really cements the friendship between the two countries. The latest example of defence co-operation is that of Israel supplying three Phalcon Airborne Warning and Control Systems

(AWACS). These are necessary to protect Indian cities from surprise missile attacks from across the borders.

We, need to know that these were cleared for delivery to India despite US expression of displeasure at the timing of decision. During his visit to Washington, DC in June this year. Musharraf made it a point to persuade the US administration to drop the idea of the Phalcon sale. Further, a similar deal with China was aborted by Israel because of the US pressure. India is also shopping for Arrow missiles from Israel though lobbies in Israel are against it. It is likely that very soon Israel will replace Russia as the number one arms seller to India. There is a tacit approval from the US towards this policy, as apart from, strategic significance of the move, it would also boost, albeit, indirectly, the US defence industries.

However the main thrust of visit clearly is cementing further existing co-operation between the two countries in the area of fighting the Islamic terrorism. Why majority of terrorists today emerge from Islamic world is a good sociological question. But the fact of the matter is: Both the countries are affected by the scourge of Islamic terrorism though underlying causes for terrorism are different. It is fashionable for men like Musharraf to equate the Kashmir cause with Palestinians as the problem's origin lies in the division of territories.

But in the case of Palestinians, the UN decision to create a Jewish state partitioned their territory. Since Palestinians did not accept the partition plan, they began to fight against the Jewish state. However, after fifty-six years, Palestinians who were trained to hate Israelis and fight them, today cannot come round to accept the reality of a Jewish state. But in the case of Jammu and Kashmir, though the state acceded to Indian Union according to the law of British Parliament that also created Pakistan by partitioning India, Pakistan cannot reconcile to the fact that a Muslim majority state can co-exist with various other communities in a pluralistic India. Having already tried thrice to capture Kashmir by war and failed, Musharraf has perfected Islamic terrorism as an instrument of achieving his goal.

While Indian experience in tackling terrorism is only two decades old, India has lot to learn from Israel. It is here that Israel has already agreed to train Indian personnel in fighting against terrorists.

In particular, Israelis have perfected the art and science of penetrating into terrorist camps and getting information on the terrorists. It is here that Indian personnel need to focus on.

As a matter of fact during Sharon's visit Israel signed six agreements on various subjects, which include co-operation in counter-terrorism. It in this area again that India, Israel and US have to learn together from one another in their war against terrorism. The strategic triangle that Russian Prime Minister Primakov spoke of between Russia, China and India in 1998 is unlikely to work, as likely partners in the triangle are not free from bilateral problems as between India and China. On the other hand, there are no bilateral problems between India, Israel and the US.

Such co-operation against terrorism between US, India and Israel should also help the US to reduce its reliance over Pakistan in its war against terrorism. More information is now coming out how Pakistan while claiming to be on the side of war against global terrorism was unable to control or eliminate domestic sources of terrorism, like Madarassas, terrorist groups like Lashkar-e-Toiba or Jaish-e-Mohammad etc. who are fountain heads of global terrorism.

39

Cross-border Terrorism now Localised: Will it Again be Internationalised?

(The Free Press Journal, 28-04-2004)

Pakistan continues to be a frontline state for the US war against terrorism. The war in one form or the other ought to continue, as it is gainful proposition for Pakistan....

After former Prime Minister A. B. Vajpayee and General Musharraf issued a joint statement in Islamabad on January 6th this year ushering in new directions in India-Pakistan relations, a totally new dimension of terrorism has arisen which is not mentioned or discussed anywhere so far. In the Joint statement General Musharraf reassured Indian Prime Minister that "he will not permit any territory under Pakistan's control to be used to support terrorism in any manner."

It is not something new but reiteration of what General Musharraf had said earlier in June 2002 to US Deputy Secretary of State, Richard Armitage that cross-border terrorism would stop and terrorist training camps would be shut down. That also goes back to his original statement to his countrymen in January 2002 his first public statement to end cross-border terrorism.

Have cases of terrorist attacks declined? Perforace Indian government had to say that they have. They had said that also after June 2002 assurance of General Musharraf. However, terrorists continue to attack every now and then targets within India. Thus for instance, the terrorists trying to disrupt first phase of parliamentary elections in J & K threw grenade at a Congress rally in Banihal in Doda district killing one and injuring at least 23. In another incident in Udhampur an assassination effort was made by hurling grenade at the Minister for Medical Education in April second week.

Though the Islamabad meeting and Joint statement made a new beginning in search of peace between the two nations, peace is fragile. Decline in cross-border terrorism is not real but controlled one. Its controlled nature is evident from the fact that suddenly while addressing a select group of journalists Musharraf said that his patience is not indefinite he cannot wait beyond July to find a solution to Jammu and Kashmir. In the past also he had gone back on his promise. Within four days of assuring US deputy Secretary of State, Richard Armitage he had denied that he gave any such assurance to cease terrorist attacks against India. Anyway he could not ensure for long a cessation of cross-border terrorism unless the core issue is resolved! After all controlling terrorists is as difficult as trying to control birds flying across the Indo-Pak borders!

What seems to have happened so far is that terrorism from across the border has turned to be domestic terrorism for India. Those who were already trained and pushed into India from across the borders were operating in Jammu and Kashmir (J& K). Thus terrorism had been localised and domesticated during the Indian elections. The old terrorist-outfits have acquired new costumes. Earlier whenever it attacked from Pakistan it was one of the several groups operating from Pakistan either Lashkar-e-Taiba or Jaise-e-Muhammad or Al Badr or something else. Now these have assumed new names in J & K. Thus Lashkar-e-Taiba has become Al Mansooran. This group tried to blow up Congress HQ on April 23.

Now that Indian elections are over and a new Congress-led coalition government has assumed power, it is likely that the screws on the terrorism door would be loosened to make India to come to terms with Pakistan on what it calls as core issue viz. J & K. After all serious talks between India and Pakistan were to begin at political level in July-August 2004. That it could happen is clear from the US approach to the question. After the euphoria of peace between India and Pakistan there were many in the US government and Indian media who attributed lot of credit to the US policy makers for the present situation in Indo-Pak relations.

Despite change in India-Pakistan equation. Pakistan continues to be a frontline state for the US war against terrorism. The War in one form or the other ought to continue, as it is gainful proposition for Pakistan and personally to its President-General Musharraf. One way it helps is to get aid from the US. In the Fiscal 05 Pakistan is to get $700 million from it against $85 million allocated to India in the State department budget. Rocca, Assistant Secretary of State defended it on the ground that India "is a growing world power" and also as a aid given to Iraq and Afghanistan falls under a "different category."

Personally for Musharraf, the US connection is important beyond concerns of US presidential elections in November 2004. In preparation to it, the US has already conferred on Pakistan Non-NATO Ally status on Pakistan. This would enable Pakistan to get military assistance from Pakistan, if necessary. Musharraf can flaunt these concessions obtained by him from the US as a personal achievement so that he can consolidate his acquired-at-gun-point position of Presidency beyond December 2004.

What does it portend to India? With the change of regime in New Delhi, US could begin a set of subtle threats to India causing a sense of insecurity, as was the case in 1991 during Narasimha Rao's tenure as PM. Thus, it could remind India of the disputed nature of J & K question, threat/fear of India-Pakistan nuclear confrontation, or come under the pressure from Pakistan to supply F-16. The point is Pakistan could revive cross-border terrorism, at will, which is presently domesticated. The US could connive at it or intervene again on behalf of India but use it to pressurise India to extend concessions to it as well as to Pakistan.

The summer in New Delhi likely to be hot with terrorism rising again. Does the Congress Party, possess a policy to tackle domestic terrorism emerging again as cross-border terrorism? Terrorism raised its head during the Congress rule. However, during the leadership crisis at 10 Janpath. Congressmen used Sonia Gandhi's ability to fight terrorism as a plea for her to agree to become the PM. Now that she has "humbly declined" she should use her skills to see that cross-border terrorism is not allowed to flourish again.

40

Don't Play Politics with National Security: UPA Soft on Terrorism?

(The Free Press Journal, 08-06-2004)

Politics behind scrapping of the POTA is clearly to consolidate Muslim vote bank of the Congress...

By and large if we say that 99 percent politicians do not hesitate to play politics with national security, you will not be farther from truth. Since acquisition of power is the single overriding motivation in them, to gain power or retain acquired power, they would go to any extent, including playing politics with vital questions of national security. Mahatma Gandhi used to say that when one thinks of national interest-national security is the first charge on national interest one should only think of the interest of the most downtrodden. In that yardstick one should say that when you think of national security you should think of the security of the entire country and not the interest of one person in power or family or the party. Examples of use of national security concept for self-aggrandisement or the aggrandisement of the party are many from various countries including India.

Iraq war is the one living example from Bush land of the United States (US). George W. Bush and his aides had seen getting rid of Saddam Hussain from Iraq as the goal that could get him a second term though it was couched in terms of national security. He won in 2000 not because he won a popular election but the Supreme Court a majority of which were Republicans installed him as the President. He learnt the trick of trade probably from another Republican -

Richard Nixon who prolonged the Vietnam War for four years-having won the presidency in 1968 on a plank of ending that very war! Only after winning the re-election in 1972 his administration signed the peace treaty in 1973 though terms were agreed much before the elections.

I have gone into these examples to show how the danger of politicians playing politics with national security is going to be a major issue in months to come in India after the United Progressive Alliance (UPA) assumed power in May. One immediate issue is of scrapping anti-terrorism law called Prevention of Terrorism Act (POTA) passed in 2002 after the Pakistani terrorists belonging to the Jaish-e-Mohammad attacked Kashmiri Legislative Assembly in October 2001 and the Indian Parliament in December 2001. Even this was in the background of the global war against terrorism in which India was a willing partner.

Thus the POTA was born out of a dire necessity of checking anti-national acts by the foreign terrorists in collaboration with anti-national elements within the country. And these activities have not disappeared. As I pointed out in my article "Cross-border Terrorism now localised: Will it again be internationalised?" terrorists were active during the elections. They had attacked Congress Party campaigners in more than one place. As a matter of fact the very first day of the new government was greeted with terrorist attacks on the Border Security Force (BSF) convoy in which more than 20 men, women and children were killed on their way to Vaishnodevi temple.

The Congress-led UPA government swears in the name of Rajiv Gandhi (For them power passed on from Rajiv Gandhi to his widow-Sonia Gandhi, totally ignoring the Congress period from 1991 to 1996). Though Rajiv Gandhi conducted a fierce national security based election campaign in the history of Indian politics in 1984. once in power he distinguished himself as the PM in putting national interest above his own or the party interest. This was best represented in his accords with the then leaders of the Akali Dal on the Punjab crisis or the Assam Students Union on the question of illegal migrants from Bangladesh. Under these accords Rajiv allowed his opponents to come to power. Though it would have been very easy for him to engineer defections and form the Congress government since it won the second highest number of seats in those legislative Assemblies.

The UPA has to be careful in responding to terrorist greetings and devising a long-term strategy to eliminate terrorists. Unfortunately the Congress track record on the subject has been extremely poor. During Narasimha Rao's tenure, the then Home Minister, late Shankar Rao Chavan was soft on terrorists as they were 'our boys'. If the economic reforms are going to be tempered with 'human face' under the UPA regime, is it also going to temper national resolve to fight against terrorism by making it to wear a human face?

The noise made by the UPA constituents so far indicates such a move. The Southern partners in the UPA like DMK and MDMK have demanded the repeal of the POTA on the ground that it is being misused by the states. Obviously that was the experience of MDMK leader Vaiko who was imprisoned by Jayalalitha. It was more a case of misuse of the act for political vendetta to hammer her political opponents than to protect national security! In that respect former Home Minister, L. K. Advani, erred in not using his abilities to extricate then an NDA constituent by making a provision for review, which was made after many months when the damage to the NDA cause and credibility was already done.

But does the fear of misuse is an alibi, justifiably strong enough to scrap a law? Was it not passed by the Parliament in the interest of national security? The threat to national security has not vanished. If misuse is the only justification, there are many laws, which are misused. There are for instance, many cases of misuse of 1998 act to prevent atrocities against untouchables. Are we going to plead for its repeal too?

The politicians who now make the demand have to remember one important principle that any law can be misused. Who misuses them? The answer is: Politicians or bureaucrats or bureaucrats under the protection of politicians. Then, isn't it better for the complaining politicians to vouchsafe that they will not misuse the laws while in power rather than complaining about its misuse? Can the Congress as a national party set a firm course on curbing any misuse of a law or power?

Hence, misuse of the POTA seems to be a lame excuse to achieve certain political goals. The politics behind scrapping of the POTA is clearly to consolidate Muslim vote bank of the Congress and its pre-election allies and post election allies. These allies like the DMK in Tamil Nadu and the Congress in Maharashtra are going to face state assembly elections within a short period. These parties have won a sizeable chunk of Muslim votes in the Parliamentary elections. Obviously the UPA wants to consolidate its Muslim vote bank. This is clear from the fact that in Maharashtra now it is stated by the Home Minister, R. R. Patil that he would like to scrap state law passed to control organised crime.

Globally the main proponents and practitioners of terrorism, hence its opponents are Muslims. When TADA was in force its main opponents were also Muslims. I have watched more than one public procession taken out by Muslims in Mumbai. But the UPA by supporting the scrapping of POTA gives an impression that they are soft on terrorism and organised crime!

41

Terrorism, a Non-issue to Pakistanis and their US Supporters

(The Free Press Journal, 15-08-2005)

Clinton administration also realised that what was going on in Kashmir is a process to create a mono-ethnic and mono-religious society in Kashmir.

India is considerably exercised over the issue of cross-border terrorism in India-Pakistan relations. Over it, in early 2002 the Indian government went to the extent of mobilising troops to international borders and line of control in Jammu and Kashmir (J & K). But it is a non-issue as far as Pakistanis, pro-Pakistan Kashmiris and their American supporters. That is something I learnt in Washington, DC where last month while attending the Fifth International Peace Conference organised by Kashmir American Council, which was co-sponsored by Association of Humanitarian Lawyers.

It was held in Capitol Hill and had a bipartisan look since Senator Tim Johnson (Democrat) and Congressman Joseph Pitts (Republican) were involved as well. I was attracted to accept Dr Ghulam Nabi Fai's invitation to attend this important Conference primarily because it focussed on the theme of "The Kashmir Dispute and Building a Peaceful South Asia." In my own presentation I placed greatest emphasis on elimination of cross-border terrorism as a prerequisite for building a peaceful South Asia.

I knew Dr Fai as a lobbyist for an independent Kashmir from the early 1993 when Indian newspapers had highlighted his getting a letter from Bill Clinton assuring him his efforts to find an early solution to Kashmir dispute. What was new to me was the fact that Pakistani representatives dominated the Conference. Among them Makdoom Faisal Hayat Khan, Minister for Kashmir Affairs, Ejazul Haq, Minister for Religious Affairs, former Foreign Secretary, Riaz Khokhar in addition to Pakistan's Ambassador in Washington, DC, Jehangir Karamat were prominent. Prime Minister of Pakistan occupied Kashmir, Sardar Sikander Hayat also was present as one of the speakers.

Other main constituent was of course large number of Kashmiris now living abroad and their sympathisers. Only other Indian who attended in his individual capacity was Dr Subramaniam Swamy. I was informed that the Indian Ambassador was invited but he could not attend because of impending visit by Indian Prime Minister Manmohan Singh. What was therefore natural was the Conference was lopsided in its presentations and the only common theme was India bashing, despite Ms Karen Parker of Association of Humanitarian Lawyers requesting the speakers not to attack any country while making their presentations!

I traced the role terrorism has played in creating current crisis in South Asia. For Pakistanis there is no cross-border terrorism, only terrorism they accept is the 'state terrorism by India. Why does India maintain, they ask, an army of 70 thousand in Kashmir? For Kashmiris, there is no terrorism in Kashmir-only freedom movement! I said, Pakistan's main instrument in achieving their policy goal of annexing Kashmir is employing cross-border terrorism. Richard A. Clarke, a counter terrorism expert, who worked in the Clinton and Bush, Jr. administrations, has come out with his latest book: *Against All Enemies: Inside America's War on Terror*. He says, I pointed out that prior to September 11, ISI Directorate "personnel had trained Kashmiri terrorists at Al Qaeda camps and worked with Al Qaeda-related terrorists to pressure on India."

India offered to Pakistan to discuss all issues including Kashmir to bring lasting peace to South Asia. As a result, after behind the scene negotiations, then Prime Minister Vajpayee and General Musharraf, Pakistani President met at the sidelines of the South Asian association of Regional Co-operation in Islamabad in January 2004. Then in the joint Declaration issued after hard bargain. Pakistan clearly stated that it would not allow territories under its control to be used for cross border terrorism against India. In the past US had extracted a commitment from General Musharraf, described as "an absolute assurance" not to permit cross border terrorism against India and also to close down all terrorist training camps.

After the change of government in New Delhi in May 2004 when he met newly appointed Prime Minister of India, Manmohan Singh in New York in September 2004 Musharraf renewed his commitment to fight against terrorism. Again in April 2005 when two heads of governments met in Delhi they declared their resolve to jointly fight against terrorism. I also pointed out that General Musharraf has himself admitted the fact that situation has changed since September 11. 2001. He had lamented on October 24, 2004 over the fact that no body accepted Pakistan's description of on going violence in Kashmir as the freedom struggle. More and more nations see it as an exhibition of Islamic terrorism. He rhetorically asked his listeners whether they would like Pakistan to be seen as fundamentalist Islamic terrorist state? Hence, I said that those who say, as some have said in the conference, that there is no terrorism in Jammu and Kashmir or equate on going violence in that state with freedom struggle only live in a make believe world. But none accept my line of presentation!

Then how do we achieve lasting peace in the region? In the Conference some of the speakers like Dr Fai, have already acknowledged the American role in bringing India and Pakistan together to talk and initiate a dialogue process since the problems amongst the two nuclear weapons states can only be resolved through a dialogue. The dialogue has already begun and two nations are moving towards creating mutual trust by introducing various Confidence Building Measures (CBMs). But we need to go beyond CBMs. We need to change our mindsets. We need to see the Kashmiri problem from non-sectarian, non-religious but humanitarian perspective.

We need to look at the American society where different ethnic and religious groups live as American citizens. In his address to Indian Parliament former US President Bill Clinton expressed his support to the right of multi-ethnic and multi-religious pluralistic societies to live as nation-states. The developments in Kashmir where terrorism is aimed at eliminating Hindus. Sikhs, and Shias were contrary to the

American ideal. Hence, his administration also realised that what was going on in Kashmir is a process to create a mono-ethnic and mono-religious society in Kashmir. Thus, they had recommended finding a non-secessionist solution to the Kashmir problem within the Indian Union.

In the light of this, it is necessary to see the Kashmir issue in a new perspective of finding a solution within a secular society of India. But so far secular ideal has been given a go by while searching for a solution. Those who talk about human rights violations in Jammu and Kashmir do so only in relation to the alleged violations of human rights by the security forces in the context of the war against terrorism. But what about violation of human rights of over 350,000 Kashmiri Pandits who were forced out of their homes by terrorists? Now most of them are languishing in refugee camps. It is ironical that a section of Kashmiris are forced to live in subhuman conditions because they belong to a religion different from those of the majority community in Kashmir! The day when all of us think in terms of a secular society inclusive of all sections of the people, human rights, peace and development will usher in. That will also enable Musharraf to reach his vision of creating a modern, moderate, Islamic Republic in Pakistan.

42

Return to the Valley

(The Indian Express, 16-09-2005)

The Pandits were a miniscule minority of 2 per cent of the population and if we can't rehabilitate them, what meaning does our secularism or Kashmiriyat have? Late Mufti Mohammed Sayeed.

In his interview published on the Op-Ed page (IE, September 14) Mufti Mohammed Sayeed asks: "The Pandits were a minuscule minority of 2 per cent of the population and if we can't rehabilitate them, then what meaning does our secularism or Kashmiriyat have?" A noble thought indeed.

But why should the Pandits be rehabilitated in new colonies? They should be empowered to go back to their old homes. The government should see to it that their homes are rebuilt and encourage local Kashmiri Muslims, who had purchased the houses the Pandits once lived in for peanuts, to return them to their earlier owners.

At an international conference on Kashmir held in Washington this July, in which I had participated, everyone spoke of the violation of human rights by Indian security forces. No one mentioned anything about the violation of human rights by the terrorists. No one mentioned the atrocities committed against the Pandits. Mine was the lone voice!

The dominant view was that there isn't any terrorism in J&K, only a freedom movement! One Kashmiri went to the extent of asserting that, under international law, indigenous people have a right to take up arms against the occupiers! These are the voices of Kashmiris who are highly intelligent and educated, but were forced out of the Valley by Delhi's politics in the 80's. They are extremely bitter about the governments in Delhi and Srinagar, and it is their bitterness that makes them violently anti-Indian.

Mufti Mohammed makes a very significant observation: "When people defeated Omar Abdullah in his bastion, they began to gain confidence that it was them and not Delhi who were responsible for his defeat. This feeling is growing in people that they—and not Delhi—can make and unmake governments." Along with the steps to rehabilitate the Pandits, the Mufti should appeal to those Kashmiris who left because of their political activities — those who were not involved in any criminal or terrorist activities — to come back to Kashmir and be a part of Kashmiriyat.

43

Why New Colonies for Pandits? Let them Go Back to their Old Homes

(The Free Press Journal, 20-09-2005)

Majority Kashmiris when speak of violation of human rights, do not speak of violence against minority Pandits.

In a recent interview Mufti Mohammed Sayeed rhetorically said that the Pandits were a minuscule minority of 2 per cent of the population and if we can't rehabilitate them, then what meaning does our secularism or Kashmiriyat have? A noble thought indeed. Hurriyat

Arms haul at LoC

leaders have also recently expressed in favour of return of the Pandits. Hurriyat is the political face of terrorist groups: hence one can assume at least some terrorist groups would welcome the return of the Pandits.

But why should the Pandits be rehabilitated in new colonies? They should be enabled to go back to their old homes; the government should see to it that their homes are rebuilt and wherever it has been purchased for peanuts by Kashmiri Muslims, the government ought to encourage them to return the homes back to the returning Pandits. I have met a large number of Pandits in India as well as in the US who have bitterly complained about how they were forced to sell their houses under adverse circumstances and leave the country.

In an international Conference on Kashmir held in the Capitol Hilt in Washington, DC, in July this year wherein I participated, every-one spoke of violation of human rights by the Indian security forces.

Obviously it meant human rights of majority Kashmiris who are Muslims. None mentioned about violation of human rights by terrorists! None mentioned about atrocities committed against the Pandits. Since Pakistanis and Kashmiris settled abroad dominate a conference, who had their own agendas, mine was a lone voice!

According to an overwhelming majority, there isn't terrorism in Jammu and Kashmir! There is only freedom movement! One Kashmiri, barrister by profession, went to the extent of asserting that under the humanitarian international law developed by the United Nations, indigenous people have a right to take up the arms against occupying people! Hence it is resistance, people resisting are freedom fighters and not terrorists. Americans right in their Legislative building were forewarned! If Red Indians take arms against the European settlers, they cannot complain!

I had to tell them to read General Musharraf's promises given at different occasions indirectly through the US officials and directly to Indian Prime Ministers to curb cross-border terrorism. How could he speak of terrorism and terrorists in Kashmir if they are freedom fighters? Way back in 1996, a former Law Minister of Pakistan, S. M. Zafar said to a pro-Pakistan congregation in London: "Everything is being done in Kashmir by Pakistan. Kashmiri movement is the official jargon for armed violence and terrorism in the state." The JKLF leader recently revealed how terrorist camps were run by information minister of Pakistan, when he travelled to Pakistan occupied Kashmir. Even now there are at least 50 terrorist training camps in POK.

The Kashmiri leaders and those Kashmiris who live abroad ought to know the hard fact that they are being used by Pakistani leaders-irrespective of whether they come from political cadres or military ranks to settle score with India for its role in the birth of Bangladesh in 1971.

At that time Kashmiri leaders had openly said that if West Pakistanis kill East Pakistanis just to rule over them, they were better off with a secular India. Of course since then Indian leadership and Kashmiri ruling elite became insensitive to problems in Kashmir. It is this lack of sensitivity in handling Kashmiri problem during the 1980s and 1990s mainly during the Congress rule and rule by the United Fronts with the Congress backing that really brought about the present problem.

Hence the voices of Kashmiris abroad are the voices of bitterness. These are the voices of Kashmiris who are highly intelligent and educated but were forced out by Delhi politics in Kashmir in the 1980s. They are extremely bitter against the governments in Delhi and Srinagar and it is their bitterness that makes them to be violently anti-Indian. Though they are personally on a one to one basis were very good to me. It is their intellectual assets combined with their anti-Indian tirade that has endeared them to Pakistanis despite their being largely in favour of an independent Kashmir.

Mufti Mohammed makes a very significant observation: "When people defeated Omar Abdullah in his bastion, they began to gain confidence that it was them and not Delhi responsible for his defeat. This feeling is growing in people that they and not Delhi can make and unmake governments." Along with the steps to rehabilitate the Pandits, he should appeal to those Kashmiris who left because of their political activities-those who were not involved in any criminal or terrorist activities-to come back to Kashmir and be part of the Kashmiriyat.

Added to it, the fact that Hurriyat leaders are in favour of a pluralistic Kashmir. Lara Rise, Senator in the Norwegian Parliament told the audience at the Kashmir Conference that Professor Bhatt had told him that Hurriyat stood for a pluralistic society. Return of Kashmiris settled, abroad would only contribute to strengthen Kashmiriyat.

44

What Maniyappan's Murder Told Us

(The Indian Express, 5-12-2005)

NSC's one major task was to achieve a fair degree of policy coordination.....The entire abduction episode has exposed India's lack of clear policy....

There's a crucial lack of coordination between the agencies handling national security

According to your news report, Defence Minister Pranab Mukherjee corrected National Security Adviser M.K. Narayanan's statement on Maniyappan's murder (IE, November 29), since he was "misquoted." The defence minister's statement raises some questions. First, is there co-ordination in security policy making within the Government of India? National security policy making is an extremely serious business, unlike determining the price of onions. The National Security Council (NSC) was created, because of public pressure, by the NDA government in 1998. The current UPA government has continued with the institution. NSC's one major task was to achieve a fair degree of policy co-ordination between the various arms of the government dealing with security.

Going by the present instance, there was apparently no co-ordination on policy at the ministerial level, let alone any meeting of the NSC. Hence, the defence minister had to "correct" the statement of the NSA, leading to a public airing of their differences over India's policy on the issue of Ramankutty Maniyappan's murder at the hands of the Taliban in Afghanistan.

Second, is the NSA a spokesman for the government on the national security policy? In the US, where the NSC concept originated in 1947, for at least the initial 20 years, the NSA role was swathed in anonymity. Even during Henry Kissinger's tenure (1969-1974), it was only after his secret China visit in 1971 that he was allowed by Richard Nixon to publicly explain the raison d'etre of that major move. The NSA ought to be considered as the additional ears, eyes and even brain of the chief policy maker—the prime minister, in our system. He should not to be seen or heard in public. Third, who is in charge of national security policy in India? Is it the foreign minister? The defence minister? Or the PM?

The entire abduction episode has exposed India's lack of a clear policy on the subject. Has Pakistan "conspired" with the Taliban to kill the Border Road Organisation's driver in order to drive a wedge between India and Afghanistan, as claimed by Narayanan? Answers to a question like this will remain elusive unless the NSC starts functioning as a collective body to discuss issues and help evolve policies. Unfortunately, the NSC never met during the NDAs tenure and has not met so far under the UPA

45

Stop Bragging, Bring to Book Blast Culprits

(The Free Press Journal, 19-08-2006)

> *"....an official ought not to speak like a politician bragging about our being better informed than the US on Mumbai Blasts in contrast to the US information about 9/11.... If we had really better information prior to 7/11, we would have been able to prevent loss of lives and property."*

National Security Adviser (NSA) M. K. Narayanan, has begun making public statements on crucial national security issues. An important concept developed in the US where the office of NSA had its early origin in the 1940s, was the anonymity of the NSA. He is supposed to be chief executive's additional eyes, ears and even brain on security issues but behind the screen. Best example is that of Henry Kissinger in the 1970s. Though he was appointed in 1969, his first ever-public appearance came only after his successful secret visit to Beijing in 1971. But when he publicly explained US policy he was doing at the instance of Richard Nixon, then President.

Narayanan said early August that Indian evidence on Pakistan's involvement in Mumbai blasts of 7/11 is 'stronger' than that of the US on 9/11. Is he speaking on the authorisation of the Prime Minister? He was obviously responding to US assistant secretary of state, Richard Boucher's statement in Washington, DC advising India to exercise extreme care before rushing on policy pronouncements to accuse Pakistan's involvement in Mumbai blasts. As he put it: "The evidence ...as far as who they were, who was responsible I don't think we've seen a lot yet....I think we need to be led by the evidence before we start trying to draw conclusions and make policy pronouncements on it." Of course, on his visit to India, he says there are anti-India terrorist groups still in Pakistan. He just proves that old habit of zigging now zagging later, a characteristic of the US foreign policy has not disappeared.

Now, be that as it may, for Narayanan's frequent forays into public diplomacy a charitable interpretation could be that in the absence of a full-fledged external affairs minister, the Prime Minister might have asked his NSA to make a response to Boucher's statement. However, an official ought not to speak like a politician bragging about our being better informed than the US on Mumbai Blasts in contrast to the US information about 9/11. One thing is pretty clear. If we had really better information prior to 7/11, we would have been able to prevent the loss of lives and property. This applies to the US as well. When we as well as the US were not able to prevent those incidents, the question of being better informed is not an objective assessment.

At what level were we better informed? Are we able to get hold of all information on who masterminded the blasts? Let us assume that Narayanan was stating that we were better informed on 7/11 than the US on 9/11 after the event. Even this contention can be easily refuted. The US had placed a price on the head of Osama Bin Laden as the chief mastermind behind 9/11 but has not been able to capture him so far. But another conspirator, of 9/11 Zacarias Moussaoui was arrested in New York and tried and given life imprisonment.

What has been our record on investigation of such acts of international terrorism? Leave aside 7/11, it took place in 2006. But serial bomb blasts took place in Mumbai in 1993, 8 years before 9/11. But we are yet to hear the judgement!

On the current investigations of 7/11, we make a statement on one day only to retract it on the next day or next week. We thundered that Abdul Karim Thunda is the brain behind 7/11; then we disowned his involvement. Many others have been arrested-Fazal Shaikh, his brother a software engineer, Muzamil and so on. But nothing is certain so far. Every one is a suspect.

It's not only on investigation of blasts that our officials assert today and retract tomorrow. Look at the claim of Indian armed forces killing a Pakistani army officer, Mohammad Hyder Turkey on Friday (July 28). Then on Saturday (July 29) Defence Ministry spokesman said: "No Pakistan army officer has been killed in Kashmir." Lt. Col. V K. Batra, the Indian army officer who had first claimed about the incident, then said that his statement was based on preliminary information! The question arises as to why should officials rush to media to make tall claims at all? This aberration apart, moving to the main issue of the claim made by NSA, real issue is, if we had more information than the Americans on 9/11, we should be able to punish the guilty much faster than the Americans. But in reaching conclusive and decisive action, we fall far more behind the Americans or their ally our erstwhile colonial rulers-British. On August 10, 2006, British discovered a plan by global terrorists-Al Qaeda to blow off flights to US in mid-Atlantic after they have taken off from Heathrow airport. What do they do? They have a list of 24 suspects of which 19 were arrested and first thing they did was to freeze their bank accounts! Have you heard our investigators doing it? Or is it a closely held secret?

George W. Bush called those terrorists conspiring to blow passenger planes over Atlantic "Islamic fascists!" Alas! We cannot call our terrorists as Islamic! Our Muslim MPs may get hurt; they have already complained to Prime Minister that terror suspects who all happen to be Muslims are being harassed! Instead of complaining, they ought to hold meetings at this stage, to educate Muslims to desist from getting involved in acts of international terrorism and spreading their terror through out India. Muslim MPs, by questioning Mumbai Police action, have contributed to further eroding the credibility of Narayanan's claim.

In this background, when Britain says terrorists arrested for 7/7/2005 train bombing included four British citizens of Pakistani origin Pakistan does not cry foul or the Americans do not raise a doubt. But in our case Pakistani President General Musharraf holds a threat against any Indian plans to attack against training camps in Pakistan occupied Kashmir. Our NSA who wants to brag about our being far ahead of Americans in the matters of investigations should see to it that Mumbai police are allowed rather made to carry on with their investigations looking at perpetrators of crime on 7/11 as terrorists and are brought to book at the earliest. It should also conclusively demonstrate involvement of Pakistan. Since it involves the questions of India's credibility.

46

Don't Give in to Blackmail

(Hindustan Times, 16-10-2006)

Clemency for Mohammad Afzal will set a bad precedent by according religion a role in the dispensation of criminal justice. It will also engender sympathy for terrorists.

India is going through a major but silent crisis as a secular nation. I call it 'silent' as there have been no major communal upheavals. My immediate concern arises from the current debate to seek to revoke the death penalty imposed on Mohammad Afzal Guru for masterminding the December 13, 2001 terrorist attack on the Parliament House.

BUT HE'S A FAMILY MAN: Afzal's wife Tabassum

Mehbooba Mufti, President of the Progressive Democratic Party — a partner in the ruling coalition in Jammu and Kashmir — has pleaded for mercy keeping in mind the delicate situation in Kashmir. Ghulam Nabi Azad, the Congress Chief Minister of the state, has also lent support to the demand for clemency. The Congress claims to be a secular party, but it has not pondered the implications of seeking clemency for a man who had a hand in the murder of several police personnel on duty.

The terrorists' effort to storm the Parliament building did not succeed fully. Had they succeeded and killed a few MPs and taken a dozen or so hostage, it is a moot question whether the Congress would have sought clemency for those responsible for planning and executing the plot.

The Central Reserve Police Force (CRPF) constables on duty saved the MPs from this fate. The government bestowed the highest civilian awards on these police persons. Delhi Police Head Constable Ghansham Patel was awarded the Kirti Chakra, the highest civilian award. A woman constable, Kamlesh Kumari, who was killed on duty, was awarded the Ashok Chakra.

But now those who try to pick holes in the judicial process that culminated in the award of the death penalty, which was confirmed by the Supreme Court, try to find various arguments to justify clemency. One story doing the rounds is that a DSP of the Special Task Force, Dravinder Singh, plotted the attack and got Afzal involved.

In such a scenario, human rights activists might demand that bravery awards given to the police personnel be withdrawn. As of now, relatives of police personnel killed while protecting MPs and the Parliament building feel cheated by the extraordinary show of sympathy for terrorists by some political parties and human rights groups.

It is worthwhile to recall the words of P.V Narasimha Rao, spoken from the ramparts of the Red Fort, on August 15, 1993: "Do they [terrorists] mean that those who have been victims of their bullets have no human rights? Do only terrorists have human rights? They have a right to kill others and they also have human rights to the effect that nobody should kill them. This is warped logic beyond comprehension and we are not prepared to accept it."

The larger issue is: Are we going to decide issues of criminal justice on grounds of religion, caste, region, language and other narrow considerations and be influenced by parochial forces? Are we going to decide criminal cases on political considerations?

If so, why attempt to get Dawood Ibrahim from Pakistan to stand trial in India for his role in the 1993 bomb blasts? If J&K has the right to seek clemency on the grounds of miscarriage of justice, Pakistan, created as a safe state for Muslims from India, has every right to deny extradition of Dawood to stand trial in India!

In light of this, it is unfortunate that the President of India, an enlightened person like Dr A.P. J. Kalam, has allowed Afzal's family members to present him with a plea for clemency. Such actions on the part of heads of state or heads of government are risky, as is clear from past experiences. In the US, for instance, President Carter's meeting with hostages' families during the Iranian crisis of 1979 had a negative effect by focusing on the human tragedy and acting as an emotional blackmail factor for decision-makers.

It was a similar situation in the case of the hijacking of the Indian Airlines flight from Kathmandu to Kandahar in December 1999, when the then Prime Minister met relatives of the hijacked passengers. The NDA government was forced to release hardcore terrorists imprisoned in Kashmir, including Jaish-e- Mohammad founder Mohammad Azher.

The President has already met the family of Afzal Guru, including his seven-year-old son. The latter reportedly told the President that he wants his father around.

There are long-term effects of the present unfortunate clamour for clemency for Afzal. It can create misplaced sympathy for those who deliberately planned and helped execute the attack.

Secondly, there is already the destructive and divisive influence of caste and religion on Indian politics, from choosing a candidate in an election to voter mobilisation. Afzal's case will set a precedent for communal dispensation of criminal justice. If the process continues, can one predict where it will stop?

47

Musharraf Warns West, Clings on to Al-Qaeda and Taliban

(The Free Press Journal, 16-10-2006)

"Let it be clear that if the ISI is not with you, you will fail" Musharraf warned the US.

Pakistani President, General Pervez Musharraf has been brutally candid when he said in his interview on the BBC on September 28 on his way back from Washington, DC. He asked US and Britain to be grateful to Pakistan's external intelligence agency Inter-State Intelligence (ISI). It is the ISI that won, according to Musharraf, the Cold War for the West. In the absence of co-operation from Pakistan and ISI West will be brought on its knees. "Let it be clear that if the ISI is not with you, you will fail" Musharraf warned.

Let me at the outset say that in its existence as an independent state since 1947, no one neither a military dictator nor an elected leader has said anything so openly and frankly like this so far. So far only the scholars had said that it was the US that first laid the seeds of terrorism by arming, training and financing Mujahideens in South West Asia to fight against the Soviet invaders in Afghanistan since 1979. Musharraf said: "We did it for you and now we are suffering. You must understand this before putting blame."

Was this bragging by Musharraf, a sign of his over confidence or a sense of desperation? It was of course, partly a direct answer to the US counter-terrorism experts and policy makers who have blamed

Pakistan for not doing enough to capture Osama Bin Laden. Undoubtedly, Osama was the creation of the CIA and not the creation of Pakistan. But Pakistan immensely benefited from its working as a conduit to pump US military and economic aid to Mujahideens. Not only part of the aid was siphoned off unofficially by the ISI, but the US also paid a huge price for Pakistan's help then in the 1980s by extending economic and military aid packages to the tune of $4 billion. Musharraf cannot forget the fact that it was during this period that Pakistan also developed its nuclear weapons-while US pretending to persuade them from going nuclear!

Thus, having got its share more than its due, why remind Americans of their indebtedness for helping it in winning the cold war against Russians? Musharraf seems to be more desperate than confident. The fact of the matter is that George Bush will be out of electoral race in 2008 but Musharraf has to face the crucial elections in 2007 as he had promised earlier. Unlike former dictators of Pakistan, he would like to fight an election and win it! He would not like to go as Yayha Khan went in 1970s or Zia-ul Haq in 1980s!

It is in this context we need to see the western criticism of Pakistani ISI and Musharraf's response. The immediate cause of western anger is based on a series of actions taken by Pakistan's ISI. First, it signed a peace agreement with Taliban insurgents that essentially cede authority to it over North Waziristan. The accord permits non-Pakistani militants to move freely in the territory as long as they maintain peace, which in effect mean as long as they do not fire on Pakistanis, Pakistanis will not disturb them. Daveed Gartenstein-Ross and Bill Roggio writing in the Weekly Standard say that Taliban has begun "to rule openly" in the area and Al Qaeda black flag was seen during the accord signing ceremony. This has not only enabled Taliban to rule over the territory but also has provided a free play to Al Qaeda terrorists to freely operate in the area and stage attacks against Afghanistan. It will not be a surprise if Taliban eventually sets up a government in exile in Waziristan for Afghanistan.

Second, President Musharraf has also preempted any US action by issuing a hands-off warning to Americans and asking them not to indulge in hot chase of terrorists on Pakistani soil. Taliban and Al Qaeda, thus have now a safe haven in Waziristan where from Taliban can stage attacks on Afghanistan and Al Qaeda could plan their global terrorist attacks.

Third, to provide manpower for the above activities, Pakistan has released in one go 2500 foreign terrorists belonging to Al Qaeda and Taliban from their prisons. This has strengthened the manpower available to Taliban. How does this help Musharraf? Bush cannot help him in winning the 2007 Presidential elections. On the other hand, his association with the US war against Islamic terrorism has created an anti-Islam image of him. Thus the Waziristan peace accord will help him in image make over from pro-west and pro-US to one of pro-Taliban. It will help a great deal to win over religious parties in Pakistan as well. Taliban has claimed their truce with Pakistan as a victory and that can deliver Musharraf a victory as well in the next election. After all, Pakistan had the dubious record as the only country to maintain diplomatic relations with Taliban in Afghanistan four years ago till its government was overthrown by the Americans.

48

Alleged Terror Link of few Muslims: All Indians Suffer

(The Free Press Journal, 24-07-2007)

...Al Qaeda in its efforts to penetrate into Indian Muslim society has been very tactful and very savvy. It has chosen Muslims from South India...

When first news appeared on June 30 indicating the alleged involvement of Indian Muslims in a failed terrorist attacks at Glasgow airport in Britain with international ramifications, there was an air of disbelief as though a high priest who was universally respected is caught in telling a lie or stealing a bowl of rice. It is extremely difficult, however, to understand such dismay and disbelief on the part of present Indian government on the involvement of Indian-Muslims in the acts of terrorism.

In my opinion, involvement in acts of international terrorism is an extension of involvement in domestic terrorism. Let me go a step further and state that there is no distinction at all between domestic terrorism and international terrorism. Take for instance, those who were involved in Mumbai train blasts or those involved in Malegaon bombings. These are all Indian Muslims well educated beyond suspicion of being involved in such crimes.

The fact of the matter was that a Bangalore-born highly educated Ph. D. in fluid dynamics, Kafeel Ahmed appeared to break a myth hitherto held dear by the Indian government, Indian peculiar secularists as well as some foreign analysts that no Indian is ever involved in an act of international terrorism. But Kafeel is an Indian of Muslim faith from the mainstream of the society and in fact involved in organised terrorism. Family of Kafeel first hesitated to admit the fact of his belonging to Bangalore-based family. Then came the more shocking news of two of his cousins-both medical doctors-Mohamed Haneef and Sabeel Ahmed detained for questioning, first in Australia and the second in London.

When the first news appeared of all the persons in this country Prime Minister Manmohan Singh had lost his sound sleep over the matter!

Prime minister Manmohan Singh said he could not sleep when he saw TV images of the family of the detained Indian doctor Mohammad Haneef and his cousins. He even recalled his memories of every Sikh being considering as a terrorist in the 1980s soon after Mrs. Gandhi's assassination by a Sikh bodyguard and post-event massacre of Sikhs in Delhi and elsewhere in the country.

The truth of an Indian being involved in an international terrorist attack is also mainly politically unacceptable to the Prime Minister and the ruling political class in the country. Because, Muslims are cultivated as a very valuable vote-bank of the Congress led UPA. The Prime Minister and the UPA government was careful in merely identifying these three alleged terrorists as of Indian origin without elaborating their Muslim identity. Though a large number of Muslim-intellectuals in the 1980s made it their trademark to claim themselves as Muslims first and Indian next. Hence, they were proclaiming themselves as Muslim-Indians rather than Indian-Muslims!

The result has been practically every Indian is made to suffer humiliation for the alleged terrorist involvement of a section of Indian Muslims. The newspapers have lucid stories of how British callers are abusing Indians in the call centre for giving them bombs in return of their giving Indians jobs! The government is not now telling these companies of Indian multiculturalism but presenting as though there is only unhyphenated and undiluted Indian!

As much as Americans and Indians in government were claiming Indian Muslim's peaceful nature, the myth has been shattered and Al-Qaeda has succeeded in denting Indian claim. Whenever, Pakistan's

ISI and their proteges have organised terrorist attacks against Indian targets like for instance, Jaish-e-Mohammad orchestrated attack on Indian Parliament in December 2001, North Indian Muslims have been recruited to carry out their dirty tasks.

But Al Qaeda in its efforts to penetrate into Indian Muslim society has been very tactful and very savvy. It has chosen Muslims from South India, from highly educated class who could maintain their real identity very secret for a long time. So far, may be, unfounded by concrete evidence, that Muslim minority in Karnataka appeared to be less doctrinaire and more assimilated in the general society.

All this seems to be over. Secular journalists have to build now on their theories as to how, Haneef or Sabeel or Kafeel are victims of international conspiracy to defame Indian Muslims.

Already Australian government is under attack for doing their duty of going to the root of international terrorism irrespective of their national origin. For the government of India the Muslim votes are more important than fighting a war against international terrorism.

49

Musharraf Under Fire from Moderates Too

(The Free Press Journal, 11-08-2007)

...American public opinion has been gradually becoming critical of Pakistan's role in the US global war against terrorism.

Musharraf is under tremendous fire from moderates as well as extreme right in Pakistan. Prior to Musharraf's usurption of power in Pakistan by engineering a military coup in October 1999 in which he deposed the then Prime Minister, Nawaz Sharif, right wing or Islamic fundamentalists were in a minority of less than 5 per cent Musharraf's support to Islamic terrorists against India enhanced power of Islamic fundamentalists by placing them in power in North West Frontier Province in the last elections.

But Musharraf demonstrated his unwillingness to cultivate Islamic fundamentalists, when in National Assembly, he needed support to form a government. He refused the support of Muttahida Majlis-e-Amal (MMA) as it was demanding the prized post of Prime Minister. But being very close to the American administration after 9/11, alliance with MMA would have been in any way suicidal. But his military action in July this year again Lal Masjid and Madrasas run by it, in his effort to flush out Al Qaeda terrorists, under the constant pressure from the Bush administration, has completely alienated religious right. This has brought suicide bombers out into open and Pakistan has seen what it means to play with terrorists! Musharraf will not be very successful in controlling the Islamic clerics and Madrasas when his Minister for Religious Affairs, Mohammad Ezaj-ul Haq is of the opinion that if some one committed a suicide bombing to protect the honour of the Prophet Mohammad, his act was justified. This, of course, he said in the context of controversy created by Islamic extremists calling for action against Salman Rushdie after he was conferred the title of Knight by the British government If that is fine with Pakistani minister in the external context, suicide bombers do not distinguish insiders from outsiders!

However, Musharraf now faces threat to his power from moderates as well. I am using the term-moderates, deliberately as it is a characteristic of Musharraf to claim himself as a moderate Muslim. However, nothing has succeeded to enhance this threat as much as Musharraf's ill-conceived step of removing Pakistani Supreme Court's Chief Justice, Iftikar Ahmed. This boom-ranged against Musharraf since not only the supporters of the Chief Justice, but practically the entire legal fraternity came down openly on the street demanding, an independent minded Chief Justice seen likely to challenge Musharraf, if he made efforts to retain his military hat in addition to civilian suit beyond December 2007, be restored to his position. And as a slap on Musharraf's face, the Supreme Court acting as the judicial council restored its Chief Justice back into his seat! Under these circumstances, naturally the question arises: Why did Musharraf do such a nasty thing? He seem to have taken a leaf from former Prime Minister, Nawaz Sharif, though Musharraf was very critical of Nawaz Sharif, for his continuous efforts after he was elected in 1998 to centralise powers in his own hands. Nawaz Sharif, then by constitutional amendment successfully took away from the then President, Farooq Leghari, power to dissolve National Assembly and dismiss the elected government. Musharraf has written in detail how there was a tussle for power between the then President Farooq Leghari and Sharif. President wanted the then Chief Justice of the Supreme Court to declare constitutional amendment passed by National Assembly unconstitutional, while Sharif manipulated through judges of the SC, known to him to isolate the Chief Justice. Musharraf, probably thought he could also succeed in playing such a game with judges of the Supreme court.

In retrospect, the then army chief, Jahangir Karamat had made a mistake of publicly suggesting that the Army be given greater role in the national affairs for which he proposed creation of a National Security Council. This had not gone well with Nawaz Sharif and he compounded Karamat's mistake by appointing Musharraf as the Army Chief to succeed General Karamat-may be for his standing firmly in support of democratically elected government of Nawaz Sharif! But that became an invitation to destroy democracy in Pakistan. Be that as it may, the strongest prop of Musharraf has been the support from the American government. However, American public opinion has been gradually becoming critical of Pakistan's role in the US global war against terrorism. This criticism became vocal after Democrats captured power in the US Congress in January 2007.

50

Why Naxals Alone? Islamic Terror is Equally a Security Threat

(The Free Press Journal, 27-02-2008)

There is growing connectivity between external security and internal security so much so that one does not know where one ends and the other begins.

During the Cold War period nations mainly focused on external aspects of national security. External security was largely taken care by the effective diplomacy conducted by the Ministry of Foreign Affairs on the one hand and on the other, by the armed forces under the control of Defence Department. The threat was always seen by

the Indian state from other nation-states inimical to its national interest-like Pakistan and China. Hence, such a threat to national security was to be met by strengthening armed forces, providing them with latest equipments and preparing them in modern warfare.

Since the end of the Cold War, a military conflict has become out of question and out of fashion-particularly after all the three-India, Pakistan along with China, became nuclear weapons states after India and Pakistan conducted their nuclear tests in May 1998. Today, mostly internal security threats emerge from largely the non-state actors active in international relations either directly or as surrogate on behalf of a state. Mostly these groups survive as surrogates, because these cannot survive for long without state patronage.

Most of national security threat perceptions today emerge from internal sources with external linkages there is vast scope for the patron-state for plausible deniability. India has taken pride in proclaiming its concept of unity in diversity. It has historically given shelter to various people from different foreign nations when they have fled their own country on the face of persecution either on the ground of race or religion. Even foreign invaders, have settled here by assimilating with local population, at the same time retaining their culture.

In a democratic system, particularly in Indian parliamentary democracy, ethnic and religious minorities have special privileges under the Indian constitution. Political parties from left to the right have exploited these provisions to create special vote banks by offering diversity-based benefits rather than emphasising unity-based perspectives. Latest is the proposal to create in states separate department of minorities. Hence, these diversities have become sources of internal security challenges, instead of strengthening national unity!

Most important one is the Islamic factor. The threat arising from this factor has undergone an interesting transformation. To begin with Pakistan sent its nationals to foment Unrest in India limited to mostly to the state of Jammu and Kashmir. This was the case during the period from 1989 to 1996. One should recall terrorists holed in Hazaratbal Mosque in Kashmir who were allowed to leave after negotiations. One condition then imposed by the terrorists was that they should not be exposed to Media!

Later, in the second phase, mostly Kashmiris were used for the same purpose. In this phase, Kashmiris were given financial support, weapons and training in the use of them. Thousands of Kashmiris were killed in this phase in anti-terrorist operations-even leading to old Kashmiris to feel that no one will be left to reach them to graves! This phase mostly lasted during the United Front governments and the NDA government (1996 to 2004).

In the third phase-now in operation since UPA came into office in 2004, for terrorism-based internal security threat, the external forces are using Indian Muslims to carry out the same design of creating unrest and spreading ill will between the communities. In this kind of domestic terrorist threat, the source of threat is from across the borders but inseparably linked to and carried out by domestic groups. Our policy makers were hasty in pronouncing and expressing their happiness at non-involvement of Indian Muslims in terrorist activities abroad. When they have so much to do at home, they need not get entangled abroad, where punishment, if caught, could be death!

External forces also provide, in addition to moral and material support, logistic support as well, more liberally. Thus for instance, bomb blasts of July 11 2006 were allegedly brought about by an Indian Muslim from Gujarat, Sheikh Faisal, who was trained, armed, funded by a Lashker-e-Toiba operative in Pakistan, known as Azam Chima. In all such cases UPA political establishment could be expected to be more sympathetic to them. The living example is the non-execution of death sentence awarded to Afzal Guru terrorism-mastermind and confirmed by the Supreme Court.

What do these various internal security threat groups work for? It is possible for us to classify their aims: (1) As acting at the behest of foreign masters, merely as mercenary groups, (2) supporting foreign powers' political aims, (3) secession of an area and creation of a new sovereign independent state or creation of a new territorial unit to enjoy a greater self-governance or autonomy, (4) overthrow of existing political arrangement for governance and (5) self-sustaining activities. Often these goals overlap in the case of many such groups. Various groups operating in Jammu and Kashmir, for instance, embrace all the above objectives in varying degree of emphasis.

Thus, what starts as terrorism or low intensity conflict promoted by external sources creates an enemy within-giving birth to internal security threats. In turn internal security issues create disaffection amongst the citizens of a state, unlike external security threats, which unite people within a state. We are accustomed to phrases like 'nation rising as one man' or 'speaking in one voice'. But internal security threats divide people on the lines of religion or caste or tribal or political affinity. These passions are much more stronger than nationalism. Thus internal security issues give rise to one man's terrorist as another man's freedom fighter.

There is growing connectivity between external security and internal security so much so that one does not know where one ends and the other begins. Therefore it is better for the Indian state to nip the problem in the bud when external terrorism begins. Since, India failed to do it, at least it should act without looking at its vote bank politics. Speaking at the CMs' Conference on December 27 last year, Prime Minister Man Mohan Singh described Naxalites as the "single biggest security challenge to the Indian state." That also aptly applies to Islamic terrorism!

51

Pak Deserves being Placed on Terror List

(The Free Press Journal, 24-05-2010)

US ought to hold a threat of placing Pakistan on Terrorism watch.... to achieve the goal of creating a moderate Islamic society and .... stop arming it through the American tax payers' money.

No country in the world can be a safe home, a financier, in-depth training centre and protector of native grown and international terrorists and yet be a strategic ally of the US, as Pakistan is today. Democrats' ascendancy to power has been a boon for Pakistan. Using its geopolitically significant location it could get American bounties on different pretexts: As a fragile democracy, as a partner in war against Terrorism, as a victim of self-promoted terrorism, as a strategic ally and now as a check against its own military leadership waiting in the wings to take over the power!

After flow of dollars in billions and lethal weapons to fight terrorists, though mostly would be used against India, Pakistan is now asking its good friends in Democratic establishment headed by President Barrack Obama to reward it with a Nuclear Deal similar to one given to India by the US. This is in the Pakistani mindset of parity with India in every field. The immediate grounds to justify their often rejected claim is that Pakistan has done enough to deserve such a reward as it has either captured or killed several of Pakistani (Bad)Taliban members-while protecting (good) Afghan Taliban leaders on their soil, so that the US could have a compromise with good Taliban.

From the American perspective, this is an imperative, yet short-term need as the US has made a public commitment to bring home American troops by mid-2011 as the US cannot shoulder an "open-ended commitment" in strife torn Afghanistan. For Pakistan it is a good investment since, if the US raises the prize amount, they could kill more of the bad Pakistani Taliban members. However, if the US fails to talk with the good Taliban and wind their Afghan venture, releasing bad Afghan Taliban could provide Pakistan strategic depth with new Taliban government in Afghanistan.

American Presidents, once elected, cannot see beyond four years as next presidential elections need to be fought on promises fulfilled, while the opponents of the President would run by pointing failures of the President. One of the slogans on which Obama won the election in November 2008 was by promising to end the War in Afghanistan and bring back troops. For him nothing is more sacrosanct if it helps him to win the next election due to be fought in November 2012.

In the past too, in addition to killing bad Taliban men-Musharraf used to throw at the Americans, whenever they said you ought to do more on terrorist front, statistics on 'most wanted' terrorists killed and dollars earned by Pakistan thereby. As he writes in his memoir, In the line of Fire, "We have captured 689 and handed over 369 to the United States...earned bounties totaling millions of dollars. Those who habitually accuse us of 'not doing enough'...should simply ask the CIA how much prize money it has paid to the government of Pakistan."

Now, elected government is following in the footsteps of Musharraf. However, Pakistani demand for Civil Nuclear Deal (CND) as offered to India is as old as the day when George W. Bush announced it for India-July 18,2005. If the US is Pakistan's outsourced gold mine, India is its measuring rod as to how much to extract at a given time. Pakistani Standard is simple: Whatever you give to India, give it to Pakistan-parity with India is the guiding principle of Pakistan!

Bush administration then had said more than once, that the CND is a mark of a unique relationship with India. As the joint declaration of July 18 said: As "responsible state with advanced nuclear technology, India should acquire the same benefits as other such states" including the US. Indian opposition to NPT is well known but Americans reluctantly agreed Indian impeccable record in the field of non proliferation without ever signing it.

Pakistan is by now well-known as the leader of global nuclear proliferation movement. Its nuclear programme was born in sin-I mean stealth from Sweden. The Father of Pakistani Bomb, Dr A. Q. Khan is the designated director of underground nuclear flea Market. He had supplied stolen nuclear technology to North Korea, Iran and Libya, among others-all those who followed anti-American policy. Nuclear programme in Pakistan has been under tight military control since Zia-ul Haq's military coup in 1978. Hence, it is impossible without the knowledge of a military regime to transfer even a piece of spent fuel. Yet, another dictator, Musharraf in 2004 fixed sole responsibility for Khan's underground nuclear Bazaar on him. Americans had accepted it. I had asked Clinton administration's non-proliferation expert-Robert Einhorn, as to how it is possible. His reply was since Pakistan was a friend in need it has to be tolerated!

Yet when Pakistan's Foreign Minister, Shah Mehmood Qureshi led delegation on strategic dialogue that included Army Chief Kayani visited Washington, DC, Secretary of State Hillary Clinton, created an illusion of serious consideration for Pakistani request for a CND by publicly stating that Pakistan's "struggles are our struggles." Knowing Democrats concern for non-proliferation, Pakistan, however, had made a strong case on the ground of its energy needs and economic compulsions as well. Secretary of State also had referred to Pakistani acute need for energy. Pakistan has a very strong Lobby to push its case. Even when Bush administration was considering the CND for India, a pro-Pakistan scholar, Stephen Cohen, had said: It should be "initial step in a process of crafting a diplomacy that addresses India's energy needs [but] America has such concerns in area that stretches from Israel to China...." Pakistan stood between Israel and China and it is this hope that made pro-Pakistani lobby not to strongly oppose CND to India!

Now that Pakistan's hopes of a CND have been put off to another period may be ten to 15 years later by a friendly American advice to improve its nonproliferation regime. Every thing in nuclear arena has a long gestation period any way. India had publicly expressed its concern on the possibilities of US consideration of a CND. Now India need to privately work on two more goals in the interest of regional peace: One, ask the US to hold a threat of placing Pakistan on Terrorism watch so as to achieve the goal of creating a moderate Islamic society in Pakistan and two, stop arming it through the American tax-payers' money. Let Pakistan buy its needs by paying hard currency it earns as is the case with India.

52

Ghulam Nabi Fai that I knew

(The Free Press Journal, weekend, 31-05-2011)

"It was ironic that some self-determination movements have very undemocratic aims, such as creation of a homogenous mono-ethnic state." James Steinberg, State Department Policy Planning Staff.

On Monday, July 18 American Federal Bureau of Investigation (FBI) arrested Dr Ghulam Nabi Fai, an American citizen of Indian origin, on the charge of working as an unregistered lobbyist for the Pakistani Government to influence US government and public in favour of Kashmir's self determination. He is supposed to have received $4 million from the Pakistan's Inter-Services Intelligence (ISI).

I first met Dr Fai on 12 October 2000 at Madison, University of Wisconsin, Wisconsin, where 29th Annual Conference on South Asia was the main reason for scholars to assemble. But one day before the commencement of the Conference there was a symposium on "Constitutional Issues" and "National Integration" as it relates to India. It was organised by the National Advisory Council on South Asian Affairs. I was invited by Professor Raju G. C. Thomas an American citizen of Indian origin, whom I had first met in American Cultural Centre in Mumbai. In this symposium I spoke on "Kashmir Conflict and Non-viability of Self Determination."

In this Symposium, Dr Fai was also a speaker who obviously spoke at length on Kashmiri Self-determination. However, before I met him at Madison, I had read in the newspapers about his Kashmir-

related lobbying particularly soon after Bill Clinton was inaugurated as President of the US in January 1993. My curiosity and interest in Clinton was more than what generally an expert on America would have for two reasons.

First, in November 1984 I had spent about two weeks watching American Presidential elections directly from Littlerock, capital of the State of Arkansas in the US of which Bill Clinton was then the Governor and had given me a certificate as 'Arkansas Traveler'. Second, as a Fulbright Scholar myself I admired him because he was a Rhodes Scholar, also considered as a prestigious scholarship.

But soon after he was inaugurated, I was very critical of Clinton's policies towards India on several grounds. I published "An open letter to Bill Clinton." Giving reference to my meeting him in Littlerock, I said in it: "Recently, I have seen your proclivity to write to those who work towards the goal of disintegration of India from the US soil. First in your letter to Dr Ghulam Nabi Fai, you expressed your desire to 'work with you and others to bring peace to Kashmir..."

Thus, I had wished to see who this Dr Fai is. At the Symposium, he gave me plenty of published material on "Self-determination of Kashmir." In my presentation I tried to bring out the fact that Kashmir is an inseparable and integral part of India. I mentioned seven dangers of self-determination and in particular, I quoted a reported statement of then member of the State Department Policy Planning staff, James Steinberg who had said: "It was ironic that some self-determination movements have very undemocratic aims, such as creation of a homogenous mono-ethnic state."

Second time I met Dr Fai is when I was invited by him to attend a two-day International Kashmir Peace Conference, at Capitol Hill, Washington, DC in July 2005. I was already in Toledo, Ohio in the US. When I knew that in the past a few Indians known to me had attended the Conference, and Dr Subramanian Swamy will also be attending it, I had no reason to decline to attend.

In this International Kashmir Peace Conference, Dr Fai had put together truly an international group who advocated Self-determination. It was a conference to fiercely advocate right to self-determination of Kashmir. It was clear right at pre-conference dinner at earlier night that India bashing had no limit. It was only Dr Subramanian Swamy in addition to this author, who presented Indian case.

With all these memories of my encounter with Dr Fai and his Kashmiri American Council, I am not surprised, as on today, that he is arrested by the US on a technical ground of not registering as a foreign lobbyist though he was getting his funds from Pakistan's ISI. My surprise is at how the US administration learnt of his illegal activities, only now as they did, in the background of growing mistrust between the two nations.

53

Terror of 13/7: Lessons to be Learnt

(One India One People, August 2011)

Today ordinary people in neighbourhood ask if the US can prevent attacks on its homeland after 9/11, why can't India do it?

Mumbai has seen once again another heinous crime of terrorism on July 13, after Pakistani promoted November 26, 2008 sea-borne international terrorism paralysed the city for three days. Terrorist attacks of 13/7 took place at three commercially busiest and all-time crowded places like Zaveri Bazaar, Opera House and Dadar (West) Kabutarkhana, killing 20 and injuring more than 131 innocent citizens. As usual, our governing politicians aided by bureaucrats have visited Mumbai city and made their tall statements. P Chidambaram, Home Minister, spoke of "coordinated attack by terrorists" as though the uncoordinated attacks could have minimised their impact. Prime Minister spoke of his determination to see that "perpetrators of the Mumbai bomb blasts shall be pursued relentlessly and brought to justice quickly." He had expressed almost identical sentiments about seven bomb blasts of 11/7 in Mumbai suburban trains that killed 181 innocent people.

Prime Minister often described as a lame duck, however, has one important unfinished agenda now in his mind: to increase the trust asset between India and Pakistan to develop "normal relations" with Pakistan and finally resolve long pending Kashmir issue during his remaining three years. In pursuance of the goal, this time in the absence of concrete evidence so far of Pakistan's involvement—

direct or indirect in 13/7, government is unwilling to name Pakistan's hand and mind; though investigators speak of it as perpetrated by banned Indian Mujahideen (IM) at the behest of Taliban. Political discussion now being raised by the government and opposition parties boil around two issues: Could terror and dialogue go together or India should refuse to talk while Pakistan directly or indirectly continues to organise or abet terrorist attacks against Indian targets.

Terror and Dialogue

Prime Minister has not even remotely hinted of involvement of Pakistan. Minister for External Affairs, S. M. Krishna, and soon retiring Foreign Secretary Nirupama Rao, reiterated that dialogue with the Pakistan will continue. S. M. Krishna also said that there would be no change in the dialogue schedule with either Pakistan or the US.

He will hold dialogue with his Pakistani counterpart on 26-27 July and also hold the strategic dialogue with the United States (US) Secretary of State, Hillary Clinton on July 20. This suits well the American purposes in the region; by increasing normalcy in India-Pakistan relations, US can work to increase Pakistan's cooperation in forcing Taliban to talk to the Karzai government, thus enabling the US to withdraw its troops from Afghanistan partially by next summer by claiming normalcy and political stability in Afghanistan. Obama naturally as of now is only interested in his next reelection in November 2012.

Opposition to Dialogue

On the other hand the main opposition party, the BJP, reiterated its opposition to the dialogue and demanded that it be called off. It is futile for India to organise dialogue on the face of continued terror carried out from Pakistani soil. The UPA government on the other hand, could claim that unlike 26/11 attacks on Mumbai, serial bomb blasts of 13/7, as of now are not directly carried out by Pakistan Army and Inter-Services Intelligence (ISI) and its protege terrorist groups like Lashker-e-Toiba (LeT) or Jaish-e-Mohammad (JeM) or several others. But this is only a superficial difference, because two terrorist attacks would rarely be identical in its origin.

In the last 30 years while Pakistan Army has supported numerous terrorist groups based in Pakistan and Pakistan Occupied Kashmir (PoK), to hit at India. It is done through military controlled ISI, which has mainly relied on LeT and JeM to carry out its heinous crimes against humanity in India. The single most important reason why the Pakistani Army is supporting terrorism in India is its intense paranoid desire to avenge its defeat at the hands of Indian Army in 1971. However, constant Indian military action on borders, international pressure against Pakistan's progressively proven involvement in organising terrorist attacks and immature Indian claims of non-involvement of Indian Muslims in such terrorist attacks has made Pakistan to make terrorism indigenous to India!

Further, particularly after 26/11 and May 2, killing of Osama Bin Laden by the US by its stealth operation right under the nose of Pakistan's Military Training Academy in Abbottabad and subsequent loss of credibility of Army and ISI, the duo has been forced to use numerous indigenous, but ISI trained, financed, controlled and brainwashed groups to believe how Indian government is against Muslims to carry out terrorist attacks. With an elected government in place in Pakistan, it gives the opportunity to the civilian facade to exercise plausible deniability. It is clearly evident in fact that after 26/11 President Zardari denied Pakistani government's role and attributed it to 'non-state actors.' But over 13/7, Zardari and PM Gilani have been very prompt in condemning terrorist attacks on July 13! Thus, the UPA government is taking a current view while Opposition is taking a long-term perspective wherein Pakistan is in one way or the other involved including in the latest terror attacks of 13/7.

Lessons to be Learnt

Today ordinary people in neighbourhood ask if the US can prevent attacks on its homeland after 9/11, why can't India do it. That is because we refuse to learn any lessons from the past experiences. What are the lessons, then to be learnt from the latest terrorist attacks, as of now, emanating indirectly from Pakistan? How can India break from this vicious circle of Pakistan directly or indirectly promoting terror attacks against India? At the cost of repetition, it must be said that the 26/11 terrorism was totally organised and implemented by Pakistani ISI through LeT with the knowledge of Pakistani Army and government probably enjoying the benefit of plausible deniability. In the absence of Indian will to self-help to protect its national security, the US has been able to extend its help by pressurising Pakistan to abandon terrorism. But neither Pakistan nor the US, can come to India's help against Pakistan promoted, trained, financed, and controlled attacks by Indian terrorist groups like IM or Students Islamic Movement in India and their sleeper cells. India needs to act on her own.

Hence, India needs to learn certain lessons and immediately act upon them. First, its time to consider terrorism linked to Pakistan as international terrorism. All externally promoted terrorism ought to be treated as an attack on the state lawfully established and governed as such. Second, international terrorism has to be seen as a central subject irrespective of whether it emanates from across the borders or from Pak promoted bodies or their active cells working within India. Since it is an attack on the state, it should be governed by a special law. Since words like POTA or TADA have become nationally divisive, call the law National Protection Law as Americans called their reply to 9/11 as Patriotic Act. The law should provide for only one appeal against the trial court. Third, the main political parties ought to depoliticise their approach to terrorism. Terrorism is a national menace which has no colour of caste or creed, or religion. If political parties cannot, at least those who are in governance should open their eyes for long-term effects of terrorism on the nation rather than think of next election. Unfortunately, in India even worst menace of international terrorism, is seen from communal angle and all political parties from the left to right try to draw political mileage from the acts of terrorism. Thus for instance, chief minister of Maharashtra could not see beyond creation of communal trouble as the purpose of 13/7. But more than one source has confirmed that Pakistan's Army wants to force Indian economic slow down if not collapse by attacking Mumbai again and again. However, all limits of political decency are crossed by former chief minister of MP, Digvijay Singh as though to avenge his loss of power to the BJP, when he blamed RSS for the latest Mumbai terror. Let us not hope for the best by praising resilience of Mumbaikars when he is in reality desperate to earn to live on the next day. Act now to save the nation and its hard working people.

54

Delhi Terror of 7/9 High Time for the Federal Government to Draw Lessons

(Freedom First, October 2011)

The main political parties ought to depoliticize their approach to terrorism. Terrorism is a national menace which has no colour of caste or creed or religion.

Terrorists had planned a dry run to attack on the Delhi High Court on 25th May this year. But policy makers in the federal government slept despite so much of experience. The Result: Delhi saw another heinous attack of terrorism on 7th September, killing 13 and wounding more than 90 at the time of writing. This, so soon after the 13/7 Mumbai attacks. Now Home Minister, P Chidambaram (PC) says Delhi police were given intelligence in July. But the Lt. Governor of Delhi, Tejinder Khanna says it was not actionable.

Assuming that PC is right, an important question arises regarding the process of policy making and administration. Since international terrorism is a subject that directly comes under the federal government, does the responsibility of the Home Minister end with the passing of the actionable intelligence? No. That is the only the beginning of action! Since the minister meets, it is said, the Delhi Police Chief almost daily, isn't it his duty to follow up on the action taken? Did PC, at any time, ask for a report?

This worked very well as an alibi for the federal government in the case of the Pakistan sponsored cross-sea terrorism of 26/11 against the financial capital of India. PC had then informed the Lok Sabha that intelligence that was available was not actionable! But

Ram Pradhan who went into the Mumbai attack of 26/11, brings out vividly the fact that intelligence received clearly identified targets of attack like the Taj and Oberoi-though in October rather than November! But there is no indication that the federal government ever followed up to enquire about action taken!

Be that as it may, policy makers and politicians waiting in the wings, aided by bureaucrats visited the Delhi High Court bomb blast site as they did earlier Mumbai after the 13/7 attacks. The Prime Minister, who flew down to Mumbai spoke of his determination to see that the "perpetrators of the Mumbai bomb blasts shall be pursued relentlessly and brought to justice quickly." He had expressed almost identical sentiments about the seven bomb blasts of 11/7 on Mumbai suburban trains that killed 181. After the latest Delhi blasts, he said: It is a cowardly act. We will deal with it. It is a long war....We will not succumb." But in nearly six cases of terrorism in the recent past, the culprits are yet to be identified!

Pakistan at the Root of Indian Terrorism

These words of Prime Minister indicate helplessness of a government that is groping in total darkness. The Prime Minister often described as a lame duck, however, has one important unfinished agenda now in his mind: to increase the trust asset between India and Pakistan, develop "normal relations" and resolve the Kashmir issue in his remaining three years in office. In pursuance of the goal, this time, as in Mumbai, 13/7, in the absence of concrete evidence of Pakistani involvement - direct or indirect in 7/9, Prime Minister was unwilling to name Pakistan's hand.

However, in the last thirty years Pakistan's Army has supported numerous terrorist groups based in Pakistan and Pakistan Occupied Kashmir (POK), to hit at India. It is done through the military controlled ISI, which has mainly relied on LeT and JeM to carry out its heinous crimes against humanity in India. The single most important reason why the Pakistani Army is supporting terrorism in India is its intense paranoid desire to avenge its defeat at the hands of Indian Army in 1971.

The duo has been forced to use numerous indigenous, but ISI trained, financed, controlled and brainwashed groups to believe how

Indian government is against Muslims to carry out terrorist attacks. With an elected government in place in Pakistan, it gives an opportunity to the civilian facade to exercise plausible deniability.

Further, particularly after 26/11 and the 2nd May, killing of Osama bin Laden by the US right under the nose of Pakistan's Military Training Academy in Abbottabad and subsequent loss of credibility the Pakistan Army and ISI, have been forced to use numerous indigenous, but ISI trained, financed, controlled and brainwashed groups to carry out terrorist attacks. With an elected government in place in Pakistan, it gives an opportunity to the civilian facade to exercise plausible deniability. Thus, Pakistani President, Zardari and PM Gilani have been very prompt in condemning terrorist attacks on 13 July! Pakistanis now point out that they too are victims of terrorism as on the very day Delhi High Court had the terrorist bomb blast, they too had a bigger bomb attack in Quetta carried out by Pakistani Taliban in which 25 were killed and at least 60 were injured! They conveniently forget the fact that indigenised Indian terrorists of Muslim faith were brainwashed, trained, funded, sheltered and used by Pakistan, while the Quetta suicide bombing had no Indian elements in it!

Lessons to be Learnt

Today ordinary people in India ask if the US can prevent attacks on its homeland in the last ten years after 9/11, why can't India do it. That is because we refuse to learn any lessons from our past experiences. What are the lessons, then to be learnt from the latest terrorist attacks? In the absence of an Indian will to self-help to protect its national security, the US has been able to extend its help by pressurising Pakistan to abandon terrorism. But neither Pakistan nor the US, can come to India's help against Pakistan promoted, trained, financed, and controlled attacks by Indian terrorist groups like IM or SIMI and their sleeper cells. India needs to act on her own.

Hence, India needs to learn certain lessons and immediately act upon them to make acts of terrorism very costly to them. First, its time to consider all terrorist attacks linked directly or indirectly to Pakistan as international terrorism. All externally promoted terrorism ought to be treated as an attack on the state lawfully established and governed as such.

Second, international terrorism has to be seen as a central subject irrespective of whether it emanates from across the borders or from Pakistan-promoted bodies or their active cells working within India. Since it is an attack on the state, it should be governed by a special law. Since words like POTA or TADA have become politically divisive, call the new law as a Nation Protection Act. Americans called their reply to 9/11 as Patriotic Act. The law should provide for separate courts for speedy justice and for only one appeal against the verdict of the trial court.

Third, the main political parties ought to depoliticise their approach to terrorism. Terrorism is a national menace which has no colour of caste or creed, or religion. If parties at the political level cannot resist the temptation, at least those who are in governance, like PC should open their eyes for long-term effects of terrorism on the nation rather than think of the next election. Unfortunately, in India even the worst menace of international terrorism, is seen from a communal angle and all political parties from the left to right try to draw political mileage from acts of terrorism. However, all limits of political decency were crossed by former chief minister of MP, Digvijay Singh, when he blamed the RSS for the latest Mumbai terror as though to avenge his loss of power to the BJP. Now people in Delhi after the recent bomb blast jeered Rahul Gandhi and asked him not to play politics with terror!

Finally, justice must be seen to be done to hundreds and thousands of innocent victims of terrorism -injured and dead - by hanging those terrorists who have been given the death sentence by trial courts and confirmed by the Supreme Court. More the nation delays carrying out these just acts, the more we are likely to see even more terrorist acts! Act now to save the nation and its hard working people, without praising them for their so-called resilience which essentially comes from concerns to ensure their bread for the next day!

55

Clemency for Terrorists - Undesirable in Every Way

(One India One People, December, 2011)

The increasing ploy of politicians to ask for clemency in case of hardcore terrorists and assassins is threatening the very root of India's integrity. This needs to be discouraged and our policy ought to be of zero tolerance to terrorists and zero tolerance of politicians supporting terrorists.

There is an emerging new threat to India and its integrity as a nation, when law makers plead/demand for clemency to hardcore international terrorists or Indian terrorists working at the behest of foreign forces on the grounds of human rights! These terrorists were tried by trial courts and given death penalty; these were confirmed by High Courts of respective states and upheld by the Supreme Court—sometimes more than once. Further, the Governors of States and the President of India under the Indian Constitution are vested with powers to grant pardon or remit or commute the sentences in certain cases. Here below, I discuss three such cases of misplaced, in my opinion, anti-national clamour for clemency to hardcore international terrorists. The perception of the threat is compounded by the fact that in all the three cases, the President of India had rejected clemency petitions!

Assassins of Rajiv Gandhi

Rajiv Gandhi had great potential to be an effective and imaginative Prime Minister—a fact similar to John F. Kennedy. Like Kennedy,

had Gandhi lived, he could have changed the course of Indian politics. But at the orders of Prabhakaran, the supreme leader of Liberation Tigers of Tamil Ealam (LTTE), Sri Lankan Tamils eliminated Rajiv Gandhi, at Sriperumpudur in Tamil Nadu (TN) on May 21, 1991, by using a human bomb. Their grouse: Allegedly, he had acted against their interest by agreeing to send Indian Peace Keeping Force (IPKF) to Sri Lanka to disarm LTTE.

After the trial court gave the death sentence to Murugan, Santhan, Perarivalan and Nalini for their conspiracy to eliminate Rajiv Gandhi, it was confirmed by the Madras High Court. The Supreme Court confirmed the death sentence on three of them but commuted Nalini's death sentence to life imprisonment in 2000. In August 2011 clemency petitions of the three conspirators were turned down by the President.

Khalistan Liberation Force

The Khalistan movement for a separate state for Sikhs in India was a brainchild of few well placed Sikhs living abroad with the full

Devinder Pal Singh Bhullar

backing of post-Bangladesh Pakistan military dictator, General Zia-ul-Haq. The sole motive of Pakistan, then as of now, was a tit for tat creation of an independent Khalistan. In Zia's calculations, an independent Khalistan will not only be a buffer state but will also provide strategic depth to a truncated Pakistan after the birth of a new state in erstwhile East Pakistan.

Devinder Pal Singh Bhullar, a former lecturer from Guru Nanak Engineering College, Ludhiana, was a member of Khalistan Liberation Force. He was involved in several cases of terrorist attacks in Punjab and New Delhi. In a car bombing on September 11, 1993 that was intended to kill Maninder Singh Bitta, then Youth Congress President and a vocal critic of Khalistani movement, killed 9 bystanders but Bitta survived. Bhullar then fled to Germany but was extradited back to Delhi to stand trial; he was convicted and given death sentence by the trial court on August 25, 2001; His appeal was dismissed by the Supreme Court on December 27, 2006 and clemency petition was also rejected by the President in May 2011.

Conspirator of attack on Parliament

Parliament is the symbol of Indian democracy; an epitome of Indian unity, integrity and sovereignty. After the 9/ 11 terrorist attack, when Pakistan was forced into the US led war against international terrorism, anti Indian terrorist groups based in Pakistan were given free hand by the then military dictator, General Pervez Musharraf. There was an attack on Kashmir Assembly in October 2001 and later on December 13, 2001, there was an attempt to storm Parliament by terrorists. Brave fight put up by the police and guards saved the Parliament from infamy of terrorist attack. Yet in the attempt to storm Parliament 15 people were killed. Afzal Guru, a Kashmiri, was tried for conspiracy whose death sentence was confirmed by the Indian Supreme Court.

Politics of pleading to save terrorists

It all started with setting September 9, 2011 as the date for the execution of Rajiv killers. Immediately the old habit of main political parties in TN of playing politics with Tamilian sentiments began. Tamil political parties asked for intervention of Jayalalitha to save the lives of Tamils—despite the fact that Murugan and Santhan were Sri

Lankans. Jayalalitha, now in power, accused Karunanidhi, DMK chief, of stage managing the show to embarrass her as the AIADMK Chief. She pointed out that while in power, he had recommended to the governor rejection of clemency pleas of three accused.However, he was now orchestrating sympathy and shedding crocodile tears for the men in death row. She, however, moved a resolution in Assembly pleading for clemency to three Tamils. She didn't explain, why should she move a resolution seeking the President to reconsider the rejection of clemency petitions. A similar unsuccessful effort was made in Jammu and Kashmir Assembly. There was also a talk of Punjab Assembly passing a resolution seeking clemency for Bhullar.

Politicians demanding commuting of death sentence because of their political compulsions have adduced different grounds as to why justice would be transgressed in the absence of it. Some of the important arguments may be briefly considered. First, abolition of death penalty is invoked. In the case of Bhullar for instance, the European Union has been kind to suggest saving of life because death penalty is inhuman. The European state system has developed during the last 400 years, hence may advocate abolition of death penalty. But it is worth remembering that the US too had abolished it only to reintroduce it later. Anyway debate on relevance of capital punishment should not be based by making international terrorists as the immediate beneficiaries.

Afzal Guru

Second, the terrorists have been languishing in jail for long, as in the case of Rajiv Gandhi assassins, for over 20 years. Hence, the pleas are made that the condemned prisoners have already suffered by waiting for so long that they deserve to have the sentence commuted to life imprisonment. However, as long as death penalty is on the statute book, delay in execution cannot be a ground for clemency. But there are two lessons to be learnt by the government. First one is not to have vote bank considerations in deciding timing of execution of a death sentence. Second lesson is: undue delay in trial or execution of terrorists convicted is likely to give rise to more terrorist attacks to get them freed. The terrorist attack in Delhi High Court on September 7, 2011 is directly linked to punish High Court for giving death sentence to Afzal Guru.

Third, human rights groups are always ready to raise voice against violation of human rights of criminals and terrorists, safely ignoring denial of right to life of victims! Thus, for instance, appearing for three terrorists involved in Rajiv killing, in Madras HC, Ram Jethmalani, Colin Gonsalves and R.Vaigai contended that the "inordinate and in explainable delay" in disposing of their mercy petitions violated Article 21 of the Constitution involving protection of life and personal liberty! It is difficult to understand how the delay, that extended the life of convicts, violated right to life! Is it because their extended life is a violation?

Finally, one can understand relatives like Bhullar's mother or Murugan's daughter asking for their loved ones' life back. But it is a travesty of law and justice by elected representatives of Tamil Nadu, Punjab or Jammu and Kashmir when law makers pass or think of passing resolution asking the federal government to show clemency to terrorists. Politicians have gone to the extent of organising protest by women in Chennai on October 30, 2011 where the leaders of the group vowed to "continue (the) struggle.. .until this death penalty is commuted."

Threat to Union of India

Current behaviour by the law makers of these legislatures is a threat to Indian nation in more than one way. First, any sympathy by lawmakers to the cause expounded by some individuals to save the lives of terrorists is likely to encourage future terrorists that one day they can still hope to live despite their involvement in heinous crime against humanity. Bitta, a terror victim and now chairman of All India Anti-Terrorist Front, rightly blamed political leaders for "encouraging activities of militants in Jammu and Kashmir." The immediate fall out could be - the only surviving Pakistani terrorist Ajmal Kasab might claim that the Indian system of giving him three judicial opportunities to prove his innocence and an added opportunity of appealing to the President of India for mercy is too cumbersome - during the period he had suffered so much of psychological pain that he be immediately be released!

Currently, Indian society is not fully well-knit one because of illiteracy, poverty, caste and regional loyalties and age-old customs and traditions. Hence, in rarest of rare cases when the nation's highest court confirms death penalty, it acts as a deterrence on a would be assassin or a terrorist. Hence any change in the death penalty, might remove deterrence effect of the death penalty. Third, clamour to save terrorists who have assassinated or attacked democratically elected representatives goes against the very root of Indian democratic state. A state comes into being because the alternative is the law of jungle. Finally, Indian union is built on the age-old concept of unity in diversity. If lawmakers and the people of different states say: "The man you want to send to gallows may be a terrorist; but he is our man, hence deserves to live," is an invitation to the disintegration of the Union. Only policy ought to be of zero tolerance to terrorists and zero tolerance of politicians supporting terrorists. The need of the hour is a law disqualifying those from contesting elections who are found to knowingly support terrorists.

56

Ajmal Kasab and Imran Khan

(One India One People, January, 2013)

It was politics at play when Imran Khan called for execution of Sarabjit Singh, soon after the hanging of terrorist Ajmal Kasab. What was the logic in Khan's demand? Two cases were so different; Kasab was a terrorist caught red-handed while Sarabjit is a case of mistaken identity.

Indian state at last mustered enough courage in November 2012 to execute Mohammad Ajmal Amir Kasab, the lone Pakistani terrorist captured by Mumbai Police for the 26/ 11 terror attacks in Mumbai, after his mercy plea was rejected by the President of India Pranab Mukherjee in early November. The Supreme Court had upheld the lower courts' death sentence imposed on Kasab.Thanks to the extraordinary courage shown by Police Constable Tukaram Ombale in capturing him live by scarifying his own life at Girgaum Chowpatty on 26 November 2008, India could for the first time get live evidence about the Pakistan's Army controlled Inter-Services Intelligence's (ISI) involvement in promoting of terrorism against India.

Kasab never ever thought that he would go back alive—because all 10 terrorists including him had landed in Mumbai to carry out 26/ 11 massacre of innocent people and go down as martyrs. Kasab was only a brain-washed pawn in the ISI's game of enforcing Pakistan Army's eternal revenge against India, for its defeat at the hands of Indian Army—executed through Lashker-e-Toiba (LeT), "non-state actor" in the words of Pakistan President Asif Ali Zardari.

However, now that Kasab is executed by India, Pakistan's Army, has maintained a studied silence. However, Pakistan, at the level of civilian government has reacted to India enforcing death sentence against a Pakistani citizen. Pakistan's Interior Minister, Rehman Malik, said that terrorists should not be spared anywhere. They deserve to be punished. Was he giving a hint to other politicians who are not bound by constrains of governance wherein as in the case of Pakistan, political wing of the government, is trying to improve relations with India, he could not possibly elaborate his thoughts?

Imran Khan's 'tit for tat' demand

But Imran Khan, cricketer turned politician, didn't have any such constraint. He wished a tit for tat and suggested that Pakistan's Indian prisoner, Sarabjit Singh be executed by Pakistan. Imran Khan has fully imbibed Pakistani Army's hatred for India. It is natural, as he is considered close to Army and expects its support whenever he contests next election. If he was a normal politician, he could have easily known that Sarabjit Singh did not stray into Pakistan as a terrorist. As Sarabjit's lawyer Awais Sheikh said that Sarabjit was mistaken for a terrorist. He was booked as Manjit Singh, who allegedly was involved in serial bomb blasts, in Lahore, which had killed 14 persons.

On the other hand Kasab was caught as a terrorist in action, and tried with the evidence rendered by eye witnesses through due process of law. While Pakistan has kept Sarabjit in Lahore prison for over two decades since 1990, Kasab was given a fair trial at the session's court with an appeal to Bombay High Court and the Supreme Court. Thus, he not only enjoyed all privileges of an Indian citizen but also exercised the right to appeal for presidential pardon.

Further, a fact of utmost importance is: While Sarabjit received and continues to receive active participation of his family and the Government of India for his release, in case of Kasab—the terrorist, neither his family was keen to meet him nor his government was interested in defending him. Pakistani government has admitted that Kasab used Pakistani territory to execute his plans for 26/11. It is further evidenced by the fact that Kasab's dead body is not claimed by either. Hence, any comparison between Kasab and Sarabjit is unwarranted, preposterous and motivated to create more ill will between Pakistan and India. That there is absolutely no comparison between the two is also stated by Pakistani human rights activist, and former Minister, Ansar Burney. It was Burney who actively worked to commute Sarabjit Singh's death sentence to life imprisonment!

Yet, as though to elaborate what Interior Minister Rehman Malik said about Kasab viz. all terrorists have to be punished, Imran Khan immediately demanded execution of Sarabjit. He never for a second paused to ponder over the difference between the two cases. This shows how much Indian media, particularly electronic media, has wrongly invested in cultivating Imran Khan, thinking that he is a liberal Pakistani and friend of India. On the other hand in all fairness, there are several Pakistani liberal scholars who have emphasised the need to bring to trial the brains behind 26/11.

Conclusion

But Pakistani civilian government will not be able to effectively try Hafiz Sayeed, founder of LeT and the founder of his front organisation, called Jamaat-ud-Dawa. Interestingly former Pakistani military dictator, Pervez Musharraf says that the government in Pakistan finds it extremely difficult to act against him as he and his organisations are very powerful and enjoy public support. He mentions his humanitarian work to help people during the 2000 earthquake in Pakistan.

The fact of the matter is: Pakistani civilian governments so far have not been able to control policy decision made by the Army. The Pakistani Army continues to desire to revenge their defeat at the hands of Indian Army. Hence it continues to use the services of terrorists groups like LeT, Jaish-e-Mohammad and Hizbul Mujahideen to carry on with anti-Indian terrorism. These terrorist outfits not only receive training, money but diplomatic cover and political and physical protection of Army through the ISI. The hatred for India is so widespread in Pakistan that a large number of Pakistanis consider India as a greater threat than terrorist groups!

In these circumstances, it is no wonder that while civilian government in Pakistan shows an eagerness to improve their relations with India, Pakistanis in general and their Army in particular are willing to promote many more Kasabs against India. Hence, Imran Khan and politicians of his ilk are willing to sacrifice many Sarabjit Singhs just to cultivate an all-powerful Army rather than take up the just cause of Sarabjit Singh with a weak government.

57

Inertia on ISIS will Prove Dear

(The Free Press Journal, 06-11-2014)

> *".....government reaction (was on 4 Indian citizens from Kalyan going to fight with ISIS) that there would be no action taken if these men came back, as they had not committed any crime in India....If what they have done in Iraq or Syria is a crime in terms of the laws of those countries, India as a UN member, also needs to consider it a crime."*

The Islamic State of Iraq and Syria (ISIS) was unheard of, until recently It first surfaced prominently in the news around May 2014. In a geographical sense, it is now a transnational concept that includes areas of western Iraq and Eastern Syria. It is neither recognised as a state, as yet, by any established state in the world nor is it a member of the UN.

What does ISIS stand for? Iraq has a Shia majority, but Saddam Hussein, a Sunni, ruled it with an iron hand for nearly 24 years (July 1979-April 2003), until his dethronement by America. After American intervention and political power moving into Shia hands, there has been an alienation of Sunnis. This was directly exploited by the Al Qaeda of Iraq (AQI), under the leadership of Abu Musab al-Zarqawi, under the banner of the Islamic State of Iraq (ISI).

But after the outbreak of civil war in Syria, the movement became transnational, with the Syrian Sunnis merging into the Iraqi group. Then it became ISIS. The ultimate goal of ISIS is the creation of an Islamic Caliphate. Another name used to describe this movement is the Islamic State of Iraq and Levant (ISIL). Generally the area described as Levant includes not only Syria, but also Lebanon and Israel. There have been some moves by the ISIS in Lebanon to mobilise marginalised Sunnis.

Thus, the ISIS is closely linked to Al Qaeda, borrowing its methods of operation. After turning into ISIS, it is led by Abu Bakr al-Baghdadi. He has designated himself Caliph of the Islamic state, which represents alienated and marginalised Sunnis. It is against the foreign occupation of any Islamic state; hence vehemently against the US. This is akin to the agenda of the Al Qaeda under Osama Bin-Laden.

Though any radicalisation of Muslims globally has its impact on Indian Muslims, had ISIS limited its ambitions to creating an Islamic Caliphate embracing the current Islamic world, it would not have been cause for alarm on the part of Indian authorities. However, there are two broad disturbing developments.

First, there have been reports that Pakistan's ISI (Inter-Services Intelligence) - the notorious instrument of the Pak Army, working against India, has established contacts with the ISIS to operate in its disputes with India, mainly in Jammu and Kashmir (J&K). By using terrorism as an instrument of its foreign policy and by promoting anti-India terrorist groups, it thought it could create a permanent problem of domestic terrorism in India.

However, it is Pakistan that is now being attacked more often by the very terrorist groups it generated internally, like the Tehreek-e-Taliban (Pakistani Taliban). The Pakistani Taliban has a one-point programme - to rule Pakistan as an Islamic state, as the Afghan Taliban did at the turn of the last century. As of now, it is puzzling that the ISI felt the need to align with the ISIS when it already had the Lashker e-Toiba, Jaish-e-Mohammad and other groups to carry out its terrorist tactics against India. This is further inexplicable in the light of the fact that the Pakistan Army has also expressed its concern over factions of the Pakistan Taliban moving over to the ISIS. Hence, India might think that the presence of the ISIS may not be a threat to our interests. But since foreign policy with regard to India is made by the Army, we must also recognise that such a conclusion could be premature as the duplicitous ways of the Pakistani Army are well-known to us.

Second, Indian Muslims are being recruited by the ISIS to fight in their current battlefields in Iraq and Syria. Already more than 30 Indians have been recruited, according to reports. More Islamic warriors seem to be needed, as Lebanon seems to be the next target, as it is embodied in the concept of ISIL. But are we as a nation, and more particularly, the government, aware of long-term consequences of Indian Muslims joining the ISIS and returning to India after their jihadi experience?

There seems to be inertia on this issue on the part of the Government. When the four young men from Kalyan went to the ISIS war zone on May 24 to fight for the Islamic cause, they must have been convinced of the legitimacy of cause for which they were going to fight. That is evident from the fact that while conveying the news of the death of one—Arif Ezaz Majeed—of the four, his friend Shaheen Tanki, who had also gone with him, reportedly told Majeed's parents: "He has sacrificed his life. He is a martyr now." That is exactly how the ISIS had also described Majeed's death on their website: "He has fulfilled his promise to God."

However, early government reaction was that there would be no action taken if these men came back, as they had not committed any crime in India. The issue before the government is: If what they have done in Iraq or Syria is a crime in terms of the laws of those countries, India as a UN member, also needs to consider it a crime. Since they have gone abroad on Indian passports, India can in the future, impound their passports to prevent them going to the ISIS even circuitously Western countries have successfully taken steps to detain men travelling to fight for the ISIS. India should also do it.

We must prepare to safeguard our country from this far more brutal terrorist group, calling itself ISIS. Its brutalities overshadow even the crimes of the Pakistani Army, like the beheading of Indian soldiers within India, or the ISI and their creation LeT, or the Mumbai attacks of November 26, 2008.

58

Terror Lessons Pak Holds Out

(The Free Press Journal, 27-12-2014)

By releasing Lakhvi, (master mind of the Mumbai attack.....) on bail Pakistan "sent a message that some militants are more equal than others." Farhatullah Babar, MP Pakistan's People's Party.

With its ghastly attack on the Army Public School in Peshawar, the Tehreek-e-Taliban (TeT) or the Pakistani Taliban on December 16, 2014, prematurely snuffed out 148 lives, 132 of whom were innocent school children. Terrorism was a tactic used in ancient times, but the credit for its use as an instrument of foreign and domestic policy in modern times goes to Pakistan. It has been rightly described as the epicentre of global terrorism! TeT spokesman, Mohammad Umar Khorasani, taking responsibility for the massacre, claimed it was revenge for the government's act of targeting their families in the North Waziristan tribal region and killing over 1,500. He said: "We want them to feel the pain." The world grieved with Pakistan over this loss. The TeT spokesman had said that the instructions were not to kill young children; but reports say that a five-year-old girl, attending school for the first time, was also killed. Spokesman Khorasani might dismiss it as collateral damage.

Pakistan has swiftly taken steps to revoke its self-imposed moratorium on the death penalty. So far, six terrorists have been executed; 500 more are in line. With great speed, the Pakistani Army has killed more than 120 suspected terrorists. The Pakistani Army

Chief visited Afghanistan the very next day of the tragedy to hold talks with officials and President Ghani. This was seen as necessary in view of the open borders between the two nations. Since the North Waziristan tribal areas are on the Afghanistan border, Pakistani Talibanis take shelter in the Afghan side while Afghan Talibanis hide on the Pakistani side. Thus the TeT leader, Mullah Fazlullah, Pakistan says, is on the Afghan side. But this time, Afghanistan has agreed to hold coordinated strikes on terrorist hideouts while rejecting joint operations.

But let alone the Americans or Indians, even the Pakistani public takes Pakistan's resolve to eliminate terrorism with a tinge of skepticism. No sooner had Pakistan announced its resolve to eliminate terrorists, its court released the terrorist, Zaki-ur-Rehman Lakhvi, mastermind of the Mumbai attack of 26/11 six years ago, on bail. Not only were Indians upset, but even Parliamentarians belonging to the Pakistan People's Party, like Farhatullah Babar said: By releasing Lakhvi, Pakistan "sent a message that some militants are more equal than others." Remember, Hafiz Saeed and Musharraf, among others, have blamed India for the Peshawar tragedy and threatened to retaliate! So it is absolutely necessary for India to watch every word and deed to evaluate options and remain ready for action based on deeds, not words. Here are a few suggestions for action.

First, emulating the swiftness with which Pakistan has acted, the government could immediately learn to change its approach to Pakistan-sponsored terrorism. Since terrorism is an instrument of foreign/national security for Pakistan, any use of it is to be considered as an act of war against the Indian state. This is exactly what Pakistan's Interior Minister, Nisar Ali Khan said to his countrymen: "We are in a state of war....Your enemies are inside your country." Follow him. Let the captured terrorists be dealt with speedily by the army courts; make necessary changes in law.

Second, as there is no distinction between good and bad terrorists, let Pakistan, in coordination with India, target Indian terrorists hiding in Pakistan or Pakistan-controlled territories; destroy terror training camps.

The likes of Syed Salahuddin, Masood Azhar, Dawood Ibrahim and now, the much wanted Lakhvi, and his leader are roaming free, as is a family friend of PM Nawaz Sharif—Hafiz Saeed, who carries a $10 million bounty on his head announced by the US. If necessary, let Pakistan and India jointly request the US to use drones to destroy terrorist hideouts and camps.

Third, the fact that nuclear weapons are not unidirectional must be impressed upon Pakistan. This is because there is considerable discussion on the possibility of JuD and its front, the anti-India terror group, LeT, buoyed by its success in the 26/11 Mumbai attacks, acquiring nuclear weapons. Pakistan should have learnt by now that the demon it created to destroy India could easily rise against it.

This was best stated by the former UN Assistant Secretary General, Giandomenico Picco, in 1993, when he wrote: "Terrorism is a criminal manifestation of intolerance....has to be addressed with speed, steadfastness and determination. But to be credible and effective, it has to be consistent...intolerance anywhere has to be tackled with determination and courage..."

59

What use this bonhomie?

(One India One People, February, 2016)

The attack on the Pathankot Airbase following PM Modi's impromptu visit to Lahore has many lessons for us. More than Modi's personal diplomacy, the need of the hour is decisions based on focused deliberations. We must also insist that Pakistan hands over the Pathankot attack mastermind Masood Azhar.

Prime Minister (PM) Narendra Modi by his decision while in Kabul to visit Lahore and join Pakistani PM Nawaz Sharif in the wedding celebration of his granddaughter on December 25, 2015, painted a masterstroke in personal diplomacy. If that was a genuinely spontaneous development, unplanned and un-designed, it was really a genius move. Incidentally, personal diplomacy is a modern development where the head of state or the head of government conducts diplomatic negotiations.

Personal diplomacy is normally built around certain personal or social occasions. The very fact that both the PMs after their successful meeting on the day cautioned the general public not to expect dramatic changes in India's Pakistan policy or Pakistan's India policy, shows they expected hurdles.

Lahore visit - gains and losses

Undoubtedly, the dramatic visit led to the growth of personal bonhomie between the leaders of the two adversarial states. Many have hailed Modi for his bold decision to visit Lahore. All those who have hailed it have a stake in lasting peace that could emerge from the success of such personal diplomacy. But has it contributed to improving India-Pakistan bilateral relations? Obviously not; because hatred generated since Partition cannot be wiped off with one act of personal diplomacy, particularly hatred based on religious differences, and not political ideologies. Even then, gains could be found, if unforeseen factors do not disturb the flow of events.

For India, the desperate issue is to find a solution to Pakistan's promotion of cross-border terrorism. That is directly related to India's economic development, achieving peaceful political conditions in the country and the region, and promoting social harmony nationally. But Pakistan has linked terrorism to resolving of dispute over Jammu and Kashmir. Earlier, it had the option of starting conventional war by stealthy means. Today that option is ruled out for Pakistan as well as India, because of possession of nuclear weapons. The possession of nuclear weapons has given rise to terrorism as an instrument of foreign policy for Pakistan, a weak nation, as opposed to India, a rising major power.

Hence, pessimists use the failure of similar earlier efforts in search of peace, to argue nothing good could emerge from a repeat

PM Modi's impromptu visit to Pakisitan set a new standard in personal diplomacy. But is this enough?

of such efforts. Let me limit to experiences gained since former prime minister A.B.Vajpayee's efforts to improve relations in 1999. His Lahore Yatra generated hopes for good neighbourly relations. But they were frustrated by General Musharraf's Kargil misadventure. For Manmohan Singh it was a personal one-point goal since 2004; but it was destroyed by the 26/11 sea-borne *Lashker-e-Toiba* terrorist attack on Mumbai, with the blessings of the Pakistani Army and its ISI (Inter-Services Intelligence).

Yet, those who call it as a mere stunt are wrong, as the meeting at Lahore has come after earlier brief meetings between the two at Modi's May 2014 swearing-in, at Kathmandu SAARC meet, the meeting at Ufa in Russia, and the follow-up by National Security Advisers (NSAs) of the two countries in 2015.

Members of the main opposition party, the Congress, have crticised PM's visit by alleging that there is no consistency in Modi's Pakistan policy or there is a U-turn in it. Consistency is not necessarily a virtue in foreign policymaking and leaders change their opinions on issues once they come to occupy a responsible position in governance.

Wasn't it also the characteristic of UPA led by the Congress under Mrs. Sonia Gandhi-Dr.Manmohan Singh rule? Classic example is: soon after 26/11, Manmohan Singh not only suspended the ongoing Composite Dialogue but informed Pakistan that terror and dialogue cannot go together; but as admitted, albeit indirectly, under American pressure, at *Sharm el Sheikh* the joint statement issued by him with Pakistani PM, Gilani after NAM summit in July 2009 said: "Action on terrorism should not be linked to the composite dialogue process..." One can give many other examples from democracies globally, but one should suffice. Candidate Richard Nixon and his Republican Party too were critical of Lyndon Johnson's efforts to end the Vietnam War in 1968, but once in office Nixon used the Vietnam peace negotiations to win a second term!

The Congress hasn't accused the BJP PM, nothing of the kind so far! On the other hand, PM Modi's hard line in the beginning in refusing to negotiate with Pakistan when it appears to take instructions from the Huriyat leaders, has permanently succeeded in denying an apparent role to them in the Kashmir dispute.

Jaish-e-Mohammed leader, Maulana Masood Azhar, is the mastermind of the Pathankot attack. Will Pakisitan yield him to India?

Attack on Pathankot Airbase

However, focus shifted from PM's personal diplomacy to cross-border terrorist attacks again. This should have been anticipated since there is a set pattern of terror attacks, though actors keep changing. This time it was by Pakistan-based, ISI-created Masood Azhar-presided, Jaish-e-Mohammad attacking Pathankot Airbase. It is in the similar mode of July 2015 Gurudaspur attack by the same terrorist group that occurred soon after two PMs had met for Shanghai Regional Cooperation meet at Ufa in Russia. The government should have been far more alert since in Ufa PMs had met in a foreign country, while in the latest case, the Indian PM visiting Pakistan had drawn considerable regional and international attention for Pakistani terrorists to strike at India to neutralise any impact on Pakistan's foreign policy.

Pathankot is more than 500 km inside Punjab from the international border. The Indian government made claims that they had intelligence on a likely attack on the airbase. They claimed to have alerted local population to close shops early by 6 pm. Punjab's deputy chief minister has said that at least 20 hours before the attack the state government had alerted all relevant authorities on the likely attack.

Thus, even a layman with rudimentary knowledge would ask: Why didn't Indian authorities sanitise and increase security rings around the outer periphery of the airbase? India-released terrorist, Azhar, has ridiculed Indian authorities for not knowing how to handle six terrorists for over 85 hours! This only shows that the Indian security establishment has not learnt any lessons after the 26/11 Mumbai terrorist attacks, even after seven years and spending crores on making India more secure!

In the aftermath of the Pathankot terrorist attack, Indian citizens felt that the Indian leadership was struggling to determine its response to terrorism emanating from Pakistan. Finally, it did demand action on the part of Pakistan against Masood Azhar. PM Sharif presented a semblance of unity within the government in Pakistan and announced that the government condemns the Pathankot attack, and reiterated the country's commitment to try to end terrorism!

Conclusion

Many are not willing to buy that 'spontaneity' was behind PM's visit to Lahore. The two PMs had met at least thrice before. But PM Modi ought to have made it a summit meeting with adequate preparations, rather than a personal diplomatic visit.

The federal government has to take following urgent steps to retrieve lost gains. It is time to make international terrorism an act of war and take all necessary consequential steps to implement it. Since Masood was handed over to Pakistani promoted terrorists responsible for hijacking the Indian Airlines plane in December 1999, India can now ask for him to be handed back to stand trial in India.

Third, an appropriate enquiry has to be instituted into the Pathankot attack. Unlike in the 26/11 investigation, where focus was only on the police role, politicians and bureaucrats have to be made accountable. Fourth, in the aftermath of the airbase attack, it is a good idea to create a Department of National Security. But that alone is not enough. The Indian Army Chief General Dalbir Singh has called for India "to change its security policy towards Pakistan." The Americans may appreciate resilience of Indian society, but as a state aspiring for major power status, we will only experience global derision.

Finally, such a policy cannot be arrived at by PM Modi deciding it in consultation with his NSA; or Defence Minister visiting arena of terror and Home Minister reiterating his determination to fight against terrorism - all in isolation. Need is for the revival of the National Security Council taking decisions after deliberations based on policy options. These steps are essential if Modi desires to make India a major power.

60

Can Pakistan Dismount the Terror-tiger?

(One India One People, September, 2016)

Pakistan is playing a singularly dangerous game of riding the tiger of terrorism. As the recent visit of Indian Home Minister Rajnath Singh to Pakistan showed, that country seems to be playing a double game, which will in the end, only hurt it the most.

On 4 August 2016, India's Home Minister (HM), Rajnath Singh, was in Islamabad to attend the seventh HMs' meet of South Asian Association of Regional Cooperation (SAARC) nations in Islamabad. Violating all norms of diplomatic protocol, Pakistan allowed anti-Singh demonstrations on the streets of Islamabad during his visit. The threat of demonstrations against the visiting Indian HM was publicised days before his visit, and these were held by none other than Hafiz Saeed, the founder of *Lashker-e-Toiba* (LeT) and *Jamaat-ud Dawa* (JuD), his so-called charity organisation. Both these groups are declared as terrorist organisations by the UN (United Nations), and the US has placed a bounty of $10 million on the head of Saeed.

The reason for the demonstrations given by the LeT chief was: 'Rajnath's hands are reddened by the blood of Kashmiris'. Ironically, that came from a person who was directly involved in spilling of blood of 166 people in Mumbai attacks (26/11) eight years ago. Though he is declared a terrorist, and internationally banned, he roams freely in the streets of Pakistan and his organisation grows in strength. Yet, Rajnath had gone to attend the SAARC making it clear that his security was Pakistan's responsibility.

India's message

Normally, in the SAARC meetings, member nations aren't supposed to raise bilateral issues. Singh was in Islamabad for twin purposes: One, to appeal to the Pakistani ruling elite to accept the fact that terror is not a remedy to resolve any issue affecting the region, and second, to appeal to Pakistan to ratify SAARC convention against terror, which has prevented regional cooperation on terror. Hence, the Indian HM alluded to the terror attacks faced by nations like Bangladesh and India. He was obviously referring to cowardly attacks in recent times - the Dhaka attack in July, 2016, at Holey Artisan Cafe in the diplomatic enclave patronised by foreigners, in which of the 20 killed, 17 were foreigners, and in Mumbai, the cross-sea attack of 26/11 and the Pathankot Airbase attack in January 2016.

Singh made it clear that for regional peace and prosperity, terrorism is the biggest challenge. Towards increased prosperity of Region's people, India has already implemented "Business Card Scheme" under which, eligible businessmen from any SAARC country can visit India to promote business interests.

Directly aiming at Pakistan but without naming it, Singh said that prosperity will be hampered if terrorism is not checked by every country. Mere condemnation of terror, but permitting it on member-

Rajanath Singh's recent visit to Pakistan was marred by hostile demonstrations

state's soil is just not enough. It is only an example of doublespeak. Patronising terrorists as patriots is unacceptable. One country's terrorist cannot be a patriot of another country. Singh made it clear that terrorism cannot be glorified and patronised. No one can distinguish between 'good' terrorism and 'bad' terrorism. Nawaz Sharif in his heart must have felt that Rajnath was stealing his words uttered at the all party conference summoned by him in his country soon after the December 2014 ghastly terrorist attacks on a military school at Peshawar, in which 148 mainly children lost their lives!

Singh also called upon Pakistan to implement SAARC Regional Convention on suppression of terrorism in pursuit of 'our common fight against terrorism.' He also asked member-states to implement additional protocol on terrorism as it includes effective measures to prosecute and punish terrorists; also if necessary, extradite terrorists to stand trial in countries where cross border terror has occurred. These important measures have not been ratified by Pakistan so far. One need not remind discerning readers how Pakistan has avoided all action to prosecute internationally acknowledged persons involved in Mumbai attacks of 26/11 like Saeed and Lakhvi.

Singh also called upon the member nations to realise the gravity of the misuse of digital technology in committing terror attacks and evading arrest and appealed to his counterparts to explore all avenues to deal with growing cyber crimes. He also urged member-states to implement the SAARC decision to create a terrorism monitoring desk.

Back home, Congressmen excelled in criticising the Home Minister's visit and his successful efforts to highlight Pakistan's perfidies and doublespeak in reducing recourse to terrorism. Mani Shankar Aiyar went to the extent of charging Singh of turning SAARC into an "Association for Regional Confrontation (instead of Cooperation)." He failed to note the insults heaped on the visiting HM. Singh was not appropriately received by his counterpart in Pakistan. The Pakistani Interior Minister hosted a lunch for visiting members, but he did not show up; thus forcing Singh to forego his lunch. Pakistan's government also denied access to Indian journalists to cover the event.

Conclusion

Pakistan's elected civilian government or its democratic facade faces two crucial issues. These will directly affect India's 'neighbourhood first' policy. First, Pakistan itself has been facing internal terror attacks. Number of such attacks inside Pakistan has become deadly; it was illustrated by the terrorist attacks by a suicide bomber at Quetta Civil Hospital on 8th August, in which over 74 were killed - mostly lawyers, who had gone to condole the death of the President of Quetta Bar Association, who was earlier gunned down by terrorists. This was soon after Rajnath Singh's fervent pleas to shun terrorism as an instrument of foreign policy.

The responsibility for the carefully executed terror attacks was taken by the Islamic State (IS) and a faction of Pakistani Taliban. The stated reason for the attacks is worth pondering. An unidentified spokesperson, on behalf of the group stated that their "objective is to establish a caliphate and diminish the basis of democracy in Pakistan which we consider an infidel system." He further added: "Lawyers were on our hit list...." They were "considered as custodians of Pakistani democratic system."

But there was a free-play of blaming India. Baluchistan's chief minister, Nawab Zehri and the mastermind of Mumbai attack, Hafiz Saeed, blamed Indian intelligence agency RAW for the attacks. This was similar to Musharraf and Saeed blaming India for killing innocent children in the military school in December 2014. This is somewhat similar to Mrs. Gandhi in the 1970s blaming whatever went against her policy towards India on American Central Intelligence Agency (CIA). In Pakistan this trend had started prominently in March 2009 when the visiting Sri Lankan cricket team was attacked by terrorists in Lahore.

Second, Pakistan's elected civil government is at crossroads. It has to decide whether to continue to permit military-ISI controlled and maneuvered international terrorist groups to operate freely against India or call the bluff by its all-powerful military. Pakistan is today riding a tiger called terrorism; it is easy to mount on it but difficult to dismount! That could lead to another military take over and face another period of military dictatorship.

India has done well in firmly asserting our disgust with Pakistani use of terror to force India to handover them Kashmir on a platter. India's HM did well to reiterate that no force on the Earth can take Kashmir away from India. We have done well to support democratic forces in Baluchistan and Pakistan occupied Kashmir (PoK). But we also need to support democratic forces in Pakistan to balance the Army. We need to remember that it is for the first time, Pakistan in 2016 began to share intelligence with India on likely terror attacks against Indian assets. It is also worth noting that after listening to Rajnath Singh on the need to control all terror, Nawaz Sharif reiterated his commitment to fight against terror.

In the context of the December 2014 attack on a military school, a member of Pakistani parliament belonging to the Pakistan People's Party, Farhatullah Babar had said: By releasing Lakhvi, the Mumbai terror-brain, Pakistan "sent a message that some militants are more equal than others." Nawaz Sharif has to decide whether his fight is only against anti-Pakistan terror groups or that includes anti-India terror groups as well. That will decide the future of democracy in Pakistan! That will also create in Pakistan necessary prodemocracy forces which will finally enable Pakistan to dismount from the Terror-Tiger!

61

Postscript: Uri Terror and Gains of Surgical Strike

As I was completing my introduction to the *Terrorism Miscellany*, there came the news of another terrorist strike—this time on military base at Uri in Jammu. My friends then told me that it should be covered with an article or a post script. The Uri strike is the game changer for the NDA II government led by PM Modi. Because even before wounds of terror attacks on Pathankot Airbase inflicted by *Jaish-e-Mohammad* (JeM) in January 2016—on a fresh contract with Pakistan's Army-ISI combo—are healed, a new terror attack came on 29 September at Uri Army command.

Earlier, Indian PM, Modi, security establishment and core public had taken a charitable approach at our neighbour's misdeeds. PM Modi had even given a long rope to Pakistani PM, Sharif to show a change of style and heart in conducting his nation's foreign policy towards India. He had given a surprise visit to Pakistani PM, prior to Pathankot. By now it is a well known fact that major foreign policy issues like nuclear weapons, relations with the United States (US), major powers like Russia, China and anti-India policy are firmly controlled by the Pakistan's Military Establishment (PME).

Hence, despite grave provocation, South Asia experts had glossed over dastardly attack on the Pathankot Airbase, by stating that it was an act of those who, in the PME wanted to scuttle India-Pakistan growing bonhomie; and any step on the part of India to retaliate might result into playing in the hands of spoilers. Despite that, anti-India elements within the PME succeeded in organising terror attacks against Uri, killing19 young soldiers in their sleep rather than engaging them in straight fight! The soldiers hailed from various states in the Indian Union and not any one state; hence there was a national uproar at PME's continued heinous crime of terror to bleed India! The nation's mood was correctly read by PM when he said that those behind the attack won't go unpunished.

Surgical Strike

The punishment came in the form of a surgical strike when it was executed by the Indian Special Force on 29 September. Details are available in tits and bits as of now.

The story of the Uri attack and successful Indian surgical strike are similar to an incident of 1962 in the Cold War period called the Cuban Missile Crisis. It is now written in every text book on American foreign policy of the post World War II period as a success story. If Uri attack is similar to the Soviets stealthily keeping missiles in Cuba and President Kennedy's response was one of risking a nuclear war to get rid of the missiles or willing to face a nuclear war. Indian response too has been one of boldly going for a surgical strike to punish terrorists and to motivate Pakistan to move away from using terrorism as an instrument of foreign policy.

Nearer at home, it is in contrast to NDA I's ultimate inaction under the leadership of Vajpayee having taken decisive action to begin with after a series of terror attacks against Indian targets culminating in an attack on Indian Parliament in December 2001. The then government first mobilised Indian troops in May 2002 on the India-Pakistan borders; Pakistan didn't blink; India ending military confrontation almost after ten months without any decisive outcome.

Be that as it may, what do we mean by surgical strike? Surgical strike is a phrase used in military science to indicate a military strike carried out against a target in a foreign country with limited weapons to achieve a specific result of removing an irritant/constant problem faced by the body-politic. Very term 'surgical' indicates that it is derived from medical science. As much as the fact that a surgery is used only when there is a crisis causing critical pain in the human body only then, surgeons will advice the option of surgery, in the like manner in the military/strategic studies when irritant in the international relations becomes unbearable, surgical strike is resorted to do away with the irritant! As in the case of human body after surgery, its form or health is never the same as before, after the surgical strike India-Pakistan relations can never be again as in the past!

Gains

First gain is that this surgical strike has helped India to make Pakistan to raise its threshold of tolerance in the use of nuclear weapons! Ever since it went publicly nuclear in May 1998, Pakistan has made it clear that its nuclear weapons are India-specific and has also advertised how its nuclear threshold of tolerance is very low! During the eyeball to eyeball confrontation after former PM, Vajpayee mobilised Indian forces on India-Pakistan borders in post-terror attack on Parliament in December 2001, Musharraf had claimed that he had conveyed to Vajpayee that if Indian troops "moved a single step across the international border or the Line of Control" India should not expect a conventional war from Pakistan. Obviously he didn't rule out use of nuclear weapons. One may recall Munir Akram's boast in UN Security Council on the same fact soon after 1998.

Recently foreign policy adviser to Pakistani PM, Sartaz Aziz had reminded India that it too has nuclear weapons. Even three days before Indian surgical strikes, Pakistan's Defence Minister, Khawaja Muhammad Asif had threatened to use tactical nuclear weapons. He had said: "We haven't kept the devices...as showpieces. But if our safety is threatened, we will annihilate them." Similar threat was held by him one day before the Uri attack as well!

This nuclear-trigger happiness of Pakistan was not taken as emerging from its inherent military weakness but theoretically as a given input in policymaking by the Indian leaders till surgical strike of September 29. Addressing members of the Indian Council of World Affairs in Godrej Bhavan former Foreign Secretary J. N. Dixit had also mentioned that as a constraint in 1999. Indian surgical strike has for once at least now has called off Pakistani nuclear bluff! Pakistan's High Commissioner, Abdul Basit, who had also echoed his superiors on the subject of their low threshold of tolerance on the use of nuclear weapons, post-surgical strike said that "to even think" of nuclear attack, "is suicidal."

As an offshoot of it, Pakistan's calculated response to India has been to deny occurrence of any such surgical strike inside its territory! This has helped to deescalate the crisis. This might help policymakers and academics to ponder over to consider Pakistan as a rational actor in international politics. Of course, any such admission would have jeopardised Pakistan's position nationally and internationally that it doesn't have terror-training-camps on its soil! Nationally it would have come under domestic pressure to retaliate against Indian surgical strike; internationally it would have amounted to Pakistan's admission such terrorist training camps do exist within their territory or territory controlled by it.

Second, Indian surgical strikes against Pakistan rationally has helped India to drive the point that terrorist attacks against Indian assets are no longer risk-free; it involves a cost and cost of each act of Uri magnitude undoubtedly will rise considerably high.

Third, surgical strike has implicitly accepted two interrelated facts: First, Jammu & Kashmir being an integral part of India, she has a right to enter into any part of the Indian Territory; second, India has asserted its right to conduct pre-emptive strike on training camps, if it has information on terrorists preparing for infiltration and attack Indian assets.

Fourth, it has also to be noted that this act of Indian surgical strike has initiated an intense internal debate in Pakistan between its all powerful Army-ISI and civil-political elected government on the need to control/eliminate all terrorist groups. First salvo was launched by PM, Sharif himself who, reportedly urged upon the need to control terrorist groups. But military pressure on the civilian government prevailed and PM denied any such move. But in a well coordinated move, the US first made a clear and unambiguous statement, asking Pakistan to act; otherwise holding a clear threat that the US will act on its own. Such a threat on the part of the US could not be ignored by the PME in the light of the US action in May 2011 to eliminate its most wanted terrorist, Osama bin Laden, which was the greatest slap on the face of Army in its relations with the US so far since its